20

to Honey
From Honey

TO:
FROM:

healing
water
FOR THE
soul

MRS. L.B. COWMAN

healing water for the soul

SELECTIONS FROM

Streams in the Desert AND *Springs in the Valley*

Healing Water for the Soul

Streams in the Desert and *Springs in the Valley* were written nearly one hundred years ago in a culturally different time than we are now in. Because of this, some of the original terms and content have been edited to properly reflect history and to respect various people groups.

ISBN 978-0-310-36518-1 (audio)
ISBN 978-0-310-36517-4 (ebook)
ISBN 978-0-310-36514-3 (hc)

Printed in Italy

22 23 24 25 26 ROT 10 9 8 7 6 5 4 3 2 1

A LETTER FROM THE EDITOR

As L. B. Cowman watched her husband slowly fade away due to declining health, she put pen to paper and wrote about the experience of fellowshipping with God in the midst of hardship, loss, and heartbreak. In 1925, Cowman published the treasure that is *Streams in the Desert*. The title of the book came from Isaiah 35:6: "Then will the lame leap like a deer, and the mute tongue shout for joy. Water will gush forth in the wilderness and streams in the desert" (NIV).

Cowman never anticipated that her devotional would be such a renowned success. She credited God for giving her *Streams in the Desert*. Fourteen years later, in 1939, she published *Springs in the Valley*.

Collectively, the devotionals have sold more than two million copies. Not only have Cowman's writings provided hope and encouragement during difficult times; the words God gave her have healed the hearts and souls of countless people.

The Cowmans founded The Oriental Missionary Society (OMS) in 1901 in Tokyo, Japan. Lettie served as president of OMS from 1928–49. The global mission organization continues to this day as One Mission Society in Greenwood, Indiana, and now has nearly 500 missionaries in 75 nations worldwide.

In honor of L. B. Cowman's contribution, we have curated entries from *Streams* and *Springs*. You can follow the compilation as a 365-day devotional or as a six-month morning and evening read. Either way, *Healing Water for the Soul* offers another generation the opportunity to experience one of the most inspirational devotionals ever written.

DAY 1

Pray continually.

1 THESSALONIANS 5:17

Is it hypocritical to pray when we don't feel like it?

Perhaps there is no more subtle hindrance to prayer than that of our moods. Nearly everybody has to meet that difficulty at times. Even God's prophets were not wholly free from it. Habakkuk felt as if he were facing a blank wall for a long time. What shall we do when moods like this come to us? Wait until we do feel like praying? It is easy to persuade ourselves that it is hypocrisy to pray when we do not feel like it; but we don't argue that way about other things in life. If you were in a room that had been tightly closed for some time you would, sooner or later, begin to feel very miserable—so miserable, perhaps, that you would not want to make the effort to open the windows, especially if they were difficult to open. But your weakness and listlessness would be proof that you were beginning to need fresh air very desperately—that you would soon be ill without it.

If the soul perseveres in a life of prayer, there will come a time when these seasons of dryness will pass away and the soul will be led out, as David says, "into a spacious place" (Ps. 18:19). Let nothing discourage you. If the soil is dry, keep cultivating it. It is said, that in a dry time this harrowing of the corn is equal to a shower of rain.

When we are listless about prayer it is the very time when we need most to pray. The only way we can overcome listlessness in anything is to put more of ourselves, not less, into the task. To pray when you do not feel like praying is not hypocrisy—it is faithfulness to the greatest duty of life. Just tell the Father that you don't feel like it—ask Him to show you what is making you listless. He will help us to overcome our moods, and give us courage to persevere in spite of them.

"When you cannot pray as you would, pray as you can."

If I feel myself disinclined to pray, then is the time when I need to pray more than ever. Possibly when the soul leaps and exults in communion with God it might more safely refrain from prayer than at those seasons when it drags heavily in devotion. CHARLES H. SPURGEON

DAY 2

He said, "This is the resting place, let the weary rest"; and, "This is the place of repose"—but they would not listen.

ISAIAH 28:12

Why do you worry? What possible use does your worrying serve? You are aboard such a large ship that you would be unable to steer even if your Captain placed you at the helm. You would not even be able to adjust the sails, yet you worry as if you were the captain or the helmsman of the vessel. Be quiet, dear soul—God is the Master!

Do you think all the commotion and the uproar of this life is evidence that God has left His throne? He has not! His mighty steeds rush furiously ahead, and His chariots are the storms themselves. But the horses have bridles, and it is God who holds the reins, guiding the chariots as He wills!

Our God Jehovah is still the Master! Believe this and you will have peace. "Don't be afraid" (Matt. 14:27).

Tonight, my soul, be still and sleep;
The storms are raging on God's deep—
God's deep, not yours; be still and sleep.
Tonight, my soul, be still and sleep;
God's hands will still the Tempter's sweep—
God's hands, not yours; be still and sleep.
Tonight, my soul, be still and sleep;

God's love is strong while night hours creep—
God's love, not yours; be still and sleep.
Tonight, my soul, be still and sleep;
God's heaven will comfort those who weep—
God's heaven, not yours; be still and sleep.
CHARLES H. SPURGEON

I implore you to not give in to despair. It is a dangerous temptation, because our Adversary has refined it to the point that it is quite subtle. Hopelessness constricts and withers the heart, rendering it unable to sense God's blessings and grace. It also causes you to exaggerate the adversities of life and makes your burdens seem too heavy for you to bear. Yet God's plans for you, and His ways of bringing about His plans, are infinitely wise.
MADAME GUYON

DAY 3

Cast all your anxiety on him.
1 PETER 5:7

Who among us has not occasionally experienced anxiety? And yet the Bible clearly prohibits it, and as clearly provides an unfailing remedy: "Blessed is the man who trusteth in Jehovah, and whose confidence Jehovah is; for he shall be like a tree . . . which stretcheth forth its roots by the water course, so that it shall not fear when heat cometh, but its leaf shall be verdant; which is not uneasy in the year of drought." SPURRELL

Not uneasy! Not uneasy in the year of drought—in a time of spiritual darkness. Not uneasy about spiritual supplies; not uneasy concerning temporal supplies—food or raiment; not uneasy concerning our lip witness—how, or what to say. Then what is there left about which we may be anxious? Nothing. For the Lord went on to say, "Why do you worry about the rest?" (Luke 12:26).

And Paul further says, "Do not be anxious about anything" (Phil. 4:6) or "In nothing be anxious." And again, Peter says, "Do not begin to be anxious."

Anxiety is therefore prohibited in the Bible. But how is it to be prevented? By hurling all your care or worry upon Him, because with Him there is care about you.

Blessed is the man who is not uneasy! APHRA WHITE

DAY 4

Against all hope, Abraham in hope believed. . . .
Without weakening in his faith.

ROMANS 4:18-19

I will never forget the statement which that great man of faith George Mueller once made to a gentleman who had asked him the best way to have strong faith: "The only way to know strong faith is to endure great trials. I have learned my faith by standing firm through severe testings."

How true this is! You must trust when all else fails.

Dear soul, you may scarcely realize the value of your present situation. If you are enduring great afflictions right now, you are at the source of the strongest faith. God will teach you during these dark hours to have the most powerful bond to His throne you could ever know, if you will only submit. "Don't be afraid; just believe" (Mark 5:36). But if you ever are afraid, simply look up and say, "When I am afraid, I will trust in You" (Ps. 56:3). Then you will be able to thank God for His school of sorrow that became for you the school of faith. A. B. SIMPSON

Great faith must first endure great trials.

God's greatest gifts come through great pain. Can we find anything of value in the spiritual or the natural realm that has come about without tremendous toil and tears? Has there ever been any great reform, any discovery benefiting humankind, or any soul-awakening revival, without the diligence and the shedding of blood of those whose sufferings were actually the pangs of its birth? For the temple of God to be built, David had to bear intense afflictions. And for the gospel of grace to be extricated from Jewish tradition, Paul's life had to be one long agony.

Take heart, O weary, burdened one, bowed down
Beneath your cross;
Remember that your greatest gain may come
Through greatest loss.
Your life is nobler for a sacrifice,
And more divine.
Acres of blooms are crushed to make a drop
Of perfume fine.
Because of storms that lash the ocean waves,
The waters there
Keep purer than if the heavens o'erhead
Were always fair.
The brightest banner of the skies floats not
At noonday warm;
The rainbow follows after thunderclouds,
And after storm.

DAY 5

Its roots may grow old in the ground and its stump die in the soil, yet at the scent of water it will bud and put forth shoots like a plant. . . . My roots will reach to the water, and the dew will lie all night on my branches. My glory will not fade; the bow will be ever new in my hand.

JOB 14:8–9; 29:29–20

Once there was an oak tree that clung to a crag on a mountainside. The wind swept its crest, and the snows and rains tore at its soil. Its roots ran along a pathway and were trampled by the feet of men. But the rain and the snows ran down the mountain, and the oak tree was dying of drought. Patiently and persistently its underground tendrils had gone forth in every direction for relief. All its power was put into the quest by which it would save its life. And, by and by, the roots reached the mountain spring. The faithful stream that touched the lips of man and beast ran up the trunk and laved the branches and gave new life to the utmost twig. The tree stood in the same place; it met the same storms; it was trodden by the same hurrying feet. But it was planted by the rivers of water and its leaf could not wither. Out into the same old life you must go today as ever, but down underneath you can be nourished by the everlasting streams of God.

Travelers returning from Palestine report that beneath the streets of Shechem there are rivers flowing. During the daytime it is impossible to hear the murmuring of the waters because of the noise. But when night comes and the clamor dies away, then can be heard the music of the hidden rivers.

Are there not "hidden rivers" flowing under the crowded streets of our lives today? If we can be assured that there is still the music of deep-flowing waters beneath all the noise and tumult of the working hours, we can walk the way of the conqueror.

Keep your roots deep in the living waters.

DAY 6

Let us go over to the other side.

MARK 4:35

Even though we follow Christ's command, we should not expect to escape the storm. In this passage of Scripture, the disciples were obeying His command, yet they encountered the fiercest of storms and were in great danger of being drowned. In their distress, they cried out for Christ's assistance.

Christ may delay coming to us during our times of distress, but it is simply so our faith may be tested and strengthened. His purpose is also that our prayers will be more powerful, our desire for deliverance will be greater, and when deliverance finally comes we will appreciate it more fully.

Gently rebuking His disciples, Christ asked, "Why are you so afraid? Do you still have no faith?" (v. 40). In effect, He was saying, "Why didn't you face the storm victoriously and shout to the raging winds and rolling waves, 'You cannot harm us, for Christ, the mighty Savior, is on board'?"

Of course, it is much easier to trust God when the sun is shining than to trust Him when the storm is raging around us.

Yet we will never know our level of genuine faith until it is tested in a fierce storm, and that is why our Savior is on board.

If you are ever to "be strong in the Lord and in his mighty power" (Eph. 6:10), your strength will be born during a storm.

With Christ in my vessel,
I smile at the storm.

Christ said, "Let us go over to the other side"—not "to the middle of the lake to be drowned." DANIEL CRAWFORD

DAY 7

And why do you worry?

MATTHEW 6:28

When a man is living on God's plan he has no need to worry himself about his trade, or about his house, or about anything that belongs to him.

Do not look at your own faith; look at God's faithfulness! Do not look around on circumstances; keep on looking at the resources of the Infinite God!

The only thing a man may be anxious about in this life is whether he is working on God's plan, doing God's work; and if that is so, all the care of everything else is back on God.

There are some things which we cannot definitely claim in prayer, because we do not know whether they are in God's mind for us. They may or may not be, but it is only by praying that we can tell. I am perfectly sure that in praying, there comes to men who dwell with God a kind of holy confidence; and when they get hold of a promise in God's Word, they look on that promise as granted.

Let us yield ourselves to God, that the living Godhead may flow through our poor, mean, frail human minds.

If the Lord careth for thee, be thyself at rest. ARCHBISHOP LEIGHTON

When we see the lilies
Spinning in distress,
Taking thought to
Manufacture loveliness;
When we see the birds all
Building barns for store,
'Twill be time for us to worry—
Not before!

If the Pilot has come on board, why should the captain also pace the deck with weary foot?

DAY 8

All that night the LORD drove the sea back.

EXODUS 14:21

In this verse, there is a comforting message showing how God works during darkness. The real work of God for the children of Israel did not happen when they awoke that morning to find they could cross the Red Sea, but it occurred "all that night."

There may be a great work occurring in your life when things seems their darkest. You may see no evidence yet, but God is at work. God was just as much at work "all that night" as He was the next day, when the Israelites finally saw the evidence. The next day simply revealed what God had done during the night.

Are you reading this from a place in your life where everything seems dark? Do you have faith to see but are still not seeing? Are you lacking continual victory in your spiritual growth? Is your daily, quiet communion gone, and there is nothing but darkness all around?

"All that night the LORD drove the sea back." Don't forget—it was "all that night." God works through the night until the morning light dawns. You may not see it yet, but through the night of your life, as you trust Him, He works. C. H. P.

"All that night" the Lord was working,
Working in the tempest blast,
Working with the swelling current,
Flooding, flowing, free and fast.
"All that night" God's children waited—
Hearts, perhaps in agony—
With the enemy behind them,
And, in front, the cruel sea.
"All that night" seemed blacker darkness
Than they ever saw before,

Though the light of God's own presence
Near them was, and sheltered o'er.
"All that night" that weary vigil
Passed; the day at last did break,
And they saw that God was working
"All that night" a path to make.
"All that night," O child of sorrow,
Can you not your heartbreak stay?
Know your God in darkest midnight
Works, as well as in the day.

L. S. P.

DAY 9

God heard their groaning and he remembered his covenant with Abraham, with Isaac and with Jacob.

EXODUS 2:24

God always hears, and He never forgets. His silence does not mean that He is not listening and is not planning. Probably it means that the best time of deliverance has not come yet, and that He is patiently waiting for the moment to arrive when He may prove His love and His power.

Cromwell said to his soldiers just before a great battle: "Know ye soldiers all, that God always comes to man's help in the nick of time."

Yes, God is always on time; never behind and never ahead. Happy the man who learns to wait as he prays, and never loses patience with God. MEN WHO PRAYED

There is a set time for putting into the furnace, and a set time for taking out of the furnace.

There is a time for pruning the branches of the vine, and there is a time when the husbandman lays aside the pruning hook.

Let us wait His time; "He that believeth shall not make haste" (Isa. 28:16 KJV). God's time is the best time. But shall we come out the same as we went in? Ah, no! We "will come forth as gold" (Job 23:10). We shall become purer vessels to hold the sweet-smelling incense of praise and prayer. We shall become holy golden vessels for the Master's use in time and in Eternity.

"When a great issue is in the balance and the path is obscure, wait; but with that waiting shirk not the work that lieth before thee, for in that task may be the solution of thy problem."

God will justify you before the universe in His own time. OTTO STOCKMAYER

• • • • • • • • • • DAY 10 • • • • • • • • • •

Ask the LORD your God for a sign, whether in the deepest depths or in the highest heights.

ISAIAH 7:11

Make your petition deep, O heart of mine,
Your God can do much more
Than you can ask;
Launch out on the Divine,
Draw from His love-filled store.
Trust Him with everything;
Begin today,
And find the joy that comes
When Jesus has His way!

We must continue to pray and "wait for the LORD" (Isa. 8:17), until we hear the sound of His mighty rain. There is no reason why we should not ask for great things. Without a doubt, we will receive them if we ask in faith, having the courage to wait with patient perseverance for Him and meanwhile doing those things that are within our power to do.

It is not within our power to create the wind or to change its direction, but we can raise our sails to catch it when it comes. We do not create electricity, yet we can tap into it with a wire that will conduct it, allowing it to work. We do not control God's Spirit, but we can place ourselves before the Lord out of obedience to what He has called us to do, and we will come under the influence and power of His mighty breath.

Can't the same great wonders be done today that were done many years ago? Where is the God of Elijah? He is waiting for today's Elijah to call on Him.

The greatest Old or New Testament saints who ever lived were on a level that is quite within our reach. The same spiritual force that was available to them, and the energy that enabled them to become our spiritual heroes are also available to us. If we exhibit the same faith, hope, and love they exhibited, we will achieve miracles as great as theirs. A simple prayer from our mouths will be powerful enough to call down from heaven God's gracious dew or the melting fire of His Spirit, just as the words from Elijah's mouth called down literal rain and fire. All that is required is to speak the words with the same complete assurance of faith with which he spoke. DR. GOULBURN, DEAN OF NORWICH

DAY 11

He gives . . . great victories; he shows unfailing love.

PSALM 18:50

Someone who knew what it was to trust God once said: "During the last two years, though I have said little about them, I have had many a crevasse open up before me. The ice has seemed to split asunder, and I have looked down into the blue depths.

"It is a glorious thing to have a big trouble, a great Atlantic billow, that takes you off your feet and sweeps you right out to sea, and lets you sink down into the depths, into old ocean's lowest caverns, till you get to the foundation of the mountains, and there see God, and then come up again to tell what a great God He is, and how graciously He delivers His people."

"He stilled the storm to a whisper" (Ps. 107:29).

Life is to be just hard enough to bring out the heroic! I shall go across battlefields and into twisting storms that I may have an experience of the Father's care, protection and glorious deliverance. I am to share in the tremendous experiences of the great!

Only when Christ opened thine ear to the storm, did He open thine ear to the stillness. GEORGE MATHESON

Prize your storms!

• • • • • • • • • DAY 12 • • • • • • • • •

Watch and pray so that you will not fall into temptation.

MATTHEW 26:41

Dear friend, never go out into the danger of the world without praying first. There is always a temptation to shorten your time in prayer. After a difficult day of work, when you kneel at night to pray with tired eyes, do not use your drowsiness as an excuse to resign yourself to early rest. Then when the morning breaks and you realize you have overslept, resist the temptation to skip your early devotion or to hurry through it.

Once again, you have not taken the time to "watch and pray." Your alertness has been sacrificed, and I firmly believe there will be irreparable damage. You have failed to pray, and you will suffer as a result.

Temptations are waiting to confront you, and you are not prepared to withstand them. Within your soul you have a sense of guilt, and you seem to be lingering some distance from God. It certainly is no coincidence that you tend to fall short of your responsibilities on those days when you have allowed your weariness to interfere with your prayer life.

When we give in to laziness, moments of prayer that are missed can never be redeemed. We may learn from the experience, but we will miss the rich freshness and strength that would have been imparted during those moments.
FREDERICK WILLIAM ROBERTSON

Jesus, the omnipotent Son of God, felt it necessary to rise each morning before dawn to pour out His heart to His Father in prayer. Should we not feel even more compelled to pray to Him who is the giver of "every good and perfect gift" (James 1:17) and who has promised to provide whatever we need?

We do not know all that Jesus gained from His time in prayer, but we do know this—a life without prayer is a powerless life. It may be a life filled with a great deal of activity and noise, but it will be far removed from Him who day and night prayed to God.

•••••••••• DAY 13 ••••••••••

God was reconciling the world to himself in Christ.
2 CORINTHIANS 5:19

There is on record a story of how a tribe of Native Americans who roamed in the neighborhood of Niagara offered, year by year, a young virgin as a sacrifice to the Spirit of the Mighty River.

She was called the Bride of the Falls.

The lot fell one year on a beautiful girl who was the only daughter of an old chieftain. The news was carried to him while he was sitting in his tent; but on hearing it the old man went on smoking his pipe, and said nothing of what he felt.

On the day fixed for the sacrifice a white canoe, full of ripe fruits and decked with beautiful flowers, was ready, waiting to receive "the Bride."

At the appointed hour she took her place in the frail bark, which was pushed out into midstream where it would be carried swiftly toward the mighty cataract.

Then, to the amazement of the crowd which had assembled to watch the sacrifice, a second canoe was seen to dart out from the river's bank a little lower down the stream. In it was seated the old chieftain. With swift strokes he paddled toward the canoe in which sat his beloved child. Upon reaching it he gripped it firmly and held it fast. The eyes of both met in one last long look of love; and then, close together, father and daughter were carried by the racing current until they plunged over the thundering cataract and perished side by side.

In their death they were not divided. The father was in it with his child!

"God was reconciling the world to himself in Christ." He did not have to do this. Nobody forced Him. The only force behind that sacrifice was the force of His seeking love for His lost world.

DAY 14

Where is God my Maker, who gives songs in the night?

JOB 35:10

Do you ever experience sleepless nights, tossing and turning and simply waiting for the first glimmer of dawn? When that happens, why not ask the Holy Spirit to fix your thoughts on God, your Maker, and believe He can fill those lonely, dreary nights with song?

Is your night one of bereavement? Focusing on God often causes Him to draw near to your grieving heart, bringing you the assurance that He needs the one who has died. The Lord will assure you He has called the eager, enthusiastic spirit of your departed loved one to stand with the invisible yet liberated, living, and radiant multitude. And as this thought enters your mind, along with the knowledge that your loved one is engaged in a great heavenly mission, a song begins in your heart.

Is your night one of discouragement or failure, whether real or imagined? Do you feel as if no one understands you, and your friends have pushed you aside? Take heart: your Maker "will come near to you" (James 4:8) and give you a song—a song of hope, which will be harmonious with the strong, resonant music of His providence. Be ready to sing the song your Maker imparts to you.

What then? Shall we sit idly down and say
The night has come; it is no longer day?
Yet as the evening twilight fades away,
The sky is filled with stars, invisible by day.

The strength of a ship is only fully demonstrated when it faces a hurricane, and the power of the gospel can only be fully exhibited when a Christian is subjected to some fiery trial. We must understand that for God to give "songs in the night," He must first make it night. NATHANIEL WILLIAM TAYLOR

DAY 15

We also glory in our sufferings, because we know that suffering produces perseverance; perseverance, character; and character, hope. And hope does not put us to shame.

ROMANS 5:3–5

A story is told of the great artist Turner, that one day he invited Charles Kingsley to his studio to see a picture of a storm at sea. Kingsley was rapt in admiration. "How did you do it, Turner?" he exclaimed. Turner answered: "I wished to paint a storm at sea; so I went to the coast of Holland, and engaged a fisherman to take me out in his boat in the next storm. The storm was brewing, and I went down to the boat and bade him bind me to its mast. Then he drove the boat out into the teeth of the storm. The storm was so furious that I longed to be down in the bottom of the boat and allow it to blow over me. But I could not: I was bound to the mast. Not only did I see that storm, and feel it, but it blew itself into me until I became part of the storm. And then I came back and painted the picture."

His experience is a parable of life: sometimes cloud and sometimes sunshine; sometimes pleasure, sometimes pain. Life is a great mixture of happiness and tragic storm. He who comes out of it rich in living, is he who dares to accept it all, face it all, and let it blow its power, mystery and tragedy into the inmost recesses of the soul. A victory so won in this life will then be an eternal possession. CHARLES LEWIS SLATTERY

•••••••• DAY 16 ••••••••

Everyone born of God overcomes the world. This is the victory that has overcome the world, even our faith.
1 JOHN 5:4

If a person allows it, he can find something at every turn of the road that will rob him of his victory and his peace of mind. Satan is far from retiring from his work of attempting to deceive and destroy God's children. At each milestone in your life, it is wise to check the temperature of your experience in order to be keenly aware of the surrounding conditions.

If you will do this and firmly exhibit your faith at the precise moment, you can sometimes actually snatch victory from the very jaws of defeat.

Faith can change any situation, no matter how dark or difficult. Lifting your heart to God in a moment of genuine faith in Him can quickly alter your circumstances.

God is still on His throne, and He can turn defeat into victory in a split second, if we will only trust Him.

God is mighty! He is able to deliver;
Faith can victor be in every trying hour;

Fear and care and sin and sorrow be defeated
By our faith in God's almighty, conquering power.
Have faith in God, the sun will shine,
Though dark the clouds may be today;
His heart has planned your path and mine,
Have faith in God, have faith always.

When you have faith, you need never retreat. You can stop the Enemy wherever you encounter him. MARSHAL FERDINAND FOCH

DAY 17

They will soar on wings like eagles.
ISAIAH 40:31

Those who wait upon the Lord shall obtain a marvelous addition to their resources: they shall obtain wings! They become endowed with power to rise above things. Men who do not soar always have small views of things. Wings are required for breadth of view. The wing-life is characterized by a sense of proportion. To see things aright we must get away from them. An affliction looked at from the lowlands may be stupendous; looked at from the heights, it may appear little or nothing. These "light and momentary troubles are achieving for us an eternal glory that far outweighs them all" (2 Cor. 4:17). What a breadth of view!

And here is another great quotation: "Our present sufferings are not worth comparing with the glory that will be revealed in us" (Rom. 8:18). This is a bird's-eye view. It sees life as a whole. How mighty the bird from which the picture is taken! "Like eagles!" What strength of wing! Such is to be ours if we wait upon the Lord. We shall be able to soar above disappointment—no matter how great—and to wing our way into the very presence of God. Let us live the wing-life!

The little bird sat on a slender limb,
Upward swinging,
And though wind and rain were rough with him,
Still kept singing.
"O little bird, quick, seek out your nest!"
I could not keep from calling;
"The bleak winds tear your tender breast,
Your tiny feet are falling."
"More need for song
When things go wrong,
I was not meant for crying;
No fear for me,"
He piped with glee,
"My wings are made for flying!"
My heart had been dark as the stormy sky
In my sorrow,
With the weight of troubles long passed by,
And the morrow.
"O little bird, sing!" I cried once more, "The sun will soon be shining.
See, there's a rainbow arching o'er
The storm cloud's silver lining."
I, too, will sing
Through everything;
It will teach blessing double;
Nor yet forget.
When rude winds fret,
To fly above my trouble.

Wing-power gives us the gift of soaring and we see how things are related one to another.

Wide soaring gives wide seeing!

DAY 18

Trust in the Lord *and do good; dwell in the land and enjoy safe pasture.*

PSALM 37:3

I once met a poor woman who earned a meager living through hard domestic labor but was a joyful, triumphant Christian. Another Christian lady, who was quite sullen, said to her one day, "Nancy, I understand your happiness today, but I would think your future prospects would sober you. Suppose, for instance, you experience a time of illness and are unable to work. Or suppose your present employers move away, and you cannot find work elsewhere. Or suppose—"

"Stop!" cried Nancy. "I never 'suppose.' 'The Lord is my shepherd, I shall not be in want' [Ps. 23:1]. And besides," she added to her gloomy friend, "it's all that 'supposing' that's making you so miserable. You'd better give that up and simply trust the Lord."

The following scripture is one that will remove all the "supposing" from a believer's life if received and acted on in childlike faith: "Be content with what you have, because God has said, 'Never will I leave you; never will I forsake you.' So we say with confidence, 'The Lord is my helper; I will not be afraid. What can man do to me?'" (Heb. 13:5–6). HANNAH WHITALL SMITH

There's a stream of trouble across my path;
It is dark and deep and wide.
Bitter the hour the future hath
When I cross its swelling tide.
But I smile and sing and say:
"I will hope and trust always;
I'll bear the sorrow that comes tomorrow,
But I'll borrow none today."

Tomorrow's bridge is a dangerous thing;
I dare not cross it now.
I can see its timbers sway and swing,
And its arches reel and bow.
O heart, you must hope always;
You must sing and trust and say:
"I'll bear the sorrow that comes tomorrow,
But I'll borrow none today."

The eagle that soars at great altitudes does not worry about how it will cross a river.

DAY 19

The LORD your God will bless you in everything you do.

DEUTERONOMY 15:18

Art thou suddenly called to occupy a difficult position full of responsibilities? Go forward, counting on Me! I am giving thee the position full of difficulties for the reason that Jehovah thy God will bless thee in all thy works, and in all the business of thy hands.

This day I place in thy hands a pot of holy oil. Draw from it freely, My child, that all the circumstances arising along thy pathway, each word that gives thee pain, each manifestation of thy feebleness, each interruption trying to thy patience, may be anointed with this oil.

Interruptions are divine instructions.

The sting will go in the measure in which thou sees Me in all things.

"Take to heart all the words I have solemnly declared to you this day. . . . They are your life" (Deut. 32:46–47).

"I will now turn aside, and see this great sight" (Ex. 3:3 KJV).

Our Father is always trying to get us to the place of spiritual discoveries.

God is not interested in getting mere information into our souls; He wants us to have a revelation of Himself. God has challenging futures for us, and will go to miracle lengths to get us to pay attention. If God calls me from ease and idleness, it will be that His undergirdings are sufficient for a great service. "I will turn aside," for it is God who calls me.

As "my expectation is from him" (Ps. 62:5 KJV), I will listen today.

DAY 20

Then Asa . . . said, "LORD, there is no one like you to help the powerless against the mighty."

2 CHRONICLES 14:11

Remind God of His exclusive responsibility: "There is no one like you to help." The odds against Asa's men were enormous. "Zerah the Cushite marched out against them with a vast army of thousands upon thousands and three hundred chariots" (v. 9). It seemed impossible for Asa to hold his own against that vast multitude. There were no allies who would come to his defense. Therefore his only hope was in God.

It may be that your difficulties have come to such an alarming level that you may be compelled to refuse all human help. In lesser trials, you may have had that recourse, but now you must cast yourself on your almighty Friend. Put God between yourself and the enemy.

Asa, realizing his lack of strength, saw Jehovah as standing between the might of Zerah and himself. And he was not mistaken. We are told that the Cushites "were crushed before the LORD *and his forces*" (v. 13, emphasis added), as though heavenly warriors threw themselves against the enemy on Israel's behalf. God's forces so overwhelmed the vast army of the enemy that they fled. Then all Israel had to do was follow up and gather the plunder. Our God is "the Lord of hosts" (Isa. 10:16 KJV) who can summon unexpected reinforcements at any moment to help His people. Believe that He is between you and your difficulty, and what troubles you will flee before Him, as clouds in the wind. F. B. MEYER

When nothing on which to lean remains,
When strongholds crumble to dust;
When nothing is sure but that God still reigns,
That is just the time to trust.
It's better to walk by faith than sight,
In this path of yours and mine;
And the darkest night, when there's no outer light
Is the time for faith to shine.

"Abraham believed God" (Rom. 4:3) and said to his eyes, "Stand back!" and to the laws of nature, "Hold your peace!" and to an unbelieving heart, "Silence, you lying tempter!" He simply "*believed* God." JOSEPH PARKER

DAY 21

I will awaken the dawn.

PSALM 57:8

Take time. Give God time to reveal Himself to you. Give yourself time to be silent and quiet before Him, waiting to receive through the Spirit the assurance of His presence with you, His power working in you. Take time to read His Word as in His presence; that from it you may know what He asks of you and what He promises you. Let the Word create around you, create within you, a holy heavenly light in which your soul will be refreshed and strengthened for the work of daily life. ANDREW MURRAY

We repeatedly come upon entries in the diary of Dr. Chalmers which express what he called the "morning grace of appropriation."

"Began my first waking moments with confident hold upon Christ as my Savior."

"A day of quietness."

"My faith took hold of the precious promises this morning."

"The morning makes the entire day. To think of morning is to think of a bloom and fragrance which, if missed, cannot be overtaken later on in the day. The Lord stands upon the shore in the morning and reveals Himself to the weary, disillusioned men who had toiled all night and taken nothing. He ever stands upon life's most dreary and time-worn shores, and as we gaze upon Him the shadows flee and it is morning."

I met God in the morning
When the day was at its best,
And His presence came like glory
Of the sunrise in my breast.
All day long the Presence lingered,
All day long He stayed with me,
And we sailed in perfect calmness
O'er a very troubled sea.
Other ships were blown and battered,
Other ships were sore distressed.
But the winds that seemed to drive them,
Brought to us a peace and rest.
Then I thought of other mornings,
With a keen remorse of mind.
When I, too, had loosed the moorings
With the Presence left behind.
And I think I know the secret,
Learned from many a troubled way;
You must seek God in the morning
If you want Him through the day.

RALPH CUSHMAN

"The early morning hour has always been a time of visions. What discoveries the saints have made while others slept!"

•••••••••• DAY 22 ••••••••••

The servant of the Lord must . . . be gentle.

2 TIMOTHY 2:24 KJV

When God finally conquers us and changes our unyielding nature, we receive deep insights into the Spirit of Jesus. Then, as never before, we see His extraordinary gentleness of spirit at work in this dark and unheavenly world. Yet the gifts of "the fruit of the Spirit" (Gal. 5:22) do not automatically become evident in our lives. If we are not discerning enough to recognize their availability to us, to desire them, and then to nourish them in our thoughts, they will never become embedded in our nature or behavior. Every further step of spiritual growth in God's grace must be preceded by acknowledging our lack of a godly attribute and then by exhibiting a prayerful determination to obtain it.

However, very few Christians are willing to endure the suffering through which complete gentleness is obtained. We must die to ourselves before we are turned into gentleness, and our crucifixion involves suffering. It will mean experiencing genuine brokenness and a crushing of self, which will be used to afflict the heart and conquer the mind.

Today many people are attempting to use their mental capacity and logical thinking to obtain sanctification, yet this is nothing but a religious fabrication. They believe that if they just mentally put themselves on the altar and believe the altar provides the gift of sanctification, they can then logically conclude they are fully sanctified. Then they go happily on their way, expressing their flippant, theological babble about the "deep" things of God.

Yet the heartstrings of their old nature have not been broken, and their unyielding character, which they inherited from Adam, has not been ground to powder. Their soul has not throbbed with the lonely, gushing groans of Gethsemane. Having no scars from their death on Calvary, they will exhibit nothing of the soft, sweet, gentle, restful, victorious, overflowing, and triumphant life that flows like a spring morning from an empty tomb. G. D. W.

And much grace was upon them all (Acts 4:33).

• • • • • • • • • • DAY 23 • • • • • • • • • •

Has your God . . . been able to rescue you from the lions?

DANIEL 6:20

Thou servant of the living God,
Whilst lions round thee roar,
Look up and trust and praise His Name,
And all His ways adore;
For even now, in peril dire,
He works to set thee free,
And in a way known but to Him,
Shall thy deliverance be.
Dost wait while lions round thee stand?
Dost wait in gloom, alone,
And looking up above thy head
See but a sealed stone?
Praise in the dark! Yea, praise His Name,
Who trusted thee to see
His mighty power displayed again
For thee, His saints, for thee.
Thou servant of the living God,
Thine but to wait and praise;
The living God, Himself, will work,
To Him thine anthem raise;

Though undelivered thou dost wait,
The God who works for thee,
When His hour strikes, will with a word
Set thee forever free.

M. E. B.

"Believe ye that I am able to do this?" . . . "Yea, Lord" (Matt. 9:28 KJV).

Strengthen yourself in the Omnipotence of God. Do not say, "Is God able?" Say, rather, "God is able." ANDREW MURRAY

"The supernatural always slumbers when faith lies sleeping, or dead."

••••••••• DAY 24 •••••••••

In him you have been enriched in every way.

1 CORINTHIANS 1:5

Have you ever seen people who through some disaster were driven to great times of prayer? And have you noticed that once the disaster was long forgotten, a spiritual sweetness remained that warmed their souls?

It reminds me of a severe storm I once saw in late spring—one in which darkness covered the sky, except where the lightning violently split the clouds with its thundering power. The wind blew and the rain fell, as though heaven had opened its windows.

What devastation there was! The storm uprooted even the strongest of oaks, and not one spiderweb escaped the wind, despite being hidden from view. But soon, after the lightning was gone, the thunder ceased and was silent, and the rain was over; a western wind arose with a sweet and gentle breath, chasing the dark clouds away. I saw the retreating storm throw a scarf of rainbows over her fair shoulders and her glowing neck. She looked back at me, smiled, and then passed from my sight.

For many weeks after the storm, the fields raised their hands, full of heavenly, fragrant flowers, toward the sky. And all summer long the grass was greener, the streams were filled, and the trees, because of their lush foliage, cast a more restful shade.

All this—because the storm had come. All this—even though the rest of the earth had long forgotten the storm, its rainbows, and its rain. THEODORE PARKER

God may not give us an easy journey to the Promised Land, but He will give us a safe one. HORATIUS BONAR

It was a storm that led to the discovery of the gold mines in India. Have we not seen storms drive people to the discovery of the priceless mines of the love of God in Christ?

Is it raining, little flower?
Be glad of rain;
Too much sun would wither one;
It will shine again.
The clouds are very dark, it's true;
But just behind them shines the blue.
Are you weary, tender heart?
Be glad of pain:
In sorrow, sweetest virtues grow,
As flowers in rain.
God watches, and you will have sun,
When clouds their perfect work have done.

LUCY LARCOM

DAY 25

For the joy set before him he endured the cross, scorning its shame.
HEBREWS 12:2

The joy of the spirit is no cheap joy. It has scars on it—radiant scars! It is joy won out of the heart of pain. Those who know it have found one of life's deepest and most transforming secrets; the transmuting of pain into a paean. Sorrow becomes not something to escape; we can make it sing. We can set our tears to music, and no music is so exquisite, so compelling. The Christians learned immediately and at once the truth which the philosopher Royce puts in these words: "Such ills we remove only as we assimilate them, take them up into the plan of our lives, give them meaning, set them in their place in the whole." When their heartstrings were stretched upon some cross of pain and the winds of persecution blew through them, then from this human aeolian harp men heard the very music of God. They did not bear pain, they used it.

Where the rain does not fall we have deserts. When the soil is not torn up by the plow and the harrow we get no crops.

Joy is a rare plant; it needs much rain for its growth and blossoming.

I heard an old farmer talk one day,
Telling his listeners how
In the wide, new country far away
The rainfall follows the plow.
"As fast as they break it up, you see,
And turn the heart to the sun,
As they open the furrow deep and free
And the tillage is begun,
The earth grows mellow, and more and more
It holds and sends to the sky

A moisture it never had before,
When its face was hard and dry.
And so wherever the plowshares run
The clouds run overhead,
And the soil that works and lets in the sun
With water is always fed."
I wonder if that old farmer knew
The half of his simple word,
Or guessed the message that, heavenly true,
Within it was hidden and heard.
It fell on my ear by chance that day,
But the gladness lingers now,
To think it is always God's dear way
That the rainfall follows the plow.
Endure with faith and courage through the frost, and you will see a glorious spring.

DAY 26

My peace I give you.
JOHN 14:27

Two painters were once asked to paint a picture illustrating his own idea of rest. The first chose for his scene a quiet, lonely lake, nestled among mountains far away. The second, using swift, broad strokes on his canvas, painted a thundering waterfall. Beneath the falls grew a fragile birch tree, bending over the foam. On its branches, nearly wet with the spray from the falls, sat a robin on its nest.

The first painting was simply a picture of stagnation and inactivity. The second, however, depicted rest.

Outwardly, Christ endured one of the most troubled lives ever lived. Storms and turmoil, turmoil and storms—wave after wave broke over Him until His worn body was laid in the tomb. Yet His inner life was as smooth as a sea of glass, and a great calm was always there.

Anyone could have gone to Him at any time and found rest. Even as the human bloodhounds were dogging Him in the streets of Jerusalem, He turned to His disciples, offering them a final legacy: "My peace."

Rest is not some holy feeling that comes upon us in church. It is a state of calm rising from a heart deeply and firmly established in God. HENRY DRUMMOND

My peace I give in times of deepest grief,
Imparting calm and trust and My relief.
My peace I give when prayer seems lost, unheard;
Know that My promises are ever in My Word.
My peace I give when you are left alone—
The nightingale at night has sweetest tone.
My peace I give in times of utter loss,
The way of glory leads right to the cross.
My peace I give when enemies will blame,
Your fellowship is sweet through cruel shame.
My peace I give in agony and sweat,
For My own brow with bloody drops was wet.
My peace I give when nearest friend betrays—
Peace that is merged in love, and for them prays.
My peace I give when there's but death for thee—
The gateway is the cross to get to Me.

L. S. P.

DAY 27

I have directed the ravens. . . . I have directed a widow there.

1 KINGS 17:4, 9

We must be where God desires. Elijah spoke of himself as always standing before the Lord God of Israel. He could as distinctly stand before God when hiding at the Kerith Ravine, or sheltering in the widow's house at Zarephath, as when he stood erect on Carmel, or listened to the voice of God at Horeb.

If we are where God wants us to be, He will see the supply of our need. It is as easy for Him to feed us by the ravens as by the widow woman. As long as God says stay here, or there, be sure that He is pledged to provide for you. Though you resemble a lonely sentinel in some distant post of missionary service God will see to you. The ravens are not less amenable to His command than of old: and out of the stores of widow women He is able to supply your need as He did Elijah's at Zarephath.

When God said to Elijah, "Hide in the Kerith Ravine" (v. 3), a carbon copy of the order was given to the ravens. They brought food morning and evening to the place of Divine appointment.

When Jesus said, "Go into all the world and preach the gospel" (Mark 16:15), He placed all the resources of heaven at the disposal of the going group.

When I was ordered toward the front in France, I got permission to remain behind ten days for letters. None came. When I reached my objective, where men were dying without a Chaplain's comfort, I found the last thirty days' post. The commanding officer said:

"In the army, the letters go where the orders read."

In the kingdom of God the blessings and equipment are found only where the orders read. Let us all go and tell the story. JOSIAH HOPKINS

It is in the path of His appointment that we shall find His Presence.

DAY 28

I have prayed for you . . . that your faith may not fail.
LUKE 22:32

Dear Christian, remember to take good care of your faith, for faith is the only way to obtain God's blessings. Prayer alone cannot bring answers down from His throne, because it is the earnest prayer of one who believes that leads to answers.

Faith is the communication link between heaven and earth. It is on this link of faith that God's messages of love travel so quickly that even before we ask, He answers. And while we are still speaking, "he hears us" (1 John 5:14). So when the connection of faith is broken, how will we obtain His promises?

Am I in trouble? I can receive help by expressing faith. Am I being battered by the Enemy? My soul will find refuge by leaning in faith upon God. But without faith, I call to Him in vain, for faith is the only road between my soul and heaven. If the road is blocked, how can I communicate with the great King?

Faith links me to Holy God and clothes me with the power of Jehovah. Faith insures me that each of His attributes will be used in my defense, helping me to defy the hosts of hell. It causes me to march triumphantly over the necks of my enemies. So without faith, how can I receive anything from the Lord?

Therefore, O Christian, carefully watch your faith. "Everything is possible for one who believes" (Mark 9:23). CHARLES H. SPURGEON

We as a people take such pride in being so practical that we want something more sure than faith. Yet Paul said, "The promise comes by faith, so that it may . . . be guaranteed" (Rom. 4:16). DANIEL CRAWFORD

Faith honors God, and God honors faith.

DAY 29

I sought the Lord, and he answered me.

PSALM 34:4

Andrew Murray says: It is one of the terrible marks of the diseased state of the Christian life in these days, that there are so many that rest content without the distinct experience of answered prayer. They pray daily, but know little of direct, definite answer to prayer as the rule of their daily life.

And it is this the Father wills. He seeks daily intercourse with His children in listening to and granting their petitions. He wills that I should come to Him day by day with distinct requests. He wills day by day to do for me what I ask.

There may be cases in which the answer is a refusal, but our Father lets His child know when He cannot give him what he requests, and like the Son in Gethsemane, he will withdraw his petition.

Whether the request be according to His will or not, God will by His Word and His Spirit teach those who are teachable and who will give Him time. Let us withdraw our requests if they are not according to God's mind, or persevere until the answer comes.

Prayer is appointed to obtain the answer!

It is in prayer and its answer that the interchange of love between the Father and His child takes place.

Are your prayers answered?

DAY 30

I have learned to be content whatever the circumstances.

PHILIPPIANS 4:11

Paul, while being denied every comfort, wrote the above words from a dark prison cell.

A story is told of a king who went to his garden one morning, only to find everything withered and dying. He asked the oak tree that stood near the gate what the trouble was. The oak said it was tired of life and determined to die because it was not tall and beautiful like the pine tree. The pine was troubled because it could not bear grapes like the grapevine. The grapevine was determined to throw its life away because it could not stand erect and produce fruit as large as peaches. The geranium was fretting because it was not tall and fragrant like the lilac.

And so it went throughout the garden. Yet coming to a violet, the king found its face as bright and happy as ever and said, "Well, violet, I'm glad to find one brave little flower in the midst of this discouragement. You don't seem to be the least disheartened." The violet responded, "No, I'm not. I know I'm small, yet I thought if you wanted an oak or a pine or a peach tree or even a lilac, you would have planted one. Since I knew you wanted a violet, I'm determined to be the best little violet I can be."

Others may do a greater work,
But you have your part to do;
And no one in all God's family
Can do it as well as you.

People who are God's without reservation "have learned to be content whatever the circumstances." His will becomes their will, and they desire to do for Him whatever He desires them to do. They strip themselves of everything, and in their nakedness find everything restored a hundredfold.

DAY 31

If only you had paid attention to my commands,
your peace would have been like a river.
ISAIAH 48:18

Do we not see how God's purposes are thwarted and deferred by human perversity? At the very time when God had determined upon the election and consecration of Aaron to the priesthood, Aaron was spending his time in molding and chiseling the golden calf.

We might have been crowned fifty years ago, but just as the coronation was about to take place we were discovered in the manufacture of an idol. The Lord was just ready to make kings of us when we made fools of ourselves.
JOSEPH PARKER

One small life in God's great plan—
How futile it seems as the ages roll,
Do what it may or strive how it can
To alter the sweep of the infinite whole!
A single stitch in the endless web,
A drop in the ocean's flow or ebb;
But the pattern is rent where the stitch is lost,
Or marred where the tangled threads have crossed:
And each life that fails of true intent
Mars the perfect plan that its Master meant.

Remember the awful truth that I can limit Christ's power in the present, although I can never alter God Almighty's order for a moment. OSWALD CHAMBERS

There is a niche in God's own Temple, it is thine;
And the hand that shapes thee for it, is Divine.

DAY 32

My hope comes from him.

PSALM 62:5

So often we simply neglect to look for the answers to what we have asked, which shows the lack of earnestness in our petitions. A farmer is never content until he reaps a harvest; a marksman observes whether or not his bullet has hit the target; and a physician examines the effect of the medicine he prescribes. Should a Christian be any less careful regarding the effect of his labor in prayer?

Every prayer of the Christian, whether for temporal or spiritual blessings, will be fully answered if it meets certain biblical requirements. It must be prayed in faith and in accordance with God's will. It must rely on God's promise, be offered up in the name of Jesus Christ, and be prayed under the influence of the Holy Spirit.

God always answers the general intent of His people's prayers. He does so not only to reveal His own glory but also to provide for the Christian's spiritual and eternal welfare. Since we see in Scripture that Jesus Christ never rejected even a single petitioner who came to Him, we can believe that no prayer made in His name will be in vain.

The answer to our prayer may be coming, although we may not discern its approach. A seed that is underground during winter, although hidden and seemingly dead and lost, is nevertheless taking root for a later spring and harvest. BICKERSTETH

Delayed answers to prayer are not only trials of faith; they also give us opportunities to honor God through our steadfast confidence in Him even when facing the apparent denial of our request. CHARLES H. SPURGEON

Feb 2nd

DAY 33

He made me into a polished arrow.

ISAIAH 49:2

Our daughters will be like pillars carved to adorn a palace.

PSALM 144:12

C*ut . . . to Shine!*

"When in Amsterdam, Holland, last summer," says a traveler, "I was much interested in a visit we made to a place then famous for polishing diamonds. We saw the men engaged in the work. When a diamond is found it is rough and dark like a common pebble. It takes a long time to polish it, and it is very hard work. It is held by means of a piece of metal close to the surface of a large wheel, which is kept going round and round. Fine diamond dust is put on this wheel, nothing else being hard enough to polish the diamond. This work is kept up for months, and sometimes for several years, before it is finished. If the diamond is intended for a king, then greater time and trouble are spent on it."

What though the precious jewel may be torn and cut until its carats are reduced tenfold! When the cutting and polishing are completed, it will shine with a thousand flashes of reflected light—every carat will be multiplied an hundredfold in value by the process of reduction and threatened destruction!

Let us *wait His time*—let us *trust His love,* that "the proven genuineness of your faith . . . may result in praise, glory and honor when Jesus Christ is revealed" (1 Pet. 1:7 KJV).

DAY 34

Then there came a voice from above the vault over their heads as they stood with lowered wings.

EZEKIEL 1:25

What is the significance of these words: "They stood with lowered wings"? People often ask, "How can I hear the voice of the Lord?" This is the secret: these "living creatures" (v. 5) heard the voice when "they stood with lowered wings."

We have all seen a bird flutter its wings while standing in place. But in this verse, we are told that "there came a voice . . . as they stood with lowered wings."

Do you ever sit, or even kneel, before the Lord and yet are conscious of a fluttering in your spirit? If so, you are not exhibiting a sense of genuine stillness while in His presence.

A dear person told me of this very thing a few days ago. "I prayed about a certain thing," she said, "but I did not wait for the answer to come." She did not get still enough to hear God speak but instead went away and followed her own thinking in the matter. The result proved disastrous, and she was forced to retrace her steps.

Oh, how much energy we waste! How much time we lose by refusing to lower the wings of our spirit and become totally quiet before Him! Imagine the calm, the rest, and the peace that will come as we wait in His presence until we hear from Him!

Then, and only then, we too may speed "back and forth like flashes of lightning" (v. 14), going directly to "wherever the spirit would go" (v. 20).

Be still! Just now be still!
Something your soul has never heard,
Something unknown to any song of bird,

Something unknown to any wind, or wave, or star,
A message from the Father's land afar,
That with sweet joy the homesick soul will thrill,
And comes to you only when you're still.
Be still! Just now be still!
There comes a presence very mild and sweet;
White are the sandals of His noiseless feet.
It is the Comforter whom Jesus sent
To teach you what the words He uttered meant.
The willing, waiting spirit, He does fill.
If you would hear His message,
Dear soul, be still!

DAY 35

He makes the clouds his chariot.

PSALM 104:3

We cannot ride in our own chariots and God's at the same time. God must burn up with the fire of His love every earthly chariot that stands in the way of our mounting into His.

Would you mount into God's chariots? Then take each thing that is wrong in your life as one of God's chariots for you. Ask Him daily to open your eyes, and you will see His unseen chariots of deliverance.

Whenever we mount into God's chariots we have a translation—not into the heavens above us as Elijah did, but into the heaven within us; away from the low, groveling plane of life, up into the heavenly places in Christ Jesus, where we shall ride in triumph over all below. But the chariot that carries the soul over this road is generally some chastening, that for the present doth not seem joyous but grievous.

Nevertheless afterward!

No matter what the source of these chastening, look upon them as God's chariots sent to carry your soul into the high planes of spiritual achievement and uplifting. You will find, to your glad surprise, that it is God's love that sends the chariots—His chariots in which you may ride prosperously over all darkness.

Let us be thankful for every trial that will help to destroy our earthly chariots, and will compel us to take refuge in the chariots of God, which always stand ready and waiting beside us in every trial.

"Yes, my soul, find rest in God; my hope comes from him. Truly he [only] is my rock and my salvation; he is my fortress, I will not be shaken" (Ps. 62:5–6).

We have to be brought to the place where all other refuges fail, before we can say He only. We say, He and my experience; He and my church relationships; He and my Christian work. All that comes after the "and" must be taken away from us, or must be proved useless, before we can come to the He only.

If we want to ride with God upon the heavens, all earth riding must be brought to an end.

He who rides with God rides above all earthborn clouds!

Oh, may no earthborn cloud arise to hide Thee from Thy servant's eyes.

No obstacle can hinder the triumphant course of God's chariots! HANNAH WHITALL SMITH

Feb-5th

DAY 36

Lift up the hands which hang down, and the feeble knees;
And make straight paths for your feet, lest that which is lame
be turned out of the way; but let it rather be healed.

HEBREWS 12:12–13 KJV

This verse is God's word of encouragement to us to lift the hands of faith and to fortify the knees of prayer. All too often our faith becomes tired, weak, and listless, and our prayers lose their power and effectiveness.

The Lord's illustration here is quite compelling. He is pointing out to us that when we become so discouraged and fearful that even one little obstacle depresses and frightens us, we are tempted to walk around it. We would rather take the easy way than face it. Perhaps there is some physical ailment that God is ready to heal, but it requires exertion on our part. The temptation is to find help from someone else or to walk around the obstacle in some other way.

We tend to find many ways of walking around emergencies instead of walking straight through them. So often we are faced with something that frightens or overwhelms us and seek to evade the problem with the excuse: "I'm not quite ready for that now." It may require some sacrifice, or demand our obedience in some area. Perhaps there is some Jericho we are facing, or we are lacking the courage to help someone else and to pray through his concern with him. Perhaps we have a prayer that awaits completion, or a physical problem that is partially healed and we continue to walk around it.

God says, "Lift up the hands that hang down." March straight through the flood, and behold! The waters will divide, the Red Sea will open, the Jordan will part, and the Lord will lead you through to victory.

Do not allow your feet to "be turned out of the way," but let your body "be healed," and your faith strengthened. Go straight ahead, leaving no Jericho unconquered behind you, and no place where Satan can boast of having overwhelmed you. This is a valuable lesson and is extremely practical. How often we find ourselves in this very situation!

Perhaps this is where you find yourself today. A. B. SIMPSON

Pay as little attention to discouragement as possible. Plow ahead like a steamship, which moves forward whether facing rough or smooth seas, and in rain or shine. Remember, the goal is simply to carry the cargo and to make it to port. MALTBIE D. BABCOCK

DAY 37

I will be like the dew.

HOSEA 14:5

Hosea leads us to the source of the dew-drenched life. It is from Him that this priceless gift comes. Those who spend much time with the Master come forth with the dew of blessing upon their lives.

The dew falls in the still night when all nature is hushed to rest. What is true in nature holds true in spiritual things: in this we have the key reason why so many of God's people are living dewless lives. They are restless, anxious, impatient, fussy, busy, with no time at all to be still before the Lord.

The finer things are being sacrificed for the coarser; the things of value for the worthless.

In Job 38:28 the question is asked, "Who fathers the drops of dew?" It is one of God's secrets. It comes quietly, and yet works so mightily. We cannot produce it, but we may receive it and live, moment by moment, in that atmosphere where the Holy Spirit may continually drench us with His presence. W. MALLIS

But the sensitive dew and the stillness are friends,
In the storm, it is true that it never descends.
Let me fuss not, nor pine, but on God cast my care,
And the dew shall be mine in the quiet of prayer.
Let Him hush the sad riot of temper and will,
Till rested and quiet the cleansed heart is still.
When the atmosphere's so, 'tis attractive to dew,
And the first thing you know 'twill be falling on you.

MAMIE PAYNE FERGUSON

"Thy dew is as the dew of herbs" (Isaiah 26:19 KJV).

God feeds the wildflowers on the lonely mountainside without the help of any man, and they are as fresh and lovely as those that are daily watched over in our gardens. So God can feed His own planted ones without the help of man, by the sweet falling dew on his spirit. ROBERT MURRAY MCCHEYNE

"Wait before the Master until your whole heart is drenched by Him, and then go forth in the power of a fresh, strong, and fragrant life."

Lord, let Thy Spirit bedew my dry fleece!

DAY 38

Grain must be ground to make bread.

ISAIAH 28:28

Many of us cannot be used as food for the world's hunger, because we have yet to be broken in Christ's hands. "Grain must be ground to make bread," and being a blessing of His often requires sorrow on our part. Yet even sorrow is not too high a price to pay for the privilege of touching other lives with Christ's blessings. The things that are most precious to us today have come to us through tears and pain. J. R. MILLER

God has made me as bread for His chosen ones, and if it is necessary for me to "be ground" in the teeth of lions in order to feed His children, then blessed be the name of the Lord. IGNATIUS

To burn brightly our lives must first experience the flame.

In other words, we cease to bless others when we cease to bleed.

Poverty, hardship, and misfortune have propelled many a life to moral heroism and spiritual greatness. Difficulties challenge our energy and our perseverance but bring the strongest qualities of the soul to life. It is the weights on the old grandfather clock that keep it running. And many a sailor has faced a strong headwind yet used it to make it to port. God has chosen opposition as a catalyst to our faith and holy service.

The most prominent characters of the Bible were broken, threshed, and ground into bread for the hungry. Because he stood at the head of the class, enduring affliction while remaining obedient, Abraham's diploma is now inscribed with these words: "The Father of Faith."

Jacob, like wheat, suffered severe threshing and grinding. Joseph was beaten and bruised, and was forced to endure Potiphar's kitchen and Egypt's prison before coming to his throne.

David, hunted like an animal of prey through the mountains, was bruised, weary, and footsore, and thereby ground into bread for a kingdom. Paul could never have been bread for Caesar's household if he had not endured the bruising of being whipped and stoned. He was ground into fine flour for the Roman royal family.

Combat comes before victory. If God has chosen special trials for you to endure, be assured He has kept a very special place in His heart just for you. A badly bruised soul is one who is chosen.

DAY 39

And the singers sang, and the trumpeters sounded: and all this continued until the burnt offering was finished.

2 CHRONICLES 29:28 KJV

There is a joy that is attained and another joy that is given. The first joy needs things to make it joy—congenial circumstances, attentive friends; the second joy joys because it is filled with a bubbling spring of internal and eternal gladness—a gladness because it is always in God, and God is always in it. It glows and grows under all circumstances—it sings because it is a song.

It sings after prayer. "Ask and you will receive, and your joy will be complete" (John 16:24). This implies that there must have been a need, a place to fill. As we believe and receive, the song sings!

It sings after faith. "Even though you do not see him now, you believe in him and are filled with an inexpressible and glorious joy" (1 Pet. 1:8). Nothing seen and nothing sensed, at least not by natural sense—yet the song sang, and with a fullness of glory not before known.

It sings after yielding. "Once more the humble will rejoice in the LORD" (Isa. 29:19). Making room for the Lord is a secret of receiving more of Himself.

It sings after sorrow. "Weeping may stay for the night, but rejoicing [singing] comes in the morning" (Ps. 30:5). He, who is Light, who gives the morning signal to every feathered songster to tune his song, will also give you a song that sings.

It sings after sacrifice. "Neither count I my life dear unto myself, so that I might finish my course with joy" (Acts 20:24 KJV).

Did you ever find the song that sang of itself in the quiet of your closet, when you heard His "Yes" to your prayer for His glory to come on earth? When nothing was seen of His working for you and your loved ones, did you hear the sweet strains of the song that sang?

The world awaits you—the singer with the new song!

DAY 40

So Jacob was left alone, and a man wrestled with him till daybreak. Then the man said, . . . "You have struggled with God and with humans and have overcome."

GENESIS 32:24, 28

If you saw one of the intimates of the King on his knees, you would marvel at the sight. Look! He is in the Audience Chamber. He has a seat set for him among the peers. He is set down among the old nobility of the Empire. The King will not put on his signet ring to seal a command, till his friend has been heard. "Command Me," the King says to him. "Ask of Me," He says, "for the things of My sons: command the things to come concerning them!" And, as if that were not enough, that man-of-all-prayer is still on his knees. He is wrestling there. There is no enemy that I can see; yet he wrestles like a mighty man. What is he doing with such a struggle? Doing? Do you not know what he is doing? He is moving Heaven and earth. He is casting this mountain, and that, into the midst of the sea. He is casting down thrones. He is smiting old empires of time to pieces. Yes, he is wrestling indeed. ALEXANDER WHYTE

Break through to God,
He fully understands
Thou art in His dear Hands,
To fulfill all His commands,
Break through to God!
Break through to God,
Be dauntless, faithful, strong,
E'en though the fight is long,
Raise to Him the victor's song,
Break through to God.
Break through to God,
Though thy heart may quail,
And the foe may rail,
Calvary's victory shall not fail,
Break through to God!

Looking back over the Welsh Revival about 1904, the Rev. Seth Joshua wrote: "The secret of the Lord was with many even before the blessing came. I know a man, who, for five years, was carried out by the Spirit, and made to weep and pray along the banks of a Welsh river. At last the travail ceased, and calm expectation followed the soul pangs of this man about whom I now write. *He lived to see the answer to his heart-cries unto the Lord.* He was present in the services in which the first historical incidents took place." *Break through to God!*

DAY 41

This God is our God.

PSALM 48:14

God is great in great things, but very great in little things," says Henry Dyer.

A party stood on the Matterhorn admiring the sublimity of the scene, when a gentleman produced a pocket microscope, and having caught a fly placed it under the glass. He reminded us that the legs of the household fly in England are naked, then called attention to the legs of this little fly which were thickly covered with hair; thus showing that the same God who made the lofty Swiss mountain attended to the comfort of His tiniest creatures, even providing socks and mittens for the little fly whose home these mountains were. This God is our God!

A doubting soul beheld a robin's nest in a gigantic elm and heard a still small voice saying, "If God spent a hundred years in creating a tree like that for a bird, He will surely take care of you." God is so interested, that He takes us one by one and arranges for every detail of our life. To Him, there are no little things.

"The God of the infinite is the God of the infinitesimal."

I saw a human life ablaze with God,
I felt a power Divine
As through an empty vessel of frail clay
I saw God's glory shine.
Then woke I from a dream, and cried aloud:
"My Father, give to me
The blessing of a life consumed by God
That I may live for Thee."

Feb- 11th

DAY 42

The people heard that he had come home.

MARK 2:1

The adult coral invertebrates, known as polyps, work underwater constructing coral reefs. They do so never even imagining they are building the foundation of a new island, which will someday support plants and animals and will be a home where the children of God will be born and equipped for eternal glory as "co-heirs with Christ" (Rom. 8:17).

Beloved, if your place in God's army is hidden and secluded, do not grumble and complain. Do not seek to run from His will and the circumstances in which He has placed you. Remember, without the polyps, the coral reefs would never be built, and God calls some people to be spiritual polyps. He is looking for those who are willing to serve in places hidden from the sight of others, yet in full view of heaven, and who are sustained by the Holy Spirit.

A day is coming when Jesus will bestow His rewards. On that day some people may wonder how you came to merit a certain reward, since they have never heard of you. But remember, He makes no mistakes.

Just where you stand in the conflict,
There is your place.
Just where you think you are useless,
Hide not your face.
God placed you there for a purpose,
Whate'er it be;
Think He has chosen you for it;
Work loyally.
Put on your armor! Be faithful
At toil or rest!
Whate'er it be, never doubting
God's way is best.

Out in the fight or on lookout,
Stand firm and true;
This is the work that your Master
Gives you to do.

With freedom from danger, we can leave a crowded meeting of believers, an inspiring mountaintop experience, or a helpful fellowship with "the righteous made perfect" (Heb. 12:23), in order to return to our modest and simple Emmaus, to the dreaded home of the Colossians, or even to the mission field of distant Macedonia. We can do so with the calm assurance that wherever God has placed us, and in every detail of our daily lives, He has ordained the land we are to possess to its very borders and has ordained the victory to be won. NORTHCOTE DECK

Feb-12th

DAY 43

Not I, but Christ.

GALATIANS 2:20 KJV

Full of the Holy Spirit.

ACTS 11:24

We would in Thee abide, in Thee be glorified, and shine as candles "lighted by the Lord."

For long the wick of my lamp had served my purpose, silently ministering as I read beside it. I felt ashamed that I had not before noticed its unobtrusive ministry. I said to the wick:

"For the service of many months I thank thee."

"What have I done for thee?"

"Hast thou not given light upon my page?"

"Indeed, no; I have no light to give, in proof whereof take me from my bath of oil, and see how quickly I expire. Thou wilt soon turn from me as a piece of smoking tow. It is not I that burns, but the oil with which my texture is saturated. It is this that lights thee. I simply mediate between the oil in the cistern and the fire on my edge. This blackened edge slowly decays, but the light continually burns."

"Dost thou not fear becoming exhausted? See how many inches of coil remain! Wilt thou be able to give light till every inch of this is slowly charred and cut away?"

"I have no fear so long as the supply of oil does not fail, if only some kindly hand will remove from time to time the charred margin . . . exposing a fresh edge to the flame. This is my twofold need: oil and trimming. Give me these and I shall burn to the end!"

God has called His children to shine as "lights in the world." Let us, then, beware of hiding our light—whether household candle, streetlamp, or lighthouse gleam—lest men stumble to their death.

It is at variance with the teaching of the wick to try to accumulate a stock of grace in a sacrament, a convention, or a night of prayer. The wick has no such stores, but is always supplied!

You may seem altogether helpless and inadequate; but a living fountain of oil is prepared to furnish you with inexhaustible supplies: Not by your might or power, but by His Spirit. Hour after hour the oil climbs up the wick to the flame! You cannot exhaust God!

Let us not flinch when the snuffers are used; they only cut away the black charred debris. He thinks so much of His work that He uses golden snuffers! And the Hand that holds the snuffers bears the nail print of Calvary!

F. B. MEYER

Feb-13th

DAY 44

Love covers over all wrongs.

PROVERBS 10:12

Follow the way of love.

1 CORINTHIANS 14:1

When you are troubled, share your problems with God alone. Recently I read the personal experience of a precious child of God. It made such an impression on me that I would like to relate it to you here.

"At midnight I found myself completely unable to sleep," she wrote. "Waves of cruel injustice were sweeping over me, and the covering of love seemed to have been unknowingly removed from my heart. In great agony I cried to God for the power to obey His admonition, 'Love covers over all wrongs.'"

"Immediately His Spirit began to work the power into me that ultimately brought about forgetfulness. I mentally dug a grave, deliberately throwing the dirt out until the hole was very deep. With sorrow, I lowered the offense that had wounded me into the grave and quickly shoveled the soil over it. Then I carefully covered the hole with green sod, planted beautiful white roses and forget-me-nots on top, and briskly walked away."

"Suddenly restful sleep came to me. And the wound that had seemed so deadly was healed without a scar. God's love has covered so completely that today I cannot remember what caused my grief."

There was a scar on yonder mountainside,
Gashed out where once the cruel storm had trod;
A barren, desolate chasm, reaching wide
Across the soft green sod.
But years crept by beneath the purple pines,

And veiled the scar with grass and moss once more,
And left it fairer now with flowers and vines
Than it had been before.
There was a wound once in a gentle heart,
From which life's sweetness seemed to ebb and die;
And love's confiding changed to bitter smart,
While slow, sad years went by.
Yet as they passed, unseen an angel stole
And laid a balm of healing on the pain,
Till love grew purer in the heart made whole,
And peace came back again.

DAY 45

Men ought always to pray, and not to faint.

LUKE 18:1 KJV

That little "ought" is emphatic. It implies obligation as high as heaven. Jesus said, "Men ought always to pray," and added, "and not to faint."

I confess I do not always feel like praying—when, judging by my feelings, there is no one listening to my prayer. And then these words have stirred me to pray: I ought to pray—I ought always to pray—I should not grow faint in praying.

Praying is a form of work. The farmer plows his field often when he does not feel like it, but he confidently expects a crop for his labors. Now, if prayer is a form of work, and our labor is not in vain in the Lord, should we not pray regardless of feelings? Once when I knelt for morning prayers I felt a sort of deadness in my soul, and just then the "accuser of the brethren" became busy reminding me of things that had long since been under the Blood. I cried to God for help, and the blessed Comforter reminded me that my Great High

Priest was pleading my case; that I must come boldly to the throne of grace. I did, and the enemy was routed! What a blessed time of communion I had with my Lord! Had I fainted instead of fighting I could not have received wages because I had not labored fervently in prayer; I could not have reaped because I had not sown. COMMISSIONER BRENGLE

DAY 46

Peter got down out of the boat, walked on the water and came toward Jesus. But when he saw the wind, he was afraid and, beginning to sink, cried out, "Lord, save me!"

MATTHEW 14:29–30

John Bunyan said that Peter did have a little faith, even in the midst of his doubts. In spite of crying out in fear, it was by getting out of the boat and walking that he got to Jesus.

In this passage of Scripture, we see that Peter's sight was actually a hindrance. Once he had stepped out of the boat, the waves were none of his business. His only concern should have been the path of light shining across the darkness from Christ Himself. Even the glow of a kingdom ten times brighter than that of ancient Egypt should not have diverted Peter's eyes.

When the Lord calls you to come across the water, step out with confidence and joy. And never glance away from Him for even a moment. You will not prevail by measuring the waves or grow strong by gauging the wind. Attempting to survey the danger may actually cause you to fall before it. Pausing at the difficulties will result in the waves breaking over your head.

"Lift up [your] eyes to the mountains" (Ps. 121:1) and go forward. There is no other way.

Do you fear to launch away?
Faith lets go to swim!
Never will He let you go;
It's by trusting you will know
Fellowship with Him.

DAY 47

In all these things we are more than conquerors through him who loved us.

ROMANS 8:37

The best steel is subjected to the alternatives of extreme heat and extreme cold. In a cutlery you will notice that knife blades are heated and beaten, and then heated again and plunged into the coldest water in order to give them the right shape and temper. You will also observe a large heap of rejected blades, rejected because they would not bear the tempering process; when put upon the grindstone little flaws appeared in some that up to that point had seemed perfect; others would not bear the tempering process.

Souls are heated in the furnace of affliction, plunged into the cold waters of tribulation, and ground between the upper and nether stones of adversity and disaster.

Some come out ready for the highest services; others are unfit for any but the lowest uses. Would you be of account among the forces which are working out the salvation of the world? Be still in the Hands of God until He tempers you.

"Stop now!" says the Knife-blade to the Cutler. "I have been in the fire often enough! Would you burn the life out of me?"

But again it goes into the glowing furnace and is heated to white heat.

"Stop hammering! I have been pounded enough already."

But down comes the sledge.

"Keep me out of this cold water! One moment in the fiery furnace, and the next in ice water. It is enough to kill one!"

But in it goes.

"Keep me off the grindstone! You'll chafe the life out of me!"

But it is made to kiss the stone until the Cutler is satisfied.

Now see! You may bend it double; yet it springs back straight as an arrow. It is as bright as polished silver, hard as a diamond, and will cut like a Damascus blade. It has been shaped, tempered, and polished; it is worth something.

Be still, and let God temper and polish you, and you will be worth something, too. Allow yourself to be prepared for usefulness. He will give you a post of holy renown if you will let Him fit you for it.

Be still in the furnace fire while the Holy Ghost molds and polishes your soul. R. V. LAWRENCE

DAY 48

Dying, and yet we live on.

2 CORINTHIANS 6:9

To one who asked him the secret of service, Mr. George Müller replied: "There was a day when I died, utterly died to George Müller"—and, as he spoke, he bent lower and lower until he almost touched the floor—"to his opinions, preferences, tastes and will; died to the world, its approval or censure; died to the approval or blame of even my brethren and friends. Since then I have studied to show myself approved only unto God."

We may not understand nor know
Just how the giant oak trees throw

Their spreading branches wide,
Nor how upon the mountainside
The dainty wildflowers grow.
We may not understand nor see
Into the depth and mystery
Of suffering and tears;
Yet, through the stress of patient years
The flowers of sympathy
Spring up and scatter everywhere
Their perfume on the fragrant air—
But lo! the seed must die,
If it would bloom and multiply
And ripened fruitage bear.

THOMAS KIMBER

Look at that splendid oak! Where was it born? In a grave. The acorn was put into the ground and in that grave it sprouted and sent up its shoots. And was it only one day that it stood in the grave? No, every day for a hundred years it has stood there, and in that place of death it has found its life. *"The creation of a thousand forests is in one acorn."*

How shall my leaves fly singing in the wind unless my roots shall wither in the dark? KAHLIL GIBRAN

Feb-18th .... DAY 49 ....

I also told them about the gracious hand of my God on me.

NEHEMIAH 2:18

Is the work God's work? Has He called you to do it, and equipped you for it? Be sure on these points. Take time to consider and pray and find what the will of the Lord is. Then, when the difficulties have been considered and the needs fairly measured, and the clear conviction remains that God calls you to rise and build, then, put your hand to the plow and never look back.

Power to endure to the end—patience to outlast all discouragements—zeal that will not die out, and that will enkindle the zeal of others—all these are given and secured to him who knows that the work and call are from God.

For every worker and every work in the kingdom of God the principles are the same. The only way to avoid being repelled and discouraged in the work, so as to give it up in irritation, disgust or despair, is to get the work put upon the right lines from the very start. These must begin in the secret place of the Most High—the Holy of Holies—alone with God. They must proceed to the Holy Place, for the light and strength contained therein—the guidance and equipment needed. Then, and not till then can they safely come out, their success secure and their permanence established, because they are thus truly "wrought in God" (John 3:21 KJV). HUBERT BROOKE

While the yoke of the Lord Jesus is easy and His burden light, nevertheless the furrow that He calls us to undertake is not always by any means easy plowing. There is no yoke that fits so smoothly and handily as His, but there is no work that requires more steady trudging and persistent faithfulness than His. Three stages of that work are strikingly set forth by Hudson Taylor when he says: "Commonly there are three stages in work for God: Impossible, Difficult, Done!"

Said General William Booth, "God loves with a special love the man who has a passion for the impossible." Are you confronting today the impossible in work for God? Praise Him for that, because you are in a way to discover the blessing of finding that work difficult, and then to experience the deep joy of finding it done, by the same Lord who started you on the furrow.

Am I Thy friend?
And canst Thou count on me,
Lord, to be true to Thee?
Canst Thou depend
On sympathy and help of mine,

In purpose, aim,
Or work of Thine,
And trust me with the honor of Thy name?

DAY 50

Feb-19th

You will sing.

ISAIAH 30:29

Someone writes of sitting one winter evening by an open wood fire, and listening to the singing of the green logs as the fire flamed about them. All manner of sounds came out of the wood as it burned, and the writer, with poetic fancy, suggests that they were imprisoned songs, long sleeping in silence in the wood, brought out now by the fire.

When the tree stood in the forest the birds came and sat on its boughs and sang their songs. The wind, too, breathed through the branches making a weird, strange music. One day a child sat on the moss by the tree's root and sang its happy gladness in a snatch of sweet melody. A penitent sat under the tree's shade and with trembling tones, amid falling leaves, sang the fifty-first Psalm. And all these notes of varied song sank into the tree as it stood there, and hid away in its trunk. There they slept until the tree was cut down and part of it became a backlog in the cheerful evening fire. Then the flames brought out the music.

This is but a poet's fancy as far as the tree and the songs of the backlog are concerned. But is there not here a little parable which may be likened to many a human life? Life has its varied notes and tones—some glad, some choked in tears. Years pass and the life gives out no music of praise, sings no songs to bless others. But, at length, grief comes, and in the flames the long-imprisoned music is set free and sings its praise to God and its notes of love to cheer and bless the world. Gathered in life's long summer and stored away in the heart, it is given out in the hours of suffering and pain.

Many a rejoicing Christian never learned to sing till the flames kindled upon him. J. R. MILLER

Gather the driftwood that will light the winter fire!

DAY 51

I am with you always, to the very end of the age.

MATTHEW 28:20

Many with lacerated feet have come back to tell the story and to testify that when the very foundations of earth seemed giving way, He remained whom no accident could take away, no chance ever change. This is the power of the Great Companionship.

Stretched on a rack, where they were torturing him piteously, one of the martyrs saw with cleansed and opened eyes, a Young Man by his side—not yet fifty years old—who kept wiping the beads of sweat from his brow.

When the fire is hottest, He is there. "And the form of the fourth is like the Son of God" (Dan. 3:25 KJV). "He that is near Me is near the fire." That is why the heart of the Divine furnace is the place of the soul's deepest peace. There is always one beside us when we go through the fire.

When John G. Paton stood beside that lonely grave in the South Sea Islands; when he with his own hands made his wife's coffin, and with his own hands dug her grave, the savages were looking on. They had never seen it in this fashion. That man must fill in the sepulcher, and soon leave it. He says, "If it had not been for Jesus and the Presence that He vouchsafed me there, I would have gone mad and died beside that lonely grave." But John G. Paton found his Master with him through the dire darkness.

Sir Ernest Shackleton and two of his companions spent thirty-six hours among the snow mountains of New Georgia, seeking for a station that meant life or death to them and their waiting crew on Elephant Island. Writing of that journey, he says, "It seemed to me, often, that we were four, not three."

He refers to the "guiding Presence" that went with them. Then in closing he writes, "A record of our journey would be incomplete without a reference to a subject so near to our hearts."

Paul was not peculiarly privileged when he saw the Living One while in route to Damascus.

Kahlil Gibran, the Syrian, explaining his remarkable modern painting of Jesus, said: "Last night I saw His face again, clearer than I have ever seen it."

Handel, composer of the "Hallelujah Chorus," declared: "I did see God on His throne."

During the terrible stress of war many affirmed positively that they saw "The White Comrade."

Phillips Brooks testified, "He is here. I know Him. He knows me. It is not a figure of speech. It is the realest thing in the world."

No distant Lord have I,
Loving afar to be;
Made flesh for me, He cannot rest
Until He rests in me.
Brother in joy or pain,
Bone of my bone was He;
Now—intimacy closer still—
He dwells Himself in me.
I need not journey far,
This dearest Friend to see;
Companionship is always mine,
He makes His home with me.

MALTBIE D. BABCOCK

Feb 21st

DAY 52

What if some were unfaithful? Will their unfaithfulness nullify God's faithfulness?

ROMANS 3:3

I suspect that the source of every bit of sorrow in my life can be traced to simple unbelief. If I truly believe the past is totally forgiven, the present is supplied with power, and the future is bright with hope, how could I be anything but completely happy?

Yes, the future is bright, because of God's faithfulness. His abiding truth does not change with my mood, and He never wavers when I stumble and fall over a promise of His through my unbelief. His faithfulness stands firm and as prominent as mountain peaks of pearl splitting the clouds of eternity. And each base of His hills is rooted at an unfathomable depth on the rock of God.

Mont Blanc does not disappear, becoming a passing vision or a whimsical mist, simply because a climber grows dizzy on its slopes. JAMES SMETHAM

Is it any wonder that we do not receive God's blessing after stumbling over His promise through unbelief? I am not saying that faith merits an answer or that we can work to earn it. But God Himself has made believing a condition of receiving, and the Giver has a sovereign right to choose His own terms for His gifts. SAMUEL HART

Unbelief continually asks, "How can this be possible?" It is always full of "hows," yet faith needs only one great answer to even ten thousand "hows." That answer is—GOD! C. H. M.

No one accomplishes so much in so little time as when he or she is praying. And the following thought certainly aligns well with all that the Lord Jesus Christ taught on prayer: If only one believer with total faith rises up, the history of the world will be changed.

Will you be that one to rise up, submitting yourself to the sovereignty and guidance of God our Father? A. E. MCADAM

Prayer without faith quickly degenerates into an aimless routine or heartless hypocrisy. However, prayer with faith brings the omnipotence of God to the support of our petitions. It is better not to pray until your entire being responds to, and understands, the power of prayer. When genuine prayer is even whispered, earth and heaven, and the past and future, say, "Amen!"

This is the kind of prayer Christ prayed. P. C. M.

Nothing lies beyond the reach of prayer except those things outside the will of God.

DAY 53

Stormy winds that do his bidding.

PSALM 148:8

Did you ever go into the woods late in the afternoon on a day of howling wind and driving rain; and did you ever see a drearier spectacle, or hear drearier sounds? The sough of the winds through the almost bare branches, the drip, drip of the rain upon the masses of withered leaves, the air filled with flying leaves fluttering down in the gloom of the forest as into a grave, the delicate colors of trunk and moss all changed and stained and blended by the soaking of the rain: how hard to believe that such dreariness is related in any way to the beauty of the summer forest!

And yet we know that it is that very wind which is rocking the trees and howling so dismally—just that streaming rain and those rotting leaves which will help to clothe the forest trees next year with verdure, and to make the woods sing with joy and pulsate with life. All winds and weathers are favorable to the development of the sturdy, well-rooted tree; even the hurricane which strips it of its leaves and branches quickens all its vital powers, challenging it to put forth greater strength.

If the tree is cut down in part, the result is a sturdier trunk and a more compact and symmetrical growth. Even if it is toppled over by a storm, its acorns are scattered and become the seeds of the forest. In its ruin it goes back to the soil from which spring other trees.

So you are better and purer and stronger today because of the tears and the sighing and the desolation. You know, and the world knows, that your life is richer, better poised, more trustful, less selfish, more detached from the things of sense—that the whole atmosphere is somehow purer and more vitalizing.

"Stormy winds that do his bidding," and the soul that hears in their tumult the rustling of Almighty Wings praises God for the storm—the storm that swings free from enervating ease; the flood that casts upon the Eternal Rock.

Storms make a strong tree—Sufferings make a strong saint!

DAY 54

Summon your power, God; show us your strength.

PSALM 68:28

The Lord imparts to me the underlying strength of character that gives me the necessary energy and decision-making ability to live my life. He strengthens me "with power through his Spirit in [my] inner being" (Eph. 3:16). And the strength He gives is continuous, for He is a source of power I cannot exhaust.

"Your strength will equal your days" (Deut. 33:25)—my strength of will, affection, judgment, ideals, and achievement will last a lifetime.

"The Lord is my strength" (Ex. 15:2) to go on. He gives me the power to walk the long, straight, and level path, even when the monotonous way has no turns or curves offering pleasant surprises and when my spirit is depressed with the terrible drudgery.

"The Lord is my strength" to go up. He is my power to climb the straight and narrow path up the Hill of Difficulty, as Christian did in Pilgrim's Progress, and not be afraid.

"The Lord is my strength" to go down. It is often once I leave the invigorating heights, where the wind and sunlight have surrounded me, and begin to descend to the more confining, humid, and stifling heat of the valley below that my heart grows faint. In fact, I recently heard someone say, referring to his own increasing physical frailty, "It is coming down that tires me most!"

"The Lord is my strength" to sit still. And what a difficult accomplishment this is! I often say to others during those times when I am compelled to be still, "If only I could do something!" I feel like the mother who stands by her sick child but is powerless to heal. What a severe test! Yet to do nothing except to sit still and wait requires tremendous strength.

"The Lord is my strength!" "Our competence comes from God" (2 Cor. 3:5). THE SILVER LINING

DAY 55

With God nothing shall be impossible.

LUKE 1:37 KJV

Those who have had the joy of climbing the Swiss mountains in springtime will have learned to love the Soldanella, with its delicate little mauve bells. Many years ago there appeared a booklet by Lilias Trotter, "The Glory of the Impossible," with a sketch of this little plant just above the snow. We have never forgotten her exquisite application of the lesson, as she traced the power of this fragile plant to melt its way through the icy covering into the sunshine overhead.

We love to see the impossible done and so does God!

"Canst thou prevail
To pierce the snow?
Thou art so frail,
And icy winds do blow!"

"I will lift up my head
And trusting, onward go."
"Now hard as rock
Frozen and dry,
Thy strength to mock,
What profits it to try?
The snow will bar thy way."
"On God I will rely."
"Thou art so weak,
Tender and fair,
Why not go, seek a balmier softer air?"
"God chose my lot for me,
And will sustain me there."
"Wilt thou keep on? Alas! the fight is stern from dawn till eve."
"'Tis not by might the victory is won;
God puts my foes to flight."
And now above in blaze of day,
Wonder of love,
We see the flower and say, "Naught is impossible To him who trusts always."

J. B. L. JUST TRUSTING

The incense buds of the kiku (chrysanthemum) will open even in the frost. JAPANESE PROVERB

DAY 56

There before me was a door standing open in heaven.

REVELATION 4:1

We should remember that John wrote these words while on the island of Patmos. He was there "because of the word of God and the testimony of Jesus" (Rev. 1:9). He had been banished to this island, which was an isolated, rocky, and inhospitable prison. Yet it was here, under difficult circumstances—separated from all his loved ones in Ephesus, excluded from worshiping with the church, and condemned to only the companionship of unpleasant fellow captives—that he was granted this vision as a special privilege. It was as a prisoner that he saw "a door standing open in heaven."

We should also remember Jacob, who laid down in the desert to sleep after leaving his father's house. "He had a dream in which he saw a stairway resting on the earth, with its top reaching to heaven, and . . . above it stood the LORD" (Gen. 28:12–13).

The doors of heaven have been opened not only for these two men but also for many others. And in the world's estimation, it seems as if their circumstances were utterly unlikely to receive such revelations. Yet how often we have seen "a door standing open in heaven" for those who are prisoners and captives, for those who suffer from a chronic illness and are bound with iron chains of pain to a bed of sickness, for those who wander the earth in lonely isolation, and for those who are kept from the Lord's house by the demands of home and family.

But there are conditions to seeing the open door. We must know what it is to be "in the Spirit" (Rev. 1:10). We must be "pure in heart" (Matt. 5:8) and obedient in faith. We must be willing to "consider everything a loss because of the surpassing worth of knowing Christ Jesus" (Phil. 3:8). Then once God is everything to us, so that "in him we live and move and have our being" (Acts 17:28), the door to heaven will stand open before us as well.

God has His mountains bleak and bare,
Where He does bid us rest awhile;
Cliffs where we breathe a purer air,
Lone peaks that catch the day's first smile.
God has His deserts broad and brown—
A solitude—a sea of sand,
Where He does let heaven's curtain down,
Unveiled by His Almighty hand.

Feb 26th

DAY 57

Thy people shall be willing in the day of thy power, in the beauties of holiness from the womb of the morning: thou hast the dew of thy youth.

PSALM 110:3 KJV

This is what the term consecration properly means. It is the voluntary surrender or self-offering of the heart, by the constraint of love to be the Lord's. Its glad expression is "I am my beloved's" (Song of Songs 6:3).

It must spring, of course, from faith. There must be the full confidence that we are safe in this abandonment; that we are not falling over a precipice, or surrendering ourselves to the hands of a judge, but that we are sinking into the Father's arms and stepping into an infinite inheritance. Oh, it is an infinite inheritance! Oh, it is an infinite privilege to be permitted thus to give ourselves up to One who pledges Himself to make us all that we would love to be; nay, all that His infinite wisdom, power, and love will delight to accomplish in us!

It is the clay yielding itself to the potter's hands, that it may be shaped into a vessel of honor, meet for the Master's use.

It is the poor street waif consenting to become the child of a prince, that he may be educated and provided for; that he may be prepared to inherit all the wealth of his guardian. DAYS OF HEAVEN UPON EARTH

He ventured all: the loss of place, and power, and love of kin—
O bitter loss! O loneliness and pain!
He gained the Christ! Who would not dare the loss
Such priceless bliss to win?
Christ for today, and each tomorrow—Christ!

J. MANNINGTON DEXTER

Make a supreme consecration!

DAY 58

He said to me: "It is done."

REVELATION 21:6

How many persons are everlastingly doing, but how few ever get through with it! How few settle a thing and know that it is accomplished and can say, "It is done"!

The moment we really believe, we are conscious that there is power. We can touch God at such times, and the fire in our souls makes us sure that something is settled forever.

Faith must be a clear-cut taking hold of God; a grasping Him with fingers of iron, with an uncompromising commitment of all to God. In learning to float you must utterly abandon yourself to the water; you must believe that the water is able to hold you up. So you must take this step of commitment, and then look up to God with confidence and say, "It is done." Our part is to commit; God's part is to work. The very moment that we commit, that very moment He undertakes. We must believe that He has undertaken what we have committed. Faith must re-echo God's promise and dare to say, "It is done."

The thing is as good as done, since He has taken it in hand.

Step out upon a bare promise right now, and "calleth those things which be not as though they were" (Rom. 4:17 KJV), and God will make your reckoning real. It will be done by actual experience. DAYS OF HEAVEN UPON EARTH

My old professor, Lord Kelvin, once said in class a very striking thing. He said that there came a point in all his great discoveries when he had to take a leap into the dark. And nobody who is afraid of such a leap from the solid ground of what is demonstrated will know the exhilaration of believing!

To commit ourselves unreservedly to Christ is just the biggest venture in the world! The wonderful thing is that when, with a certain daring, we take Lord Kelvin's "leap into the dark" we discover it is not dark at all, but life abundant, and liberty and peace. GEORGE H. MORRISON

Believe that it is settled because God says so!

Feb 28th DAY 59

Then there came a voice from above the vault . . .
as they stood with lowered wings.

EZEKIEL 1:25

If in God's starry universe there throbbed
No heart but His and mine, I would not plod
With eyes earthbound, hungry of soul, and robbed
Of a sweet sense of nearness to my God.
For mystic notes that issue from His soul
Would wing their shining way in singing showers
Into my waiting heart, when spared the toll
Of intercourse with men that wastes my powers.
Alone with God! My soul, invite the art,
As One who climbed the heights alone to pray,
And in the gentle stillness, heart to heart,
Let Heaven's dew transform this house of clay.

Oh, God is everywhere. Yes, God is here!
Only my faith is dim . . . the world too near.

EDITH ALICE BANG

In the silences I make in the midst of the turmoil of life I have appointments with God. From these silences I come forth with spirit refreshed, and with a renewed sense of power. I hear a Voice in the silences, and become increasingly aware that it is the Voice of God.

Oh, how comfortable is a little glimpse of God! DAVID BRAINERD

DAY 60

I heard a hushed voice.

JOB 4:16

Some twenty years ago a friend gave me a book entitled *True Peace.* It had an old medieval message and this one primary thought—that God was waiting in the depths of my being to speak to me if I would only be still enough to hear His voice.

I assumed this would not be a difficult thing to do, so I tried to be still. No sooner had I begun to do so than complete pandemonium seemed to break loose. Suddenly I heard a thousand voices and sounds from without and within, until I could hear nothing except these incredible noises. Some were my own words, my own questions, and even my own prayers, while others were temptations of the Enemy, and the voices of the world's turmoil.

In every direction I turned, I was pushed, pulled, and confronted with indescribable unrest and overwhelming noises. I seemed compelled to listen to some of them and to respond in some way. But God said, "Be still, and know that I am God" (Ps. 46:10). Then my mind was filled with worries over my responsibilities and plans for tomorrow, and God said again, "Be still."

As I listened and slowly learned to obey, I shut my ears to every other sound. Soon I discovered that once the other voices ceased, or once I ceased to hear them, "a gentle whisper" (1 Kings 19:12) began to speak in the depths of my being. And it spoke to me with an inexpressible tenderness, power, and comfort.

This "gentle whisper" became for me the voice of prayer, wisdom, and service. No longer did I need to work so hard to think, pray, or trust, because the Holy Spirit's "gentle whisper" in my heart was God's prayer in the secret places of my soul. It was His answer to all my questions, and His life and strength for my soul and body. His voice became the essence of all knowledge, prayer, and blessings, for it was the living God Himself as my life and my all.

This is precisely how our spirit drinks in the life of our risen Lord. And then we are enabled to face life's conflicts and responsibilities, like a flower that has absorbed the cool and refreshing drops of dew through the darkness of the night. Yet just as dew never falls on a stormy night, the dew of His grace never covers a restless soul. A. B. SIMPSON

DAY 61

Having disarmed the powers and authorities, he made a public spectacle of them, triumphing over them.

COLOSSIANS 2:15

Here Satan is represented as a conquered foe, and even as a degraded antagonist. He has been "disarmed." One is reminded of the figure of a scarecrow on a farmer's field where the dead birds are hung up as warnings against other depredators. He cannot harm us although he may alarm us. He is beaten before the battle begins. We enter the fray with the prestige of victors. Let us hold this high place as we meet our adversary. Let us treat him as a defeated enemy. Let us not honor him by our doubts and fears. It is not our valor or our victory. It is our confidence in Christ, the Victor, that wins.

"This is the victory that has overcome the world, even our faith" (1 John 5:4). Our triumph has already been won by our Leader, but we must identify ourselves with His victory. Let us never dare to doubt!

"And the hostile princes and rulers He shook off from Himself, and boldly displayed them as His conquests, when by the Cross He triumphed over them" (Col. 2:15 WNT).

Says Dr. Weymouth: "Stand your ground in the day of battle, and having fought to the end, remain victors on the field!" "Victors on the field"—I am thrilled by the inspiring word. After every temptation—the temptation which comes to me in sunshine or the temptation that comes to me in the gloom—after every fight, victors on the field, the Lord's banner flying, and the evil one and all his hosts in utter rout, and in full and dire retreat! J. H. JOWETT

Describing the force of the waves which beat on the Eddystone Lighthouse, a writer says: "But without a quiver the lighthouse supports those terrible attacks. Yet it bends toward them as if to render homage to the power of its adversaries."

Let us meet the storms of life with the fixedness and plasticity with which the lighthouse overcomes the wild tempest.

Fastened to the Rock of Ages, I shall not be moved.

DAY 62

My words . . . will come true at their proper time.

LUKE 1:20

The Lord is sure to accomplish those things
A loving heart has waited long to see;
Those words will be fulfilled to which she clings,
Because her God has promised faithfully;

And, knowing Him, she ne'er can doubt His Word;
He speaks and it is done. The mighty Lord!
The Lord is sure to accomplish those things,
O burdened heart, rest ever in His care;
In quietness beneath His shadowing wings
Await the answer to your longing prayer.
When you have "cast your cares," the heart then sings,
The Lord is sure to accomplish those things.
The Lord is sure to accomplish those things,
O tired heart, believe and wait and pray;
Peacefully, the evening chime still rings,
Though cloud and rain and storm have filled the day.
Faith pierces through the mist of doubt that bars
The coming night sometimes, and finds the stars.
The Lord is sure to accomplish those things,
O trusting heart, the Lord to you has told;
Let Faith and Hope arise, and lift their wings,
To soar toward the sunrise clouds of gold;
The doorways of the rosy dawn swing wide,
Revealing joys the darkness of night did hide.

BESSIE PORTER

Matthew Henry said, "We can depend on God to fulfill His promise, even when all the roads leading to it are closed. 'For no matter how many promises God has made, they are "Yes" in Christ. And so through him the "Amen" [so be it] is spoken by us to the glory of God' [2 Cor. 1:20]."

March 4th

DAY 63

My faithful God, answer me when I call out to you. Give me rest from my trouble. Have mercy on me. Hear my prayer.

PSALM 4:1 NIRV

It is a little thing to trust God as far as we can see Him, as far as the way lies open before us; but to trust Him when we are hedged in on every side and can see no way to escape, this is good and acceptable with God. This is the faith of Abraham, our father.

"Under . . . hopeless circumstances he hopefully believed" (Rom. 4:18 WNT).

Abraham Lincoln, during the Civil War, once said: "I have been driven many times to my knees by the overwhelming conviction that I had nowhere else to go. My own wisdom and that of all about me seemed insufficient for the day."

The greatest men, without God, are nothing but dismal failures.

The devil may wall you 'round
But he cannot roof you in;
He may fetter your feet and tie your hands
And strive to hamper your soul with bands
As his way has ever been;
But he cannot hide the face of God
And the Lord shall be your light,
And your eyes and your thoughts can rise to the sky,
Where His clouds and His winds and His birds go by,
And His stars shine out at night.
The devil may wall you 'round;
He may rob you of all things dear,
He may bring his hardest and roughest stone
And thinks to cage you and keep you alone,

But he may not press too near;
For the Lord has planted a hedge inside,
And has made it strong and tall,
A hedge of living and growing green;
And ever it mounts and keeps between
The trusting soul and the devil's wall.
The devil may wall you 'round,
But the Lord's hand covers you,
And His hedge is a thick and thorny hedge,
And the devil can find no entering wedge
Nor get his finger through;
He may circle about you all day long,
But he cannot work as he would,
For the will of the Lord restrains his hand,
And he cannot pass the Lord's command
And his evil turns to good.
The devil may wall you 'round,
With his gray stones, row on row,
But the green of the hedge is fresh and fair,
And within its circle is space to spare,
And room for your soul to grow;
The wall that shuts you in
May be hard and high and stout,
But the Lord is sun and the Lord is dew,
And His hedge is coolness and shade for you,
And no wall can shut Him out.

ANNIE JOHNSON FLINT

DAY 64

When you walk, your steps will not be hampered;
when you run, you will not stumble.

PROVERBS 4:12

The Lord only builds a bridge of faith directly under the feet of a faithful traveler. He never builds the bridge a few steps ahead, for then it would not be one of faith. "We live by faith, not by sight" (2 Cor. 5:7).

Years ago automatic gates were sometimes used on country roads. They would securely block the road as a vehicle approached, and if the traveler stopped before coming to the gate, it would not open. But if the traveler drove straight toward it, the weight of the vehicle would compress the springs below the roadway, and the gate would swing back to let him pass. The vehicle had to keep moving forward, or the gate would remain closed.

This illustrates the way to pass through every barrier that blocks the road of service for God. Whether the barrier is a river, a mountain, or a gate, all a child of Jesus must do is head directly toward it. If it is a river, it will dry up as he comes near it, as long as he still forges ahead. If it is a mountain, it will be removed and "cast into the sea" (Mark 11:23 KJV), providing he approaches it with unflinching confidence.

Is some great barrier blocking your path of service right now? Then head straight for it, in the name of the Lord, and it will no longer be there. HENRY CLAY TRUMBULL

We sit and weep in vain, while the voice of the Almighty tells us to never stop moving upward and onward. Let us advance boldly, whether it is dark and we can barely see the forest in front of us, or our road leads us through the mountain pass, where from any vantage point we can only see a few steps ahead.

Press on! And if necessary, like the ancient Israelites we will find a pillar of clouds and fire to lead the way on our journey through the wilderness. God will provide guides and inns along the road, and we will discover food, clothing, and friends at every stage of our journey. And as Samuel Rutherford, the great Scottish minister, once stated so simply, "Whatever happens, the worst will only be a weary traveler receiving a joyful and heavenly welcome home."

I'm going by the upper road, for that still holds the sun,
I'm climbing through night's pastures where the starry rivers run:
If you should think to seek me in my old dark abode,
You'll find this writing on the door,
"He's on the Upper Road."

DAY 65

Your true and proper worship. Your reasonable service.

ROMANS 12:1 NIV; KJV

Why are we saved? We are saved in order to be sacrificed. There is a striking lesson in God's saving certain of the clean beasts and clean fowl at the time of the flood. At God's direction, Noah brought these, as well as other beasts and fowl that were not clean, into the ark of salvation. These clean creatures were favored above those that were lost in the flood. It must have been a wonderful experience to step out from the ark onto dry land again. But what happened then?

"Then Noah built an altar to the Lord and, taking some of all the clean animals and clean birds, he sacrificed burnt offerings on it" (Gen. 8:20).

Thus it appears that certain of these creatures were saved in order to be sacrificed after their salvation was complete. If this surprises us, have we realized that we who believe in Christ are saved for exactly that purpose?

"I urge you, brothers and sisters, in view of God's mercy, to offer your bodies as a living sacrifice" (Rom. 12:1).

This is acceptable unto God, and it is our reasonable service.

Noah's sacrifice of the clean animals brought great blessing to the earth, as the record goes on to show us; and the "living sacrifice" of God's children brings great blessing to mankind.

Let us thank God, indeed, that we are saved to be sacrificed. SUNDAY SCHOOL TIMES

Laid on Thine altar, O my Lord, Divine,
Accept this day my gift for Jesus' sake.
I have no jewels to adorn Thy shrine,
Nor any world-famed sacrifice to make;
But here I bring within my trembling hand
This will of mine: a thing that seemeth small;
And only Thou dear Lord, canst understand
That when I yield Thee this, I yield Thee all.
It hath been wet with tears and dimmed with sighs,
Clenched in my clasp, till beauty it hath none.
Now from Thy footstool, where it vanquished lies,
The prayer ascendeth: "Let Thy will be done."
Take it, O Father, ere my courage fail,
And blend it so with Thine own will, that e'en
If in some desperate hour my cry prevail,
And Thou giv'st back my gift, it may have been
So changed, so purified, so fair have grown,
So one with Thee, so filled with peace Divine,
I may not know nor feel it as my own,
But gaining back my will may find it Thine.
All I have I am bringing to Thee!

DAY 66

When a farmer plows for planting, does he plow continually?

ISAIAH 28:24

One day in early summer I walked past a lovely meadow. The grass was as soft, thick, and beautiful as an immense green oriental rug. At one end of the meadow stood a fine old tree that served as a sanctuary for countless wild birds, whose happy songs seemed to fill the crisp, sweet air. I saw two cows who lay in the shade as the very picture of contentment. And down by the road, eye-catching dandelions mingled their gold with the royal purple of the wild violets. I leaned against the fence for a long time, feasting my hungry eyes and thinking in my soul that God never made a more beautiful place than this lovely meadow.

The next day I passed that way again, and to my great dismay, the hand of the destroyer had been there. A farmer with a large tractor, which was now sitting idle in the meadow, had in one day inflicted terrible devastation. Instead of seeing the soft, green grass, I now saw the ugly, bare, and brown earth. Gone were the dandelions and the pretty violets. And instead of the multitude of singing birds, there were now only a few, who were industriously scratching the ground for worms. In my grief I said, "How could anyone spoil something so beautiful?"

Then suddenly my eyes were opened, as if by some unseen hand, and I saw a vision. The vision was that of a field of ripe corn ready for harvest. I could see the giant, heavily laden stalks in the autumn sun, and I could almost hear the music of the wind as it swept across the golden tassels. And before I realized it, the bare earth took on a splendor it did not have the day before.

Oh, if only we would always catch the vision of the abundant harvest when the great Master Farmer comes, as He often does, to plow through our very souls—uprooting and turning under that which we thought most beautiful and leaving only the bare and the unlovely before our agonizing eyes.

Why should I be frightened and surprised by the plow of the Lord, which makes deep furrows in my soul? I know He is not some arbitrary or irrational farmer—His purpose is to yield a harvest. SAMUEL RUTHERFORD

March 8th

DAY 67

They are the ones who will dwell on the heights,
whose refuge will be the mountain fortress. . . . Your
eyes will . . . view a land that stretches afar.

ISAIAH 33:16–17

Up yonder on the rocky cliff in a rough nest of sticks lies an egg. The eagle's breast-feathers warm it; the sky bends down and invites it; the abysses of the air beckon it, saying: All our heights and depths are for you; come and occupy them.

And all the peaks and the roomy places up under the rafters of the sky, where the twinkling stars sit sheltered like twittering sparrows, call down to the pent-up little life, "Come up hither!" and the live germ inside hears through the thin walls of its prison, and is coaxed out of its shell, and out of the nest, and off the cliff, and then up and away into the wide ranges of sunlit air, and down into the deep gulfs that gash mountains apart. A PILGRIM OF THE INFINITE

I stand upon the mount of God
With sunlight in my soul;
I hear the storms in vales beneath,
I hear the thunders roll.
But I am calm with Thee, my God,
Beneath these glorious skies;
And to the height on which I stand,
No storms, nor clouds, can rise.

Oh, this is life! Oh, this is joy!
My God, to find Thee so;
Thy face to see, Thy voice to hear,
And all Thy love to know.

HORATIUS BONAR

DAY 68

The revelation awaits an appointed time. . . . Though it linger, wait for it; it will certainly come and will not delay.

HABAKKUK 2:3

In the captivating booklet Expectation Corner, one of the characters, Adam Slowman, was led into the Lord's treasure house. Among the many wonders revealed to him there was the "Delayed Blessing Office," where God stored the answers to certain prayers until it was wise to send them.

For some who pray expecting an answer, it takes a long time to learn that delays of answers are not denials. In fact, in the "Delayed Blessing Office," there are deep secrets of love and wisdom that we have never imagined! We tend to want to pick our blessings from the tree while they are still green, yet God wants us to wait until they are fully ripe.

"The Lord longs to be gracious to you. . . . Blessed are all who wait for him!" (Isa. 30:18). The Lord watches over us in all the difficult places, and He will not allow even one trial that is too much for us. He will use His refining fire to burn away our impurities and will then gloriously come to our rescue.

Do not grieve Him by doubting His love. Instead, lift up your eyes and begin praising Him right now for the deliverance that is on its way to you. Then you will be abundantly rewarded for the delay that has tried your faith.

O you of little faith,
God has not failed you yet!
When all looks dark and gloomy,
You do so soon forget—
Forget that He has led you,
And gently cleared your way;
On clouds has poured His sunshine,
And turned your night to day.
And if He's helped you to this point,
He will not fail you now;
How it must wound His loving heart
To see your anxious brow!
Oh! doubt not any longer,
To Him commit your way,
Whom in the past you trusted,
And is just the same today.

DAY 69

I will not fear though tens of thousands assail me on every side.

PSALM 3:6

Evening. Felt much turmoil of spirit, in prospect of having all my plans for the welfare of this great region and this teeming population, knocked on the head tomorrow. But I read that Jesus said: "All power is given unto me in heaven and in earth. Go ye therefore, and teach all nations. . . . and, lo, I am with you always, even unto the end of the world" (Matt. 28:18–20 KJV)! It is the word of a Gentleman, of the strictest and most sacred honor. So there's an end of it! I will not cross furtively tonight as I intended. Should such a man as I flee? Nay, verily, I shall take observations for latitude and longitude tonight, though they may be the last. I feel quite calm now, thank God! DIARY OF DAVID LIVINGSTONE

During the terrible days of the Boxer uprising in China, as one report followed another of mission stations destroyed and missionaries massacred, Hudson Taylor sat quietly at his desk singing softly the hymn he loved so dearly: Jesus, I am resting, resting, In the joy of what Thou art.

When our confidence is in God, we may be superior to circumstances. "If God is for us, who can be against us?" (Rom. 8:31). However impossible it may seem to the reasoning of the earthly-minded, it is nevertheless a blessed reality to the trustful child of God, that "Faith can sing through days of sorrow: 'All, all is well!'"

"Though I was afraid of many things," said John Buchan, "the thing I feared most mortally was being afraid."

Fierce was the wild billow,
Dark was the night;
Oars labored heavily;
Foam glimmered white.
Trembled the mariners,
Peril was night;
Then said the God of Gods,
"Peace! It is I."
Ridge of the mountain wave,
Lower thy crest.
Wail of the stormy wind,
Be thou at rest.
Peril there none can be;
Sorrow must fly,
Where saith the Light of Life, "Peace! It is I."

Come into port greatly, or sail with God the seas! RALPH WALDO EMERSON

March 11th

DAY 70

I am now going to allure her; I will lead her into the [desert]. . . . There I will give her back her vineyards.

HOSEA 2:14–15

The desert is certainly a strange place to find vineyards! Can it be true that the riches of life that we need can be found in the desert—a place that symbolizes loneliness, and through which we can seldom find our way? Not only is this true but verse 15 goes on to say, "I . . . will make the Valley of Achor a door of hope. There she will [sing] as in the days of her youth." "Achor" means "troubled," yet the Valley of Achor is called "a door of hope."

Yes, God knows our need for a desert experience. He knows exactly where and how to produce enduring qualities in us. The person who has been idolatrous, has been rebellious, has forgotten God, and has said with total self-will, "I will go after my lovers" (Hos. 2:5), will find her path blocked by God. "She will chase after her lovers but not catch them; she will look for them but not find them" (Hos. 2:7). And once she feels totally hopeless and abandoned, God will say, "I am now going to allure her; I will lead her into the [desert] and speak tenderly to her."

What a loving God we have!

We never know where God has hidden His streams. We see a large stone and have no idea that it covers the source of a spring. We see a rocky area and never imagine that it is hiding a fountain. God leads me into hard and difficult places, and it is there I realize I am where eternal streams abide.

DAY 71

I consider that our present sufferings are not worth comparing with the glory that will be revealed in us.

ROMANS 8:18

For developing character an imperfect man needs the stimulus and discipline of a developing environment, not yet perfected—a world of struggle and resistance: obstacles to be overcome, battles to be won, baffling problems to be solved. He needs not a soft world of ease to lull him to sleep, but a changing environment of action and reaction: cold and heat, summer and winter, sunshine and shadow, light and darkness, pleasure and pain, prosperity and adversity.

As Dr. Hillis said: "He who would ask release from suffering would take the winter out of the seasons, the glory of the night out of the round of day, the cloud and rainstorms out of the summer; would expel the furrows from the face of Lincoln; would rob Socrates of his dignity and majesty; would make Saint Paul a mere esthetic feeling; would steal the sweetness from maternity; would rob the Divine Sufferer of His sanctity."

When the little girl told her music teacher that it hurt her fingers to practice the piano, the teacher answered: "I know it hurts, but it strengthens them, too." Then the child packed the philosophy of the ages in her reply: "Teacher, it seems that everything that strengthens, hurts."

God never wastes His children's pain!

God loves much those whom He trusts with sorrow, and designs some precious soul enrichment which comes only through the channel of suffering.

There are things which even God cannot do for us unless He allows us to suffer. He cannot have the result of the process without the process.

If you are among "them that love God" (Rom. 8:28 KJV), all things are yours! The stars in their courses fight for you. Every wind that blows can only fill your sails.

God does not test worthless souls!

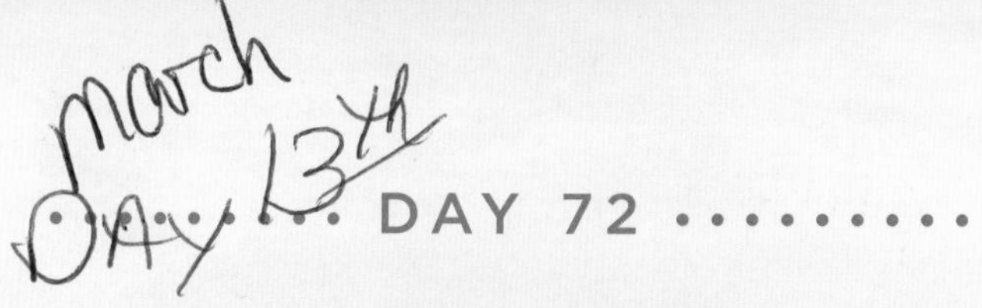

DAY 72

We do not know what to do, but our eyes are on you.

2 CHRONICLES 20:12

An Israelite named Uzzah lost his life because he "reached out and took hold of the ark of God" (2 Sam. 6:6). He placed his hands on it with the best of intentions—to steady it, "because the oxen stumbled" (2 Sam. 6:6)—but nevertheless, he had overstepped his bounds by touching the Lord's work, and "therefore God struck him down" (2 Sam. 6:7). Living a life of faith often requires us to leave things alone.

If we have completely entrusted something to God, we must keep our hands off it. He can guard it better than we can, and He does not need our help. "Be still before the LORD and wait patiently for him; do not fret when people succeed in their ways, when they carry out their wicked schemes" (Ps. 37:7).

Things in our lives may seem to be going all wrong, but God knows our circumstances better than we do. And He will work at the perfect moment, if we will completely trust Him to work in His own way and in His own time. Often there is nothing as godly as inactivity on our part, or nothing as harmful as restless working, for God has promised to work His sovereign will. A. B. SIMPSON

Being perplexed, I say,
"Lord, make it right!
Night is as day to You,
Darkness as light.
I am afraid to touch
Things that involve so much;
My trembling hand may shake,
My skilless hand may break;
Yours can make no mistake."
Being in doubt I say,

"Lord, make it plain;
Which is the true, safe way?
Which would be gain?
I am not wise to know,
Nor sure of foot to go;
What is so clear to Thee,
Lord, make it clear to me!"

It is such a comfort to drop the entanglements and perplexities of life into God's hands and leave them there.

DAY 73

He performeth the thing that is appointed for me.

JOB 23:14 KJV

Let us have confidence in the purposes of God. The thought occurs in the writings of Goulburn, Adolph Monod, and others, that the Lord owed that wonderful calmness which marked His life—a calmness which never forsook Him, whether teaching, or traveling, however engaged, however tried—very much to the fact that His Father had a plan for Him; not a plan for a lifetime merely, but a plan for each day; and that He had but to discover what the plan was, and then carry it out; and so, however puzzling and perplexing the maze of duties through which He had to thread His way, nothing ever perplexed or puzzled Him, because, putting His hand in His Father's, He just walked in the paths prepared for Him.

Well, now, what if God should have a plan for everyone? What if God should have a plan for you? In such a case—surely it is the true case—everything we have to do, everything we have to bear, comes to us as part of a prearranged plan. Things that disturb our work, things that upset our purposes, things that thwart our wishes, interruptions, annoyances—these may all be a part of the plan—God's plan—and should be met accordingly. LIVING WATERS

I doubt not through the ages One Eternal purpose runs.

There's a throne above the world. There's a Man on the throne. He has a plan for things down here during this time of turmoil and strife. His Spirit is down here to get that plan done. He needs each one of us. He puts His Hand on each Christian life and says, "Separate yourself from all else for the bit I need you to do." His Hand is on you. Are you doing it? Anything else classes as failure. THE BENT-KNEE TIME BY S. D. GORDON

DAY 74

He made me into a polished arrow.

ISAIAH 49:2

Pebble Beach, on the California coast, has become quite famous for the beautiful pebbles found there. The raging white surf continually roars, thundering and pounding against the rocks on the shore. These stones are trapped in the arms of the merciless waves. They are tossed, rolled, rubbed together, and ground against the sharp edges of the cliffs. Both day and night, this process of grinding continues relentlessly. And what is the result?

Tourists from around the world flock there to collect the beautiful round stones. They display them in cabinets and use them to decorate their homes. Yet a little farther up the coast, just around the point of the cliff, is a quiet cove. Protected from the face of the ocean, sheltered from the storms, and always in the sun, the sands are covered with an abundance of pebbles never sought by the travelers.

So why have these stones been left untouched through all the years? Simply because they have escaped all the turmoil and the grinding of the waves. The quietness and peace have left them as they have always been—rough, unpolished, and devoid of beauty—for polish is the result of difficulties.

Since God knows what niche we are to fill, let us trust Him to shape us to it. And since He knows what work we are to do, let us trust Him to grind us so we will be properly prepared.

O blows that strike! O hurts that pierce
This fainting heart of mine!
What are you but the Master's tools
Forming a work Divine?
Nearly all of God's jewels are crystallized tears.

DAY 75

We were under great pressure.

2 CORINTHIANS 1:8

You smell delightfully fragrant," said the Gravel Walk to the bed of Camomile flowers under the window.

"We have been trodden on," replied the Camomiles.

"Does that cause it?" asked the Gravel Walk. "Treading on me produces no sweetness."

"Our natures are different," answered the Camomiles. "Gravel walks become only the harder by being trodden upon; but the effect on our own selves is that, if pressed and bruised when the dew is upon us, we give forth the sweet smell you now delight in."

"Very delightful," replied the Gravel Walk. Trials come alike to the Christian and to the man of the world. The one grows bitter and hardened under the experience, while the other becomes mellow and Christlike. It is because their natures are different.

Oh, beautiful rose, please tell me,
For I would like to know,

Why I must crush your petals
That sweet perfume may flow.
Oh, life that is clothed in beauty,
Perhaps like that beautiful rose,
You will need to be crushed by suffering
Ere you give out your best; who knows?
A life that is crushed by sorrow
Can feel for another's grief,
And send out that sweet perfume of love
That will bring some heart relief.
Oh, do not repine at your testing,
When called to pass under the rod,
It is that life might the sweeter be,
And comes from the Hand of God.
He knows how much we are needing,
Of sorrow, or suffering, or test,
And only gives to His children
The things that He knoweth are best.
Then let us rejoice when He sendeth
Some sorrow or hardship that tries,
And be glad to be crushed as the rose leaf,
That a sweeter perfume may arise.

FLORA L. OSGOOD

DAY 76

They will soar on wings like eagles.

ISAIAH 40:31

There is a fable about the way birds first got their wings. The story goes that initially they were made without them. Then God made the wings, set them down before the wingless birds, and said to them, "Take up these burdens and carry them."

The birds had sweet voices for singing, and lovely feathers that glistened in the sunshine, but they could not soar in the air. When asked to pick up the burdens that lay at their feet, they hesitated at first. Yet soon they obeyed, picked up the wings with their beaks, and set them on their shoulders to carry them.

For a short time the load seemed heavy and difficult to bear, but soon, as they continued to carry the burden and to fold the wings over their hearts, the wings grew attached to their little bodies. They quickly discovered how to use them and were lifted by the wings high into the air. The weights had become wings.

This is a parable for us. We are the wingless birds, and our duties and tasks are the wings God uses to lift us up and carry us heavenward. We look at our burdens and heavy loads, and try to run from them, but if we will carry them and tie them to our hearts, they will become wings. And on them we can then rise and soar toward God.

There is no burden so heavy that when lifted cheerfully with love in our hearts will not become a blessing to us. God intends for our tasks to be our helpers; to refuse to bend our shoulders to carry a load is to miss a new opportunity for growth. J. R. MILLER

No matter how overwhelming, any burden God has lovingly placed with His own hands on our shoulders is a blessing. FREDERICK WILLIAM FABER

DAY 77

Set a guard over my mouth, LORD; keep watch over the door of my lips.

PSALM 141:3

Unthinking say;
Set Thou a seal upon my lips—
Just for today.

Keep still! When trouble is brewing, keep still! When slander is getting on its legs, keep still! When your feelings are hurt, keep still till you recover from your excitement at any rate! Things look different through an unagitated eye.

In a commotion once I wrote a letter and sent it, and wished I had not. In my later years I had another commotion and wrote another long letter; my life had rubbed a little sense into me, and I kept that letter in my pocket until I could look it over without agitation, and without tears, and I was glad I did—less and less it seemed necessary to send it. I was not sure it would do any harm, but in my doubtfulness I learned reticence, and eventually it was destroyed.

Time works wonders! Wait till you can speak calmly and then perhaps you will not need to speak. Silence is the most powerful thing conceivable, sometimes. It is strength in its grandeur; it is like a regiment ordered to stand still in the mad fury of battle. To plunge in were twice as easy. Nothing is lost by learning to keep still. HANNAH WHITALL SMITH

Lord, keep me still,
Though stormy winds may blow,
And waves my little bark may overflow,
Or even if in darkness I must go,
Yet keep me still, yet keep me still.
Lord, keep me still,
The waves are in Thy hand,
The roughest winds subside at Thy command.
Steer Thou my bark in safety to the land,
And keep me still, and keep me still.
Lord, keep me still,
And may I ever hear Thy still small voice
To comfort and to cheer;
So shall I know and feel Thee ever near.
And keep me still, and keep me still.

Silence is a great peacemaker. HENRY WADSWORTH LONGFELLOW

DAY 78

I have chosen thee in the furnace of affliction.

ISAIAH 48:10 KJV

Doesn't God's Word come to us like a soft rain shower, dispelling the fury of the flames? Isn't it like fireproof armor, against which the heat is powerless? Then let afflictions come, for God has chosen me. Poverty, you may walk through my door, but God is already in my house, and He has chosen me. Sickness, you may intrude into my life, but I have a cure standing ready—God has chosen me. Whatever occurs in the valley of tears, I know He has chosen me.

Dear Christian, do not be afraid, for Jesus is with you. Through all your fiery trials, His presence is both your comfort and safety. He will never forsake those He has chosen for His own. "Do not be afraid, for I am with you" (Gen. 26:24) is His unfailing word of promise to His chosen ones who are experiencing "the furnace of affliction." CHARLES H. SPURGEON

Pain's furnace heat within me quivers,
God's breath upon the flame does blow;
And all my heart in anguish shivers
And trembles at the fiery glow; And yet I whisper,
"As God will!" And in the hottest fire hold still.
He comes and lays my heart, all heated,
On the hard anvil, minded so
Into His own fair shape to beat it
With His great hammer, blow on blow;
And yet I whisper, "As God will!"
And at His heaviest blows hold still.
He takes my softened heart and beats it;
The sparks fly off at every blow;
He turns it o'er and o'er and heats it,

And lets it cool, and makes it glow;
And yet I whisper, "As God will!"
And in His mighty hand hold still.
Why should I complain? for the sorrow
Then only longer-lived would be;
The end may come, and will tomorrow,
When God has done His work in me;
So I say trusting, "As God will!"
And, trusting to the end, hold still.

JULIUS STURM

The burden of suffering seems to be a tombstone hung around our necks. Yet in reality it is simply the weight necessary to hold the diver down while he is searching for pearls. JULIUS RICHTER

DAY 79

The Lord *took me from tending the flock.*

AMOS 7:15

Whom have You left behind to carry out the work?" asked the angels. "A little band of men and women who love Me," replied the Lord Jesus.

"But what if they should fail when the trial comes? Will all You have done be defeated?"

"Yes, if they should fail all I have done will be defeated; but they will not fail!"

And the angels wondered as they saw the sublime confidence of love which this betokened!

"Wilt thou follow Me?"
The Savior asked.

The road looked bright and fair,
And filled with youthful hope and zeal
I answered, "Anywhere."
"Wilt thou follow Me?" Again He asked.
The road looked dim ahead;
But I gave one glance at His glowing face "To the end, dear Lord," I said.
"Wilt thou follow Me?" I almost blanched,
For the road was rough and new,
But I felt the grip of His steady Hand,
And it thrilled me through and through.
"Still followest thou?" 'Twas a tender tone,
And it thrilled my inmost heart.
I answered not, but He drew me close,
And I knew we would never part.

The way lies through Gethsemane, through the city gate, outside the camp. The way lies alone, and the way lies until there is no trace of a footstep, only the Voice, "Follow Me!" But in the end it leads to "the joy set before him" (Heb. 12:2) and to the Mount of God.

The hour is desperately dark; your flame is needed.

DAY 80

I called him but he did not answer.

SONG OF SONGS 5:6

Once the Lord has given us great faith, He has been known to test it with long delays. He has allowed His servants' voices to echo in their ears, as if their prayers were rebounding from a contemptuous sky. Believers have knocked at the heavenly gate, but it has remained immovable, as though its hinges had rusted. And like Jeremiah, they have cried, "You have covered yourself with a cloud so that no prayer can get through" (Lam. 3:44).

True saints of God have endured lengthy times of patient waiting with no reply, not because their prayers were prayed without intensity, nor because God did not accept their pleas. They were required to wait because it pleased Him who is sovereign and who gives "according to his good purpose" (Phil. 2:13 CSB). And if it pleases Him to cause our patience to be exercised, should He not do as He desires with His own?

No prayer is ever lost, or any prayer ever breathed in vain. There is no such thing as prayer unanswered or unnoticed by God, and some things we see as refusals or denials are simply delays. HORATIUS BONAR

Christ sometimes delays His help so He may test our faith and energize our prayers. Our boat may be tossed by the waves while He continues to sleep, but He will awake before it sinks. He sleeps but He never oversleeps, for He is never too late. ALEXANDER MACLAREN

Be still, sad soul! lift up no passionate cry,
But spread the desert of your being bare
To the full searching of the All-seeing eye;
Wait! and through dark misgiving, deep despair,
God will come down in pity, and fill the dry
Dead place with light, and life, and springlike air.

JOHN CAMPBELL SHAIRP

DAY 81

In the year that King Uzziah died, I saw the Lord.

ISAIAH 6:1

We have to get our eyes off others before we can have the full vision of Jesus. Moses and Elijah had to pass to make possible the vision of

Jesus only. In the year that King Uzziah died, Isaiah says, I saw the Lord. His eyes and hopes had been upon the mighty and victorious earthly leader, and with his death all these hopes had sunk in despair. But the stars come out when the lights of earth fade. It was then Isaiah's true vision and life began.

It is not enough to see Jesus along with other things and persons. What we need is to have Him fill all our vision, all our sky, all our heart, all our plans, and all our future. What He wants from us is "first love," that is, the supreme place; and He cannot really be anything to us satisfactorily until He is everything. He is able to fill every capacity of our being and without displacing any rightful affection or occupation, yet so blend with all, so control all, so become the very essence of all thought and all delight that we can truly say, "For to me to live is Christ" (Phil. 1:21 KJV), for "the love of Christ constraineth" me (2 Cor. 5:14 KJV), shuts me up and in from everything else as a pent-up torrent in its narrow course, to live not unto myself but unto him "who loved me, and gave himself for me" (Gal. 2:20 KJV).

Holy Spirit, bring us our transfiguration, take us apart to our Mount of vision, let Moses and Elijah pass, and let us see no man save Jesus only.

ECHOES OF A NEW CREATION

Am I not enough, Mine own? Enough,
Mine own, for thee?
Hath the world its palace towers,
Garden glades of magic flowers,
Where thou wouldst be?
Fair things and false are there,
False things but fair,
All things thou findst at last
Only in Me.
Am I not enough, Mine own? I, forever
and alone? I, needing thee?

SUSO

DAY 82

Some time later the brook dried up because there had been no rain in the land.

1 KINGS 17:7

Week after week, with an unwavering and steadfast spirit, Elijah watched the brook dwindle and finally dry up. Often tempted to stumble in unbelief, he nevertheless refused to allow his circumstances to come between himself and God. Unbelief looks at God through the circumstances, just as we often see the sun dimmed by clouds or smoke. But faith puts God between itself and its circumstances, and looks at them through Him.

Elijah's brook dwindled to only a silver thread, which formed pools at the base of the largest rocks. Then the pools evaporated, the birds flew away, and the wild animals of the fields and forests no longer came to drink, for the brook became completely dry. And only then, to Elijah's patient and faithful spirit, did the word of the Lord come and say, "Go at once to Zarephath" (v. 9).

Most of us would have become anxious and tired, and would have made other plans long before God spoke. Our singing would have stopped as soon as the stream flowed less musically over its rocky bed. We would have hung our harps on the willows nearby and begun pacing back and forth on the withering grass, worrying about our predicament. And probably, long before the brook actually dried up, we would have devised some plan, asked God to bless it, and headed elsewhere.

God will often extricate us from the mess we have made, because "his love endures forever" (1 Chron. 16:34). Yet if we had only been patient and waited to see the unfolding of His plan, we would never have found ourselves in such an impossible maze, seeing no way out. We would also never have had to turn back and retrace our way, with wasted steps and so many tears of shame.

"Wait for the LORD" (Ps. 27:14). Patiently wait! F. B. MEYER

DAY 83

I press on. . . . Forgetting what is behind.

PHILIPPIANS 3:12–13

In the very depths of yourself, dig a grave. Let it be like some forgotten spot to which no path leads; and there, in the eternal silence, bury the wrongs that you have suffered. Your heart will feel as if a weight had fallen from it, and a Divine peace come to abide with you. CHARLES WAGNER

To be misunderstood even by those whom one loves is the cross and bitterness of life. It is the secret of that sad melancholy smile on the lips of great men which so few understand. It is what must have oftenest wrung the heart of the Son of Man. AMIEL

Blasted rock and broken stone,
Ordinary earth,
Rolled and rammed and trampled on,
Forgotten, nothing worth,
And blamed, but used day after day;
An open road—the king's highway.
Often left outside the door,
Sometimes in the rain,
Always lying on the floor,
And made for mud and stain:
Men wipe their feet, and tread it flat,
And beat it clean—the master's mat.
Thou wast broken, left alone,
Thou wast blamed, and worse,
Thou wast scourged and spat upon,
Thou didst become my curse—

Lord Jesus, as I think of that
I pray, make me Thy road, Thy mat.

GOLD CORD

"The power to help others depends upon the acceptance of a trampled life."

DAY 84

He knows the way that I take; when he has tested me, I will come forth as gold.

JOB 23:10

Faith grows during storms. These are just four little words, but what significance they have to someone who has endured life-threatening storms!

Faith is that God-given ability that, when exercised, brings the unseen into plain view. It deals with the supernatural and makes impossible things possible. And yes, it grows during storms—that is, it grows through disturbances in the spiritual atmosphere. Storms are caused by conflicts between the physical elements, and the storms of the spiritual world are conflicts with supernatural, hostile elements. And it is in this atmosphere of conflict that faith finds its most fertile soil and grows most rapidly to maturity.

The strongest trees are found not in the thick shelter of the forest but out in the open, where winds from every direction bear down upon them. The fierce winds bend and twist them until they become giant in stature. These are the trees that toolmakers seek for handles for their tools, because of the wood's great strength.

It is the same in the spiritual world. Remember, when you see a person of great spiritual stature, the road you must travel to walk with him is not one where the sun always shines and wildflowers always bloom. Instead, the way is a steep, rocky, and narrow path, where the winds of hell will try to knock you off your feet, and where sharp rocks will cut you, prickly thorns will scratch your face, and poisonous snakes will slither and hiss all around you.

The path of faith is one of sorrow and joy, suffering and healing comfort, tears and smiles, trials and victories, conflicts and triumphs, and also hardships, dangers, beatings, persecutions, misunderstanding, trouble, and distress. Yet "in all these things we are more than conquerors through him who loved us" (Rom. 8:37).

Yes, "in all these"—even during storms, when the winds are the most intense—"we are more than conquerors." You may be tempted to run from the ordeal of a fierce storm of testing, but head straight for it! God is there to meet you in the center of each trial. And He will whisper to you His secrets, which will bring you out with a radiant face and such an invincible faith that all the demons of hell will never be able to shake it. E. A. KILBOURNE

DAY 85

The place where you are standing is holy ground.

EXODUS 3:5

We cannot depend upon great events, striking circumstances, exalted moments and great occasions to measure our zeal, courage, faith, and love. These are measured by the commonplace, workaday tasks, the homely hidden paths of common life.

Thank God for the new vision, the beautiful idea, the glowing experience of the mountain; but unless we bring it down to the level of life, and teach it to walk with feet, work with hands, and stand the strain of daily life, we have worse than lost it—we have been hurt by it. The uncommon life is the product of the day lived in the uncommon way.

Conspicuous efficiency in a lowly sphere is the best preparation for a higher one.

The incidents of which Jesus' work was made up are, humanly speaking, very humble and unpretentious. Human details fill the compass of His vast experience and work. He might have stilled a tempest every night. He could have walked upon the sea or flown over it, had the need existed. He could have transfigured Himself before Pilate and the astonished multitude in the Temple. He could have made visible ascensions at noon every day, had He been minded so to do.

The most faithful cannot compare with Jesus in lowliness of manner: He taught only one woman at Jacob's well; He noticed a finger-touch on the hem of His garment; He stooped to take little children up in his arms and bless them; even so small a thing as a cup of cold water, He said, would yield its recompense of a heavenly reward.

It may be on a kitchen floor,
Or in a busy shopping store,
Or teaching, nursing, day by day,
Till limb and brain almost give way;
Yet if, just there, by Jesus thou art found,
The place thou standest on is Holy Ground.

M. COLLEY

"I will make the place of my feet glorious" (Isa. 60:13 KJV) said the Lord. Be it never so rough, be it never so steep, be it never so miry—the place of His feet is glorious!

Take God on thy route and thou shalt banish wrinkles from thy brow. Gethsemane itself shall not age thee if thou tread by the side of Jesus; for it is not the place of thy travel that makes thee weary—it is the heaviness of thy step. GEORGE MATHESON

DAY 86

I have come down from heaven not to do my will
but to do the will of him who sent me.

JOHN 6:38

When he was crossing the Irish Channel one dark starless night, says Dr. F. B. Meyer, he stood on the deck by the captain and asked him, "How do you know Holyhead Harbor on so dark a night as this?" He said, "You see those three lights? Those three must line up behind each other as one, and when we see them so united we know the exact position of the harbor's mouth."

When we want to know God's will there are three things which always concur: the inward impulse, the Word of God, and the trend of circumstances! God in the heart, impelling you forward; God in the Book, corroborating whatever He says in the heart; and God in circumstances, which are always indicative of His will. Never start until these three things agree.

Stand still at the crossroads ready to walk or run, and you will not be kept waiting long.

When we're not quite certain if we turn to left or right—isn't it a blessing when a signpost looms in sight! If there were no signposts we should wander miles astray—in the wrong direction if we didn't know the way.

God has set His signposts on Life's strange and winding road. When we're blindly stumbling with the burden of our load—He will lead our footsteps though the pathway twist and bend—in some form He guides us, through The Book, a song, a friend. . . . In the dark uncertain hours, we need not be afraid—when we're at the crossroads, and decisions must be made. . . . Though the track is unfamiliar, and the light is gray—rest assured, there's bound to be a signpost on the way.

Let us be silent unto Him, and believe that, even now, messengers are hastening along the road with the summons, or direction, or help which we need.

DAY 87

Then Jesus told his disciples . . . that they should always pray and not give up.

LUKE 18:1

Observe the ant," the great Turkic conqueror Tamerlane told his friends. In relating a story from his early life, he said, "I once was forced to take shelter from my enemies in a dilapidated building, where I sat alone for many hours. Wishing to divert my mind from my hopeless situation, I fixed my eyes on an ant carrying a kernel of corn larger than itself up a high wall. I counted its attempts to accomplish this feat. The corn fell sixty-nine times to the ground, but the insect persevered. The seventieth time it reached the top. The ant's accomplishment gave me courage for the moment, and I never forgot the lesson." THE KING'S BUSINESS

Prayer that uses previously unanswered prayers as an excuse for laziness has already ceased to be a prayer of faith. To someone who prays in faith, unanswered prayers are simply the evidence that the answer is much closer. From beginning to end, our Lord's lessons and examples teach us that prayer that is not steadfast and persistent, nor revived and refreshed, and does not gather strength from previous prayers is not the prayer that will triumph. WILLIAM ARTHUR

Arthur Rubinstein, the great pianist, once said, "If I neglect practicing one day, I notice; two days, my friends notice; three days, the public notices." It is the old principle "Practice makes perfect." We must continue believing, praying, and doing His will. In any of the arts, when the artist ceases to practice, we know the result. If we would only use the same level of common sense in our faith that we use in our everyday life, we would be moving on toward perfection.

David Livingstone's motto was, "I resolved never to stop until I had come to the goal and achieved my purpose." He was victorious through unwavering persistence and faith in God.

DAY 88

Bind the festival sacrifice with cords to the horns of the altar.

PSALM 118:27 NASB

Is the altar of sacrifice calling you? Why not ask God to bind you to it, so you will never be tempted to turn away from a life of consecration, or dedication, to Him? There are times when life is full of promise and light, and we choose the cross; yet at other times, when the sky is gray, we run from it. Therefore it is wise to be bound to the altar.

Dear blessed Holy Spirit, will You bind us to the cross and fill us with such love for it that we will never abandon it? Please bind us with Your scarlet cord of redemption, Your gold cord of love, and the silver cord of hope in Christ's second coming. We ask this so we will not turn from the cross of sacrifice, or desire becoming anything but humble partners with our Lord in His pain and sorrow!

"The horns of the altar" are inviting you. Will you come? Are you willing to continually live a life of total surrender, giving yourself completely to the Lord?

I once heard a story of a man who attended a tent revival meeting and tried to give himself to God. Every night at the altar, he would dedicate himself to the Lord. Yet as he left each evening, the Devil would come to him and convince him that since he did not feel changed, he was not truly redeemed.

Again and again he was defeated by the Adversary. Finally one evening he came to the meeting carrying an ax and a large wooden stake. After dedicating himself once more, he drove the stake into the ground where he had knelt to pray. As he was leaving the tent, the Devil came to him as usual, trying to make him believe that his commitment to God was not genuine. He quickly returned to the stake, pointed to it, and said, "Devil, do you see this stake? This is my witness that God has forever accepted me."

Immediately the Devil left him, and he never experienced doubts again.

THE STILL SMALL VOICE

Beloved, if you are tempted to doubt the finality of your salvation experience, drive a stake into the ground and then let it be your witness before God, and even the Devil, that you have settled the question forever.

Are you groping for a blessing,
Never getting there?
Listen to a word of wisdom,
Get somewhere.
Are you struggling for salvation
By your anxious prayer?
Stop your struggling, simply trust, and—
Get somewhere.
Does the answer seem to linger
To your earnest prayer?
Turn your praying into praise, and—
Get somewhere.
You will never know His fullness
Till you boldly dare
To commit your all to Him, and—
Get somewhere.

SONGS OF THE SPIRIT

DAY 89

That person will receive the crown of life . . . promised.

JAMES 1:12

The greatest helpers of humanity have been its cross-bearers. The leaders of men have suffered in loneliness; the prophets have learned their lessons in the school of pain. The corals in the sheltered lagoon grow rank and useless; those that are broken and crushed by the surf form the living rock and the foundations of continents. Ease has not produced greatness.

Men who have had to struggle with an unfavorable environment, to fight cold, to buffet the storm, to blast the rock or wring a livelihood from barren soil, have won character by their pains.

The bird rises against a strong head wind, not only in spite of the wind, but because of it. The opposing force becomes a lifting force if faced at the right angle.

The storm may buffet ships and rend the rigging, but it makes strong hands and brave hearts. Oh, fellow-voyager amid the storms and calms of life's wide sea, "Spread thy sails to catch the favoring breezes of adversity."

If the greatest character of all time, even He who was the very touchstone of destiny, could be made perfect only through suffering, is it not probable that you and I must be also?

The best things all lie beyond some battle plain: you must fight your way across the field to get them!

High natures must be thunder-scarred
With many a scarring wrong!
Naught unmarred with struggle hard
Can make the soul's sinews strong.

LOWELL

Take the hardest thing in your life—the place of difficulty, outward or inward, and expect God to triumph gloriously in that very spot. Just there He can bring your soul into blossom. LILIAS TROTTER

DAY 90

This is the victory that has overcome the world, even our faith.

1 JOHN 5:4

It is easy to love Him when the blue is in the sky,
When the summer winds are blowing, and we smell the roses nigh;
There is little effort needed to obey His precious will
When it leads through flower-decked valley, or over sun-kissed hill.
It is when the rain is falling, or the mist hangs in the air,
When the road is dark and rugged, and the wind no longer fair,
When the rosy dawn has settled in a shadowland of gray,
That we find it hard to trust Him, and are slower to obey.
It is easy to trust Him when the singing birds have come,
And their songs of praise are echoed in our heart and in our home;
But it's when we miss the music, and the days are dull and drear,
That we need a faith triumphant over every doubt and fear.
And our blessed Lord will give it; what we lack He will supply;
Let us ask in faith believing—on His promises rely;
He will ever be our Leader, whether smooth or rough the way,
And will prove Himself sufficient for the needs of every day.

Trusting even when it appears you have been forsaken; praying when it seems your words are simply entering a vast expanse where no one hears and no voice answers; believing that God's love is complete and that He is aware of your circumstances, even when your world seems to grind on as if setting its own direction and not caring for life or moving one inch in response to your petitions; desiring only what God's hands have planned for you; waiting patiently while seemingly starving to death, with your only fear being that your faith might fail—"This is the victory that has overcome the world"; this is genuine faith indeed. GEORGE MACDONALD

DAY 91

In the LORD *I take refuge.*

PSALM 11:1

That is a jubilant bird note, but the bird is singing, not on some fair dewy spring morning, but in a cloudy heaven, and in the very midst of a destructive tempest. A little while ago I listened to a concert of mingled thunder and birdsong. Between the crashing peals of thunder, I heard the clear thrilling note of the lark. The melody seemed to come out of the very heart of the tempest. The environment of this Psalm is stormy. The sun is down. The stars are hid. The waters are out. The roads are broken up. And in the very midst of the darkness and desolation one hears the triumphant cry of the psalmist, "In the LORD I take refuge." The singer is a soul in difficulty. He is the victim of relentless antagonists. He is pursued by implacable foes. The fight would appear to be going against him. The enemies are overwhelming, and, just at this point of seeming defeat and imminent disaster, there emerges this note of joyful confidence in God. "In the LORD I take refuge." It is a song in the night. J. H. JOWETT

There is a bird of the thrush family found in the South of Ireland, called "The Storm Thrush," from its peculiar love of storms. In the wildest storms of rain and wind it betakes itself to the very topmost twig of the highest tree and there pours out its beautiful song—its frail perch swaying in the wind.

A beautiful story is told of some little birds whose nest had been ruined. As the poet walked among the trees in his garden after the storm, he found a torn nest lying on the ground. He began to brood sadly over it, pitying the birds whose home had thus been wrecked. But as he stood there and mused he heard a twittering and chattering over his head; looking up he saw the birds busy building again their ruined nest!

I heard a bird at break of day
Sing from the autumn trees
A song so musical and calm,
So full of certainties,
No man, I think, could listen long
Except upon his knees.
Yet this was but a simple bird
Alone among dead trees.

Robert Louis Stevenson closes one of his prayers with these words: "Help us with the grace of courage that we be none of us cast down while we sit lamenting over the ruins of our happiness. Touch us with the fire of Thine altar, that we may be up and doing, to rebuild our city."

Begin to build anew!

DAY 92

Because you have done this and have not withheld your son, your only son, I will . . . make your descendants as numerous as the stars in the sky . . . because you have obeyed me.

GENESIS 22:16–18

From the time of Abraham, people have been learning that when they obey God's voice and surrender to Him whatever they hold most precious, He multiplies it thousands of times. Abraham gave up his one and only son at the Lord's command, and in doing so, all his desires and dreams for Isaac's life, as well as his own hope for a notable heritage, disappeared. Yet God restored Isaac to his father, and Abraham's family became "as numerous as the stars in the sky and as the sand on the seashore" (v. 17). And through his descendants, "when the set time had fully come, God sent his Son" (Gal. 4:4).

This is exactly how God deals with every child of His when we truly sacrifice. We surrender everything we own and accept poverty—then He sends wealth. We leave a growing area of ministry at His command—then He provides one better than we had ever dreamed. We surrender all our cherished hopes and die to self—then He sends overflowing joy and His "life . . . that [we] might have it more abundantly" (John 10:10 KJV).

The greatest gift of all was Jesus Christ Himself, and we can never fully comprehend the enormity of His sacrifice. Abraham, as the earthly father of the family of Christ, had to begin by surrendering himself and his only son, just as our heavenly Father sacrificed His only Son, Jesus. We could never have come to enjoy the privileges and joys as members of God's family through any other way. CHARLES GALLAUDET TRUMBULL

We sometimes seem to forget that what God takes from us, He takes with fire, and that the only road to a life of resurrection and ascension power leads us first to Gethsemane, the cross, and the tomb.

Dear soul, do you believe that Abraham's experience was unique and isolated? It is only an example and a pattern of how God deals with those who are prepared to obey Him whatever the cost. "After waiting patiently, Abraham received what was promised" (Heb. 6:15), and so will you. The moment of your greatest sacrifice will also be the precise moment of your greatest and most miraculous blessing. God's river, which never runs dry, will overflow its banks, bringing you a flood of wealth and grace.

Indeed, there is nothing God will not do for those who will dare to step out in faith onto what appears to be only a mist. As they take their first step, they will find a rock beneath their feet. F. B. MEYER

DAY 93

God remembered Noah . . . and he sent a wind over the earth, and the waters receded. Now the springs of the deep and the floodgates of the heavens had been closed, and the rain had stopped falling from the sky. The water receded steadily from the earth.

GENESIS 8:1–3

All this because God remembered Noah! The forces of heaven and earth were enlisted, reversed, ordered about, solely because God remembered Noah and had plans for him. We may forget; God does not!

God's time is never wrong,
Never too fast nor too slow;
The planets move to its steady pace
As the centuries come and go.
Stars rise and set by that time,
The punctual comets come back
With never a second's variance,
From the round of their viewless track.
Men space their years by the sun,
And reckon their months by the moon,
Which never arrive too late
And never depart too soon.
Let us set our clocks by God's,
And order our lives by His ways,
And nothing can come and nothing can go
Too soon or too late in our day.

ANNIE JOHNSON FLINT

"There are no dates in His fine leisure."

DAY 94

I will remain quiet and will look on from my dwelling place.

ISAIAH 18:4

In this passage, Assyria is marching against Ethiopia. As the army advances, God makes no effort to stop them, and it appears as though they will be allowed to do as they wish. The Lord is watching from His "dwelling place" while the sun continues to shine on them, yet "before the harvest" (v. 5) the entire proud army is defeated as easily as new growth is pruned from a vine.

Isn't this a beautiful picture of God—remaining quiet and watching? Yet His silence is not to be confused with passive agreement or consent. He is simply biding His time and will arise at the most opportune moment, just when the plans of the wicked are on the verge of success, in order to overwhelm the enemy with disaster. And as we see the evil of this world, as we watch the apparent success of wrongdoers, and as we suffer the oppression of those who hate us, let us remember those miraculous words of God—"I will remain quiet and will look on."

Yes, God does have another point of view, and there is wisdom behind His words. Why did Jesus watch His disciples straining at the oars through the stormy night? Why did He, though unseen by others, watch the sequence of anguishing events unfold in Bethany as Lazarus slowly passed through the stages of his terminal illness, succumbed to death, and was finally buried in a rocky tomb? Jesus was simply waiting for the perfect moment when He could intercede most effectively.

Is the Lord being quiet with you? Nevertheless, He is attentive and still sees everything. He has His finger on your pulse and is extremely sensitive to even the slightest change. And He will come to save you when the perfect moment has arrived.

Whatever the Lord may ask of us or however slow He may seem to work, we can be absolutely sure He is never a confused or fearful Savior.

O troubled soul, beneath the rod,
Your Father speaks, be still, be still;
Learn to be silent unto God,
And let Him mold you to His will.
O praying soul, be still, be still,
He cannot break His promised Word;
Sink down into His blessed will,
And wait in patience on the Lord.
O waiting soul, be still, be strong,
And though He tarry, trust and wait;
Doubt not, He will not wait too long,
Fear not, He will not come too late.

april 5th

DAY 95

"Sovereign LORD, how can I know that I will gain possession of it?" So the LORD said to him, "Bring me a heifer." . . . Then birds of prey came down on the carcasses, but Abram drove them away.

GENESIS 15:8–9, 11

When God promises us a great blessing, and we ask how we may know that we shall have it, the answer is always the same: By your own sacrifice to Me. God cannot fulfill His richest promises to any of us until we have offered up to Him, in utter completeness of surrender, ourselves. Then He can do glorious things for and with our lives.

And then, also, "the birds of prey" attack a life as never before. The devil does not like to see any life sacrificed to God, for he knows how mightily God will use that life to defeat the works of darkness. So the birds of prey come down. We must expect to be attacked and tempted more fiercely and continuously after our life has been wholly surrendered to God than we ever were before. MESSAGES FOR THE MORNING WATCH

There is a Chinese legend of a potter who sought for many years to put a certain tint on the vases he made, but all his efforts failed. At last discouraged and in despair he threw himself into his furnace and his body was consumed in the fire; then, when the vases were taken out they bore the exquisite color which he had striven so long to produce.

The legend illustrates that truth that we can do our noblest and best work only at cost of self. The alabaster box must be broken before its odors can flow out.

Christ lifted up and saved the world not by an easy, pleasant, successful life in it; but by suffering and dying for it. And we can never bless the world merely by having a good time in it; but only by giving our lives for it.

It takes heart's blood to heal hearts. Saving of life proves, in the end, the losing of it.

My wild will was captured, yet under the yoke
There was pain and not peace at the press of the load;
Till the glorious burden the last fiber broke,
And I melted like wax in the furnace of God.
And now I have flung myself recklessly out,
Like a chip on the stream of His infinite will;
I pass the rough rocks with a smile and a shout,
And just let my God His dear purpose fulfill.

DAY 96

The eyes of the LORD range throughout the earth to strengthen those whose hearts are fully committed to him.

2 CHRONICLES 16:9

God is looking for men and women whose hearts are firmly fixed on Him and who will continually trust Him for all He desires to do with their lives. God is ready and eager to work more powerfully than ever through His people, and the clock of the centuries is striking the eleventh hour.

The world is watching and waiting to see what God can do through a life committed to Him. And not only is the world waiting but God Himself awaits to see who will be the most completely devoted person who has ever lived: willing to be nothing so Christ may be everything; fully accepting God's purposes as his own; receiving Christ's humility, faith, love, and power yet never hindering God's plan but always allowing Him to continue His miraculous work. C. H. P.

There is no limit to what God can do through you, provided you do not seek your own glory.

George Mueller, at more than ninety years of age, in an address to ministers and other Christian workers, said, "I was converted in November 1825, but I didn't come to the point of total surrender of my heart until four years later, in July 1829. It was then I realized my love for money, prominence, position, power, and worldly pleasure was gone. God, and He alone, became my all in all. In Him I found everything I needed, and I desired nothing else. By God's grace, my understanding of His sufficiency has remained to this day, making me an exceedingly happy man. It has led me to care only about the things of God.

"And so, dear believers, I kindly ask if you have totally surrendered your heart to God, or is there something in your life you refuse to release, in spite of God's call?

"Before the point at which I surrendered my life, I read a little of the Scriptures but preferred other books. Yet since that time, the truth He has revealed to me of Himself has become an inexpressible blessing. Now I can honestly say from the depth of my heart that God is an infinitely wonderful Being.

"Please, never be satisfied until you too can express from your innermost soul, 'God is an infinitely wonderful Being!'"

My prayer today is that God would make me an extraordinary Christian. GEORGE WHITEFIELD

DAY 97

For no matter how many promises God has made, they are "Yes" in Christ.

2 CORINTHIANS 1:20

Sometimes Christians go for a good while in trouble, not realizing that riches are laid up for them in a familiar promise.

When Christian and Hopeful strayed out of the path upon forbidden ground, and found themselves locked up in Doubting Castle by Giant Despair for their carelessness, there they lay for days, until one night they began to pray. "Now a little before it was day, Good Christian, as one half-amazed, broke out in passionate speech: 'What a fool!' quoth he, 'am I, thus to lie in this horrible dungeon, when I may as well walk at liberty. I have a key in my bosom called Promise, that will, I am persuaded, open any lock in Doubting Castle.' Then said Hopeful, 'That's good news good brother; pluck it out of thy bosom and try.' Then Christian pulled it out of his bosom, and began to try the dungeon door, whose bolts gave back, and the door flew open with ease, and Christian and Hopeful came out." THE PILGRIM'S PROGRESS BY JOHN BUNYAN

Often you cannot get at a difficulty so as to deal with it aright and find your way to a happy result. You pray, but have not the liberty in prayer which you desire. A definite promise is what you want. You try one and another of the inspired words, but they do not fit. You try again, and in due season a promise presents itself which seems to have been made for the occasion; it fits exactly as a well-made key fits the lock for which it was prepared. Having found the identical word of the living God you hasten to plead it at the throne of grace, saying, "O Lord, Thou hast promised this good thing unto Thy servant; be pleased to grant it!" The matter is ended: sorrow is turned to joy; prayer is heard. CHARLES H. SPURGEON

Faith, mighty faith, the promise sees
And looks to God alone,

Laughs at impossibilities,
And cries, "It shall be done."

Try all your keys! Never despair! God leaves no treasure-house locked against us!

DAY 98

Shall I not drink the cup the Father has given me?

JOHN 18:11

To "drink the cup" was a greater thing than calming the seas or raising the dead. The prophets and apostles could do amazing miracles, but they did not always do the will of God and thereby suffered as a result. Doing God's will and thus experiencing suffering is still the highest form of faith, and the most glorious Christian achievement.

Having your brightest aspirations as a young person forever crushed; bearing burdens daily that are always difficult, and never seeing relief; finding yourself worn down by poverty while simply desiring to do good for others and provide a comfortable living for those you love; being shackled by an incurable physical disability; being completely alone, separated from all those you love, to face the trauma of life alone; yet in all these, still being able to say through such a difficult school of discipline, "Shall I not drink the cup the Father has given me?"—this is faith at its highest, and spiritual success at its crowning point.

Great faith is exhibited not so much in doing as in suffering. CHARLES PARKHURST

In order to have a sympathetic God, we must have a suffering Savior, for true sympathy comes from understanding another person's hurt by suffering the same affliction. Therefore we cannot help others who suffer without paying a price ourselves, because afflictions are the cost we pay for our ability to sympathize. Those who wish to help others must first suffer. If we wish to rescue others, we must be willing to face the cross; experiencing the greatest happiness in life through ministering to others is impossible without drinking the cup Jesus drank and without submitting to the baptism He endured.

The most comforting of David's psalms were squeezed from his life by suffering, and if Paul had not been given "a thorn in the flesh" (2 Cor. 12:7 KJV), we would have missed much of the heartbeat of tenderness that resonates through so many of his letters.

If you have surrendered yourself to Christ, your present circumstances that seem to be pressing so hard against you are the perfect tool in the Father's hand to chisel you into shape for eternity. So trust Him and never push away the instrument He is using, or you will miss the result of His work in your life.

Strange and difficult indeed
We may find it,
But the blessing that we need
Is behind it.

The school of suffering graduates exceptional scholars.

DAY 99

Until now you have not asked for anything in my name. Ask and you will receive, and your joy will be complete.

JOHN 16:24

Alexander the Great had a famous, but indigent, philosopher in his court. This man adept in science was once particularly straightened in his circumstances. To whom should he apply but to his patron, the conqueror of the world? His request was no sooner made than granted. Alexander gave him a commission to receive of his treasury whatever he wanted. He immediately demanded in his sovereign's name ten thousand pounds. The treasurer, surprised at so large a demand, refused to comply, but waited upon the king and represented to him the affair, adding withal how unreasonable he thought the petition and how exorbitant the sum. Alexander listened with patience, but as soon as he heard the remonstrance replied, "Let the money be instantly paid. I am delighted with this philosopher's way of thinking; he has done me a singular honor: by the largeness of his request he shows the high idea he has conceived both of my superior wealth and my royal munificence."

Saints have never yet reached the limit to the possibilities of prayer. Whatever has been attained or achieved has touched but the fringe of the garment of a prayer-hearing God. We honor the riches both of His power and love only by large demands. A. T. PIERSON

You cannot think of a prayer so large that God, in answering it, will not wish that you had made it larger. Pray not for crutches, but for wings! PHILLIPS BROOKS

Make thy petition deep.
It is thy God who speaks with love o'erflowing,
Thy God who claims the rapture of bestowing,
Thy God who whispers, all thy weakness knowing,
"Wouldst thou in full reap?
Make thy petition deep."
Now to the fountainhead thy vessel bringing,
Claim all the fullness of its glad upspringing;
At Calvary was proclaimed its boundless measure;
Who spared not then, withholds from thee no treasure;
This word—His token, keep:
Make thy petition deep.

If Alexander gave like a King, shall not Jehovah give like a God?

DAY 100

Since we have a great high priest . . . , Jesus the Son of God, let us hold firmly to the faith we profess. . . . Let us then approach the throne of grace with confidence, so that we may receive mercy and find grace to help us in our time of need.

HEBREWS 4:14, 16

Our great Helper in prayer is the Lord Jesus Christ. He is our Advocate, ever pleading our case before the Father. He is our "great high priest," whose primary ministry has for centuries been intercession and prayer on our behalf. It is He who receives our imperfect petitions from our hands, cleanses them of their defects, corrects their error, and then claims their answer from His Father. And He does so strictly on the basis of His worth and righteousness through the sufficiency of His atonement.

Believer, are you lacking power in prayer? Look to Christ, for your blessed Advocate has already claimed your answer. And if you give up the fight just as the moment of victory approaches, you will grieve and disappoint Him. He has already entered "the Most Holy Place" (Ex. 26:33) on your behalf, holding up your name on the palms of His hands. The messenger is now on his way to bring you your blessing, and the Holy Spirit simply awaits your act of trust, so He may whisper in your heart the echo of the answer from the throne of God, "It is done" (Rev. 21:6). A. B. SIMPSON

The Holy Spirit is the one who works to make our prayers acceptable, yet we often forget this truth. He enlightens our mind so we may clearly see our desires, then softens our heart so we may feel them, and finally He awakens and focuses those desires toward godly things. He gives us a clear view of God's power and wisdom, provides grace "in our time of need," and strengthens our confidence in His truth so we will never waver.

Prayer is a wonderful thing, and each person of the Trinity is involved in every acceptable prayer. J. ANGELL JAMES

DAY 101

Whatever you ask for in prayer . . . it will be yours.

MARK 11:24

Oh, the victories of prayer! They are the mountaintops of the Bible. They take us back to the plains of Mamre, to the fords of Peniel, to the prison of Joseph, to the triumphs of Moses, to the victories of Joshua, to the deliverances of David, to the miracles of Elijah and Elisha, to the holy story of the Master's life, to the secret of Pentecost, to the keynote of Paul's unparalleled ministry, to the lives of saints and the deaths of martyrs, to all that is most sacred and sweet in the history of the church and the experience of the children of God.

And when for us the last conflict shall have passed, and the footstool of prayer shall have given place to the harp of praise, the scenes of time that shall be gilded with eternal radiance shall be those linked with deepest sorrow and darkest night, over which we have written Jehovah Shammah (the Lord was there).

Beyond thy utmost wants,
His power can love and bless;
To trusting souls He loves to grant
More than they can express.

DAY 102

Do not move an ancient boundary stone set up by your ancestors.

PROVERBS 22:28

Among the property owned jointly by two young brothers who were carpenters was the old tumbledown place of their birth. One of the brothers was soon to be married and the old house was to be torn down and a new one erected on its site. For years neither of the brothers had visited the cottage, as it had been leased.

As they entered now and started the work of demolishing the place, again and again floods of tender memories swept over them. By the time they reached the kitchen they were well-nigh overcome with their emotions. There was the place where the old kitchen table had stood—with the family Bible—where they had knelt every evening. They were recalling now with a pang how in later years they had felt a little superior to that time-honored custom carefully observed by their father.

Said one: "We're better off than he was, but we're not better men."

The other agreed, saying, "I'm going back to the old church and the old ways, and in my new home I'm going to make room for worship as Dad did."

The strength of a nation lies in the homes of its people. ABRAHAM LINCOLN

Says Dr. J. G. Paton: "No hurry for market, no rush for business, no arrival of friends or guests, no trouble or sorrow, no joy or excitement, ever prevented us from kneeling around the family altar while our high priest offered himself and his children to God." And on his father's life in his home was based Dr. Paton's decision to follow the Lord wholly. "He walked with God—why not I?"

"Stand ye in the . . . old paths, where is the good way" (Jer. 6:16 KJV).

DAY 103

For you who revere my name, the sun of righteousness will rise with healing in its rays. Unto you that fear my name shall the Sun of righteousness arise with healing in his wings.

MALACHI 4:2 NIV; KJV

A South American traveler tells of a curious conflict which he once witnessed between a little quadruped and a poisonous reptile of great size. The little creature seemed no match for its antagonist that threatened to destroy it by a blow, as well as its helpless young, but it fearlessly faced its mighty enemy and rushing at him, struck him with a succession of fierce and telling blows, but received at the onset a deep and apparently fatal wound from the poisonous fangs, which flashed for a moment with an angry fire, and then fastened themselves deep into the flesh of the daring little assailant.

For a moment it seemed as if all were over, but the wise little creature immediately retired into the forest, and hastening to the plantain tree eagerly devoured some of its leaves, and then hurried back, seemingly fresh and restored, to renew the fray with vigor and determination. Again and again this strange spectacle was repeated: the serpent, although greatly exhausted, ferociously attacked, and again and again wounded its antagonist to death, as it seemed; but the little creature each time repaired to its simple prescription, and returned to renewed victory. In the course of an hour or two the battle was over—the mammoth reptile lay still and dead and the little victor was unharmed, in the midst of the nest and the helpless little ones.

How often we are wounded by the dragon's sting—wounded, it would seem to death! and if we had to go through some long ceremony to reach the source of life, we must faint and die. But blessed be His Name as near at hand as that which the forest holds in its shade, there is ever for us a plant of healing to which we may continually repair and come back refreshed, invigorated, transfigured—like Him who shone with the brightness of celestial light as He prayed in the mount; who, as He prayed in the garden arose triumphant over the fear of death, strengthened from on high to accomplish the mighty battle of our redemption. A. B. SIMPSON

It is His wings that heal our pains,
And soothe the serpent's poisoned stings;
Close to His bosom we must press
To feel His healing wings.

DAY 104

Therefore will the LORD wait, that he may be gracious unto you . . . blessed are all they that wait for him.

ISAIAH 30:18 KJV

We should not only understand the importance of our waiting on God but also realize something even more wonderful—the Lord waits on us. And the very thought of His waiting on us will give us renewed motivation and inspiration to "wait for him." It will also provide inexpressible confidence that our waiting will never be in vain. Therefore, in the spirit of waiting on God, let us seek to discover exactly what it means right now.

The Lord has an inconceivably glorious purpose for each of His children. "If this is true," you ask, "why is it that He continues to wait longer and longer to offer His grace and to provide the help I seek, even after I have come and waited on Him?" He does so because He is a wise gardener who "waits for the land to yield its valuable crop" and is "patiently waiting for the autumn and spring rains" (James 5:7). God knows He cannot gather the fruit until it is ripe, and He knows precisely when we are spiritually ready to receive blessings for our gain and His glory. And waiting in the sunshine of His love is what will ripen our soul for His blessings. Also, waiting under the clouds of trials is as important, for they will ultimately produce showers of blessings.

Rest assured that if God waits longer than we desire, it is simply to make the blessings doubly precious. Remember, He waited four thousand years, "but when the set time had fully come, God sent his Son" (Gal. 4:4). Our time is in His hands, and He will quickly avenge those He has chosen, swiftly coming to our support without ever delaying even one hour too long.

ANDREW MURRAY

DAY 105

Whatever . . . that the Father may be glorified in the Son.

JOHN 14:13

Do we pray for His glory?

This is the privilege and possibility for every man who can speak to God "in His Name."

In the Lone Star Mission at Ongole, India, a faithful few had held on believingly and courageously year after year. Now the mission was about to be abandoned. The work had apparently failed; money had failed. The only hope now was God.

Dr. Jowett and his wife took with them that famous old Hindu woman, Julia, nearly one hundred years of age, and ascended the hills above Ongole to ask God to save the Lone Star Mission. The old Hindu saint mingled her tears with her description of the most important and most thrilling moment of her life—that memorable sunrise meeting on "Prayer Meeting Hill," as she rehearsed the story one night in Nellore, India, to Dr. Cortland Myers.

They all prayed, and they all believed! They talked and then they prayed again! They wrestled before heaven's throne in the face of a heathen world, like Elijah on Carmel. At last the day dawned. Just as the sun rose above the horizon Dr. Jowett arose out of darkness and seemed to see a great light. He lifted his hand heavenward and turned his tear-stained face toward the great Heart of Love. He declared that his vision saw the cactus field below transformed into a church and mission buildings!

His faith grasped and gripped the great fact! He claimed the promise and challenged God to answer a prayer that was entirely for His own glory and the salvation of men!

The money came immediately, and clearly from God's hand!

The man—God's choice, came immediately! Clearly it was of God that Dr. Clough was called to put new life and hope into the almost abandoned mission.

Today on that very cactus field stands the Christian church with the largest membership of any church on earth—20,000 members! If it had not been divided by necessity there would now be 50,000 members—the greatest miracle of the modern missionary world.

On that well-nigh abandoned field, Dr. Clough baptized 10,000 persons in one year; 2,222 in one day!

"Prayer Meeting Hill moved the throne of God, and made the world tremble! The battlements of heaven must have been crowded to watch these many workings of a prayer for His glory!"

DAY 106

Sing . . . to the Lord, always giving thanks
to God the Father for everything.

EPHESIANS 5:19–20

No matter the source of the evil confronting you, if you are in God and thereby completely surrounded by Him, you must realize that it has first passed through Him before coming to you. Because of this, you can thank Him for everything that comes your way. This does not mean thanking Him for the sin that accompanies evil, but offering thanks for what He will bring out of it and through it. May God make our life one of continual thanksgiving and praise, so He will then make everything a blessing.

I once saw a man draw some black dots on a piece of paper. Several of us looked at it yet saw nothing but an irregular arrangement of dots. Then he also drew a few lines, put in a few rests, and added a treble clef at the beginning. Suddenly we realized that the dots were musical notes, and as we began to sound them out, we were singing,

Praise God from whom all blessings flow,
Praise Him all creatures here below.

Each of us has many black dots or spots in our life, and we cannot understand why they are there or why God permitted them. But when we allow Him into our life to adjust the dots in the proper way, to draw the lines He desires, and to put rests at the proper places to separate us from certain things, then from the black dots and spots He will compose a glorious harmony.

So let us not hinder Him in His glorious work! C. H. P.

Would we know that the major chords were sweet,
If there were no minor key?
Would the painter's work be fair to our eyes,
Without shade on land or sea?
Would we know the meaning of happiness,
Would we feel that the day was bright,
If we'd never known what it was to grieve,
Nor gazed on the dark of night?

Many people owe the grandeur of their lives to their tremendous difficulties. CHARLES H. SPURGEON

When an organist presses the black keys of a great organ, the notes are just as beautiful as when he presses the white ones. Yet to fully demonstrate the capabilities of the instrument, he must press them all.

DAY 107

Blessed are those who have not seen and yet have believed.

JOHN 20:29

There are those to whom no visions come, no moments upon the mount suffused with a glory that never was on land or sea. Let not such envy the men of vision. It may be that the vision is given to strengthen a faith that else were weak. It is to the people who can live along the line of what others call the commonplace, and yet trust, that the Master says, "Blessed."

Beware of a life of fitful impulse. Live and act on sustained principle. It is a poor thing—the flash of summer lightning, compared with the steady luster of moon and star.

"The darkest night has stars in it!"

When the low mood comes, open your New Testament. Read it imaginatively: stand on the shore at Capernaum; visit the home at Bethany; sit by Jacob's well and in the Upper Room; look into the eyes of Jesus; listen to His voice; take a walk around by Calvary; remember the crown of thorns; then tell yourself (for it is true), "All this was for me! The Son of God loved me, and gave Himself for me." And see if a passion of praise does not send the low mood flying.

"Praise and service are great healers." When life grows sore and wounding, and it is difficult to be brave, praise God! Sing something, and you will rally your own heart with the song!

You must learn to swim and hold your head above the water even when the sense of His Presence is not with you to hold up your chin.

Do not depend on frames or feelings. You cannot always live in the tropics.

April 18th

DAY 108

Then they believed his promises and sang his praise. But they soon forgot what he had done and did not wait for his plan to unfold. In the desert they gave in to their craving; in the wilderness they put God to the test. So he gave them what they asked for, but sent a wasting disease upon them.

PSALM 106:12–15

In Hebrews 11:27, we read that Moses "persevered because he saw him who is invisible." Yet in the above passage, exactly the opposite was true of the children of Israel. They persevered only when their circumstances were favorable, because they were primarily influenced by whatever appealed to their senses, instead of trusting in the invisible and eternal God.

Even today we have people who live an inconsistent Christian life because they have become preoccupied with things that are external. Therefore they focus on their circumstances rather than focusing on God. And God desires that we grow in our ability to see Him in everything and to realize the importance of seemingly insignificant circumstances if they are used to deliver a message from Him.

We read of the children of Israel, "Then they believed his promises." They did not believe until after they saw—once they saw Him work, "then they believed." They unabashedly doubted God when they came to the Red Sea, but when He opened the way and led them across and they saw Pharaoh and his army drowned—"Then they believed." The Israelites continued to live this kind of up-and-down existence, because their faith was dependent on their circumstances. And this is certainly not the kind of faith God wants us to have.

The world says that "seeing is believing," but God wants us to believe in order to see. The psalmist said, "I would have despaired unless I had believed that I would see the goodness of the LORD in the land of the living" (Ps. 27:13 NASB).

Do you believe God only when your circumstances are favorable, or do you believe no matter what your circumstances may be? C. H. P.

Faith is believing what we do not see, and the reward for this kind of faith is to see what we believe. SAINT AUGUSTINE

DAY 109

You must go to everyone I send you to.

JEREMIAH 1:7

Have you ever read George Eliot's poem called "Stradivarius"? Stradivari was the famous old violin maker whose violins, nearly two centuries old, are almost worth their weight in gold today. Says Stradivari in the poem:

If my hand slacked,
I should rob God—since He is fullest good,
Leaving a blank instead of violins.
He could not make Antonio Stradivari's violins
Without Antonio.

You are God's opportunity in your day. He has waited for ages for a person just like you. If you refuse Him, then God loses His opportunity which He sought through you, and He will never have another for there will never be another person on the earth just like you.

Bring to God your gift, my brother,
He'll not need to call another,
You will do;
He will add His blessing to it,
And the two of you will do it,
God and you.

R. E. NEIGHBOUR

Get taken clear out into the purpose of God and let Him lade you with merchandise for others.

We find scores of people in middle life who are in the unhappy position of doing everyday work which they hate and which does not express the personality, when each one might have done brilliantly in another sphere if he had given a day's prayerful thought to a decision which affected half a century.

DAY 110

And when they climbed into the boat, the wind died down.

MATTHEW 14:32

Faith can conquer every obstacle! Some people insist upon holding Christ at a distance, waiting before going to Him until obstacles have been removed. When economic skies are brighter; when doubts have been cleared; when the edge of sorrow has been dulled: then they will go to Jesus.

Peter, knowing that the Master was near, in sublime faith asked to be permitted to go to Him across the surging waters. Fear almost conquered him, but even then Jesus lifted him by the hand.

There are always storms of difficulty and of assailing doubts. Unanswered questions and the problems of hideous wrongs are always battling against the good purposes of Christ. Do not let the storms keep you from the consoling presence of Christ. Build a bridge out of the storms, and go to Him!

"Get into the boat!" Thou didst whisper.
At first how I feared to obey;
I looked not at Thee, but the storm clouds,
The darkness, the waves, and the spray.
But then came the words, "Will you trust Him?
Will you claim and receive at His hand
All His definite fullness of blessing?
Launch out at thy Master's command!"

Thou art willing, my Lord, could I doubt Thee?
Hast Thou ever proved untrue?
Nay! out at Thy word I have ventured,
I have trusted. Thy part is to do.

LAURA A. BARTER-SNOW

When Jesus rises, the storm stops. The calm comes from the power of His Presence. As a strong quiet man steps in majestically among a crowd of noisy brawlers, his very appearance makes them ashamed and hushes their noise; so Jesus steps in among the elements, and they are still in a moment.

DAY 111

When I called him he was only
one man, and I blessed him.

ISAIAH 51:2

A celebrated Scottish nobleman and statesman once replied to a correspondent that he was "plowing his lonely furrow." Whenever God has required someone to do a big thing for Him, He has sent him to a lonely furrow. He has called him to go alone.

You may have to become the loneliest person on earth, but if you do you will be able always to see around you the chariots of God, even twenty thousand, and thousands of thousands, and then you will forget your loneliness.

The soil is hard,
And the plow goes heavily.
The wind is fierce
And I toil on wearily—
But His hands made the yoke!
Ah wonder—that I should bear His yoke—

It is enough, if I may but plow the furrow,
For the Sower to sow the seed.

If you have taken hold of the plow, hold on until the field is finished. "Let us not cave in" (fall out and leave a gap) (Gal. 6:9, Greek).

Says Theodore L. Cuyler, "After long and painful perplexities about accepting a certain attractive call, I opened the Book and read: 'Why gaddest thou about so much to change thy way?'" (Jer. 2:36 KJV).

"Your present field may be limited, but you are not limited by your field. Great men have sprung from the furrows. Great men have plowed and harrowed, and leaving these things have written their names deep in history. There are heights undreamed of, ecstasies unthought of for the one who follows on. So follow on in the valley, looking for hills. One day you will look back with surprise, and then turning go forward with fresh courage."

You were made to mount and not to crawl!

"One lonely soul on fire with the love of God may set the whole universe ablaze" (Acts 2:41; Rev. 5:11).

April 22nd

DAY 112

For through the Spirit we eagerly await by faith
the righteousness for which we hope.

GALATIANS 5:5

There are times when everything looks very dark to me—so dark that I have to wait before I have hope. Waiting with hope is very difficult, but true patience is expressed when we must even wait for hope. When we see no hint of success yet refuse to despair, when we see nothing but the darkness of night through our window yet keep the shutters open because stars may appear in the sky, and when we have an empty place in our heart yet will not allow it to be filled with anything less than God's best—that is the greatest kind of patience in the universe. It is the story of Job in the midst of the storm, Abraham on the road to Moriah, Moses in the desert of Midian, and the Son of Man in the Garden of Gethsemane. And there is no patience as strong as that which endures because we see "him who is invisible" (Heb. 11:27). It is the kind of patience that waits for hope.

Dear Lord, You have made waiting beautiful and patience divine. You have taught us that Your will should be accepted, simply because it is Your will. You have revealed to us that a person may see nothing but sorrow in his cup yet still be willing to drink it because of a conviction that Your eyes see further than his own.

Father, give me Your divine power—the power of Gethsemane. Give me the strength to wait for hope—to look through the window when there are no stars. Even when my joy is gone, give me the strength to stand victoriously in the darkest night and say, "To my heavenly Father, the sun still shines."

I will have reached the point of greatest strength once I have learned to wait for hope. GEORGE MATHESON

Strive to be one of the few who walk this earth with the ever present realization—every morning, noon, and night—that the unknown that people call heaven is directly behind those things that are visible.

DAY 113

Your name will no longer be Jacob, but Israel, because you have struggled with God and with humans and have overcome.

GENESIS 32:28

Napoleon was once reviewing his troops near Paris. The horse on which he sat was restless, and the Emperor having thoughtlessly dropped the reins from his hand in the eagerness of giving a command, the spirited animal bounded away and the rider was in danger of being hurled to the ground. A young private standing in the lines leaped forward and, seizing the bridle, saved his beloved Commander from a fall. The Emperor glancing at him said in his quick abrupt way, “Thank you, Captain.” The private looked up with a smile and asked, “Of what regiment, sir?” “Of my guards,” answered Napoleon, and instantly galloped to another part of the field.

The young soldier laid down his musket with the remark, “Whoever will may carry that gun; I am done with it,” and proceeded at once to join a group of officers who stood conversing at a little distance. One of them, a General, observing his self-possessed approach, angrily said, “What is this insolent fellow doing here?”

“This insolent fellow,” answered the young soldier looking the other steadily in the eye, “is a Captain of the Guards.” “Why, man,” responded the officer, “you are insane; why do you speak thus?” “He said it,” replied the soldier, pointing to the Emperor, who was far down the lines. “I beg your pardon, Captain,” politely returned the General, “I was not aware of your promotion.”

To those looking on he was still a private, dressed in the coarse rough garb of a common soldier; but in the bold assertion of his dignity, he could meet all the jeers of his comrades and all the scoffs of his superiors with the ready reply, “He said it.”

He said it! He said it!!

DAY 114

Test me in this . . . and see if I will not throw open the floodgates of heaven and pour out so much blessing that there will not be room enough to store it.

MALACHI 3:10

Here is what God is saying in this verse: “My dear child, I still have floodgates in heaven, and they are still in service. The locks open as easily as before, and the hinges have not grown rusty. In fact, I would rather throw them open to pour out the blessings than hold them back. I opened them for Moses, and the sea parted. I opened them for Joshua, and the Jordan River was stopped. I opened them for Gideon, and the armies of the enemy fled. And I will open them for you—if you will only let Me.

"On My side of the floodgates, heaven is still the same rich storehouse as always. The fountains and streams still overflow, and the treasure-rooms are still bursting with gifts. The need is not on My side but on yours. I am waiting for you to 'test me in this.' But you must first meet the condition I have set to 'bring the whole tithe into the storehouse' [Mal. 3:10], and thereby give Me the opportunity to act."

I will never forget my mother's concise paraphrase of Malachi 3:10. The actual Bible text begins with the words "Bring the whole tithe into the storehouse" and ends with "I will . . . pour out so much blessing that," in effect, "you will be embarrassed over your lack of space to receive it." But my mother's paraphrase was this: "Give all He asks and take all He promises." SAMUEL DICKEY GORDON

God's ability to perform is far beyond our prayers—even our greatest prayers! I have recently been thinking of some of the requests I have made of Him innumerable times in my prayers. And what have I requested? I have asked for a cupful, while He owns the entire ocean! I have asked for one simple ray of light, while He holds the sun! My best asking falls immeasurably short of my Father's ability to give, which is far beyond what we could ever ask. JOHN HENRY JOWETT

All the rivers of Your grace I claim,
Over every promise write my name.

EPH. 1:8–19

DAY 115

Why this waste?

MARK 14:4

There is nothing that seems more prodigal than the waste of nature. The showers fall and sink into the ground, and seem to be lost. The rain cometh down from heaven and returneth not thither; the rivers run into the sea, and become absorbed in the ocean's brine. All this seems like a waste of precious material; and yet, science has taught us that no force is ever wasted, but simply converted into another form in which it goes on its way with an altered ministry, but an undiminished force.

Someone has represented in a sort of poetic parable a little raindrop trembling in the air, and questioning with the Genius of the sky whether it should fall upon the earth or still linger in the beautiful cloud.

"Why should I be lost and buried in the dirty soil? Why should I disappear in the dark mud, when I may glisten like a diamond or shine like an emerald or ruby in the rainbow's arch?"

"Yes," the Genius agrees; "but, if you fall in the earth you will come forth with a better resurrection in the petal of the flower, in the fragrance of the rose, in the hanging cluster of the vine."

And so, at last, the timid crystal drops one tear of regret, disappears beneath the soil, and is speedily drunk by the parched ground; it has gone out of sight—apparently out of existence. But lo! the root of yonder lily drinks in the moisture; the sap vessels of that damask rose absorb its refreshing draft; the far-reaching rootlet of yonder vine has found that fountain of life—and in a little while that raindrop comes forth in the snowy blossom of the lily, in the rich perfume of the rose, in the purple cluster of the vine, and as it meets once more the Genius of the air it answers back its glad acknowledgment: "Yes, I died, but I have risen, and now I live in a higher ministry, in a larger life, in a better resurrection." A. B. SIMPSON

Pour out thy love like the rush of a river,
Wasting its waters forever and ever,
Through the burnt sands that reward not the giver:
Silent or songful, thou nearest the sea.
Scatter thy life as the summer's shower pouring;
What if no bird through the pearl rain is soaring?
What if no blossom looks upward adoring?
Look to the life that was lavished for thee!
So the wild wind strews its perfumed caresses:
Evil and thankless the desert it blesses;
Bitter the wave that its soft pinion presses;
Never it ceases to whisper and sing.
What if the hard heart give thorns for thy roses?
What if on rocks thy tired bosom reposes?
Sweeter is music with minor-keyed closes,
Fairest the vines that on ruin will cling.

DAY 116

His way is in the whirlwind and the storm.

NAHUM 1:3

I remember when I was a young person attending school in the vicinity of Mount Pleasant. One day I sat on the side of the mountain and watched a storm as it moved through the valley. The skies were filled with darkness, and thunder began to shake the earth. It seemed as though the lush landscape were completely changed, and its beauty gone forever. But the storm passed quickly and soon moved out of the valley.

If I had sat in the same place the following day and said, "Where is that intense storm and all its terrible darkness?" the grass would have said, "Part of it is in me." The beautiful daisy would have said, "Part of it is in me." And all the other flowers, fruits, and everything that grows in the ground would have said, "Part of the storm has produced the radiance in me."

Have you ever asked the Lord to make you like Him? Have you ever desired the fruit of the Spirit and prayed for sweetness, gentleness, and love? If so, then never fear the fierce storms that even now may be blowing through your life. Storms bring blessings, and rich fruit will be harvested later. HENRY WARD BEECHER

The flowers live by the tears that fall
From the sad face of the skies;
And life would have no joys at all,
Were there no watery eyes.
Love the sorrow, for grief will bring
Its own reward in later years;
The rainbow! See how fair a thing
God has built up from tears.

HENRY S. SUTTON

April 27th

DAY 117

Do you not know that your bodies are temples of the Holy Spirit, who is in you, whom you have received from God? You are not your own; you were bought at a price. Therefore honor God with your bodies.

1 CORINTHIANS 6:19–20

The Christian who truly enters into these two verses has solved some of the deepest problems in life. Those who recognize God's absolute proprietorship of their bodies are not long in doubt as to where they should go, or what they should do. Consecration is simply a matter of letting God have what He has paid for, or returning stolen property.

"You were bought at a price." It was an infinite price that God paid. It was something more than silver and gold—the precious Blood of His only begotten Son (see 1 Peter 1:18–19). God emphasizes the tremendous cost of redemption as an appeal to the heart of the redeemed. The price He has paid measures His estimate of us. He does not give a life so dear to Him for a soul that is worth nothing to Him. He has laid down the gold of His heart—even Jesus Christ. If we would go and stand on Calvary's hill, and consider what it has cost heaven to purchase our salvation, we could not long withhold from Him what He rightfully owns—the full service of spirit, soul, and body. Yet how many are satisfied to say, "Jesus is mine," who never go on to say, "I am His." One who takes this higher ground is bound to be careful what he does with property which belongs to another.

When the thought of His proprietorship becomes uppermost, then we will simultaneously recognize the fact that being His, we are temples of the Holy Spirit. Conscious of God's ownership, and thoughtful of our Divine Guest—the Holy Spirit—it is only natural that we should glorify God in our bodies and in our spirits, which are His. To glorify Him thus is simply to exhibit the power and character of God in that which is His.

The Christian's greatest joy is found in letting God possess His own property.

DAY 118

Have you entered the storehouses . . . which I reserve for times of trouble?

JOB 38:22–23

Our trials are great opportunities, but all too often we simply see them as large obstacles. If only we would recognize every difficult situation as something God has chosen to prove His love to us, each obstacle would then become a place of shelter and rest, and a demonstration to others of His inexpressible power. If we would look for the signs of His glorious handiwork, then every cloud would indeed become a rainbow, and every difficult mountain path would become one of ascension, transformation, and glorification.

If we would look at our past, most of us would realize that the times we endured the greatest stress and felt that every path was blocked were the very times our heavenly Father chose to do the kindest things for us and bestow His richest blessings.

God's most beautiful jewels are often delivered in rough packages by very difficult people, but within the package we will find the very treasures of the King's palace and the Bridegroom's love. A. B. SIMPSON

We must trust the Lord through the darkness, and honor Him with unwavering confidence even in the midst of difficult situations. The reward of this kind of faith will be like that of an eagle shedding its feathers is said to receive—a renewed sense of youth and strength. J. R. MACDUFF

If we could see beyond today
As God can see;
If all the clouds should roll away,
The shadows flee;
O'er present griefs we would not fret.
Each sorrow we would soon forget,
For many joys are waiting yet
For you and me.
If we could know beyond today
As God does know,
Why dearest treasures pass away
And tears must flow;
And why the darkness leads to light,
Why dreary paths will soon grow bright;
Some day life's wrongs will be made right,
Faith tells us so.

"If we could see, if we could know,"
We often say,
But God in love a veil does throw
Across our way;
We cannot see what lies before,
And so we cling to Him the more,
He leads us till this life is o'er;
Trust and obey.

april 29th

DAY 119

But the LORD will be a refuge for his people,
a stronghold for the people of Israel.
JOEL 3:16

Soldiers may be wounded in battle and sent to the hospital. A hospital isn't a shelf; it is a place of repair.

A soldier on service in the spiritual army is never off his battlefield. He is only removed to another part of the field when a wound interrupts what he meant to do, and sets him doing something else.

Is it not joy, pure joy, that there is no question of the shelf? No soldier on service is ever "laid aside"; he is only given another commission to fight among the unseen forces of the field. Never is he shelved as of no further use to his beloved Captain! The soldier must let his Captain say when and for what He needs him most, and he must not cloud his mind with questions. A wise master never wastes his servant's time, nor a commander his soldiers'. So let us settle it once for all and find heart's ease in doing so. There is no discharge in warfare—no, not for a single day. We may be called to serve on the visible field, going continually into the invisible both to renew our strength and to fight the kind of battle that can only be fought there. Or, we may be called off the visible altogether for a while and drawn deep into the invisible. That dreary word "laid aside" is never for us. We are soldiers of the King! ROSE FROM BRIER

Place of repair: O blessed place of refuge!
How gladly will I come to meet Him there,
To cease awhile from all the joy of service
To find a deeper joy with Him to share.
Place of repair: for tired brain and body!
How much I need that place just out of sight
Where only He can talk, and be beside me,
Until again made strong by His great might.
Place of repair: when trials press upon me
And God permits the unexpected test,
'Tis there I learn some lesson sweet and precious
As simply on His faithfulness I rest.
Place of repair: the place to take my sorrow,
The thing that hurts and would be hard to bear,
But somehow in the secret place I'm finding
That all the hurt is healed since He is there.
Place of repair: to wait for fresh enduement
I silently with Him alone would stay
Until He speaks again, and says,
"Go forward to help some other sheep to find the way."
Place of repair: O trysting-place most hallowed,
The Lord Himself is just that place to me,
His grace, His strength, His glory and His triumph,
Himself alone my all-sufficiency.

April 30th

DAY 120

Why, Lord, do you stand far off?

PSALM 10:1

God is . . . an ever-present help in trouble" (Ps. 46:1). But He allows trouble to pursue us, as though He were indifferent to its overwhelming pressure, so we may be brought to the end of ourselves. Through the trial, we are led to discover the treasure of darkness and the immeasurable wealth of tribulation.

We may be sure that He who allows the suffering is with us throughout it. It may be that we will only see Him once the ordeal is nearly passed, but we must dare to believe that He never leaves our trial. Our eyes are blinded so we cannot see the One our soul loves. The darkness and our bandages blind us so that we cannot see the form of our High Priest. Yet He is there and is deeply touched. Let us not rely on our feelings but trust in His unswerving faithfulness. And though we cannot see Him, let us talk to Him. Although His presence is veiled, once we begin to speak to Jesus as if He were literally present, an answering voice comes to show us He is in the shadow, keeping watch over His own. Your Father is as close to you when you journey through the darkest tunnel as He is when you are under the open heaven! DAILY DEVOTIONAL COMMENTARY

Although the path be all unknown?
Although the way be drear?
Its shades I travel not alone
When steps of Yours are near.

DAY 121

"Present your case," says the Lord. "Set forth your arguments," says Jacob's King.

ISAIAH 41:21

Over in Canada there lived an Irish saint called "Holy Ann." She lived to be one hundred years old. When she was a young girl, she was working in a family for very small wages under a very cruel master and mistress. They made her carry water for a mile up a steep hill. At one time there had been a well dug there; it had gone dry, but it stood there year after year. One night she was very tired, and she fell on her knees and cried to God; and while on her knees she read these words: "I will open . . . fountains in the midst of the valleys: I will make . . . the dry land springs of water" (Isa. 41:18 KJV). "Produce your cause, saith the Lord; bring forth your strong reasons" (v. 21). These words struck Holy Ann, and she produced her cause before the Lord. She told Him how badly they needed the water and how hard it was for her to carry the water up the steep hill; then she lay down and fell asleep. She had pleaded her cause and brought forth her strong reasons. The next morning early she was seen to take a bucket and start for the well. Someone asked her where she was going, and she replied, "I am going to draw water from the well." "Why, it is dry," was the answer. But that did not stop Holy Ann. She knew whom she had believed, and on she went; and, lo and behold, there in the well was eighty-three feet of pure, cold water, and she told me that the well never did run dry! That is the way the Lord can fulfill His promises. "Produce your cause . . . bring forth your strong reasons," and see Him work in your behalf.

How little we use this method of holy argument in prayer; and yet there are many examples of it in Scripture: Abraham, Jacob, Moses, Elijah, Daniel—all used arguments in prayer, and claimed the Divine interposition on the ground of the pleas which they presented.

DAY 122

May 2nd

With skillful hands he led them.

PSALM 78:72

When you are unsure which course to take, totally submit your own judgment to that of the Spirit of God, asking Him to shut every door except the right one. But meanwhile keep moving ahead and consider the absence of a direct indication from God to be the evidence of His will that you are on His path. And as you continue down the long road, you will find that He has gone before you, locking doors you otherwise would have been inclined to enter. Yet you can be sure that somewhere beyond the locked doors is one He has left unlocked. And when you open it and walk through, you will find yourself face to face with a turn in the river of opportunity—one that is broader and deeper than anything you ever dared to imagine, even in your wildest dreams. So set sail on it, because it flows to the open sea.

God often guides us through our circumstances. One moment, our way may seem totally blocked, but then suddenly some seemingly trivial incident occurs, appearing as nothing to others but speaking volumes to the keen eye of faith. And sometimes these events are repeated in various ways in response to our prayers. They certainly are not haphazard results of chance but are God opening up the way we should walk, by directing our circumstances. And they begin to multiply as we advance toward our goal, just as the lights of a city seem to increase as we speed toward it while traveling at night. F. B. MEYER

If you go to God for guidance, He will guide you. But do not expect Him to console you by showing you His list of purposes concerning you, when you have displayed distrust or even half-trust in Him. What He will do, if you will trust Him and go cheerfully ahead when He shows you the way, is to guide you still farther. HORACE BUSHNELL

As moves my fragile boat across the storm-swept sea,
Great waves beat o'er her side, as north wind blows;
Deep in the darkness hid lie threat'ning rocks and reefs;
But all of these, and more, my Pilot knows.
Sometimes when darkness falls, and every light's gone out,
I wonder to what port my frail ship goes;
Although the night be long, and restless all my hours,
My distant goal, I'm sure, my Pilot knows.

THOMAS CURTIS CLARK

DAY 123

I being in the way, the LORD led me.

GENESIS 24:27 KJV

The way" means God's way, the pathway prepared for us; not our way; not any kind of way (Proverbs 14:12); not man's way; but the direct way of duty and command. In such a way the Lord will be sure to lead and guide us. The Lord answered the servant's prayer *exactly* as he prayed, step by step.

"God never gives guidance for two steps at a time. I must take one step, and then I receive light for the next."

As thou dost travel down the corridor of Time
Thou wilt find many doors of usefulness;
To gain some there are many weary steps to climb,
And then they will not yield! but onward press,
For there before thee, in the distance just beyond
Lies one which yet will open; enter there,
And thou shalt find all realized thy visions fair
Of fields more vast than thou hast yet conceived.

Press on, faint not; though briars strew thy way,
The greatest things are yet to be achieved;
And he who falters not will win the day.
No man can shut the door which God sets wide,
He bids thee enter there—thy work awaits inside.

FAIRELIE THORNTON

Keep to your post and watch His signals! Implicitly rely on the methods of His guidance.

DAY 124

May 4th

Offer yourselves to God as those who have been brought from death to life.

ROMANS 6:13

One night I went to hear a sermon on consecration. Nothing special came to me from the message, but as the preacher knelt to pray, he said, "O Lord, You know we can trust the Man who died for us." That was my message. As I rose from my knees and walked down the street to catch the train, I deeply pondered all that consecration would mean to my life. I was afraid as I considered the personal cost, and suddenly, above the noise of the street traffic, came this message: "You can trust the Man who died for you." I boarded the train, and as I traveled toward home, I thought of the changes, sacrifices, and disappointments that consecration might mean in my life—and I was still afraid.

Upon arriving home, I went straight to my room, fell on my knees, and saw my life pass before my eyes. I was a Christian, an officer in the church, and a Sunday school superintendent, but I had never yielded my life to God with a definite act of my will. Yet as I thought of my own "precious" plans that might be thwarted, my beloved hopes to be surrendered, and my chosen profession that I might have to abandon—I was afraid.

I completely failed to see the better things God had for me, so my soul was running from Him. And then for the last time, with a swift force of convicting power to my inmost heart, came that searching message: "My child, you can trust the Man who died for you. If you cannot trust Him, then whom can you trust?" Finally that settled it for me, for in a flash of light I realized that the Man who loved me enough to die for me could be absolutely trusted with the total concerns of the life He had saved.

Dear friend, you can trust the Man who died for you. You can trust Him to thwart each plan that should be stopped and to complete each one that results in His greatest glory and your highest good. You can trust Him to lead you down the path that is the very best in this world for you. J. H. M.

Just as I am, Thy love unknown,
Has broken every barrier down,
Now to be Thine, yea, Thine alone,
O Lamb of God, I come!

Life is not wreckage to be saved out of the world but an investment to be used in the world.

DAY 125

And a light shone in the cell. [The angel] struck Peter on the side and woke him up. "Quick, get up!"
ACTS 12:7

If we fear the Lord, we may look for timely interpositions when our case is at its worst. Angels are not kept from us by storms, nor hindered by darkness. Seraphs think it no humiliation to visit the poorest of the heavenly family. If angels' visits are few and far between at ordinary times, they shall be frequent in our nights of tempest and tossing. Dear reader, is this an hour of distress with you? Then ask for peculiar help. Jesus is the Angel of the Covenant, and if His presence be now earnestly sought it will not be denied. What that presence brings is heart cheer. CHARLES H. SPURGEON

And a light shined in my cell,
And there was not any wall,
And there was no dark at all,
Only Thou, Emmanuel.
Light of love shined in my cell,
Turned to gold the iron bars,
Opened windows to the stars,
Peace stood there as sentinel.
Dearest Lord, how can it be
That Thou art so kind to me?
Love is shining in my cell,
Jesus, my Emmanuel.

A. W. C.

DAY 126

I will turn all my mountains into roads.

ISAIAH 49:11

God will make our obstacles serve His purposes. We all have mountains in our lives, and often they are people and things that threaten to block the progress of our spiritual life. The obstacles may be untruths told about us; a difficult occupation; "a thorn in [the] flesh" (2 Cor. 12:7); or our daily cross. And often we pray for their removal, for we tend to think that if only these were removed, we would live a more tender, pure, and holy life.

"How foolish you are, and how slow to believe!" (Luke 24:25). These are the very conditions we need for achievement, and they have been put in our lives as the means of producing the gifts and qualities for which we have been praying so long. We pray for patience for many years, and when something begins to test us beyond our endurance, we run from it. We try to avoid it, we see it as some insurmountable obstacle to our desired goal, and we believe that if it was removed, we would experience immediate deliverance and victory.

This is not true! We would simply see the temptations to be impatient end. This would not be patience. The only way genuine patience can be acquired is by enduring the very trials that seem so unbearable today.

Turn from your running and submit. Claim by faith to be a partaker in the patience of Jesus and face your trials in Him. There is nothing in your life that distresses or concerns you that cannot become submissive to the highest purpose. Remember, they are God's mountains. He puts them there for a reason, and we know He will never fail to keep His promise.

"God understands the way to it and he alone knows where it dwells, for he views the ends of the earth and sees everything under the heavens" (Job 28:23–24). So when we come to the foot of the mountains, we will find our way. F. B. MEYER CHRIST IN ISAIAH

The purpose of our trials is not only to test our worthiness but also to increase it, just as the mighty oak is tested by the storms as well as strengthened by them.

May 7th

DAY 127

Christ in you, the hope of glory.

COLOSSIANS 1:27

The greatest thing that any of us can do is not to live for Christ but to live Christ. What is holy living? It is Christ-life. It is not to be Christians, but Christ-ones. It is not to try to do or be some great thing but simply to have Him and let Him live His own life in us; abiding in Him and He in us, and letting Him reflect His own graces, His own faith, His own consecration, His own love, His own patience, His own gentleness, His own words in us, while we "declare the praises of him who called [us] out of darkness into his wonderful light" (1 Pet. 2:9). This is at once the sublimest and the simplest life that it is possible to live. It is a higher standard than human perfection, and yet it is possible for a poor, sinful, imperfect man to realize it through the perfect Christ who comes to live within us.

God help us so to live, and thus to make real to those around us the simplicity, the beauty, the glory, and the power of the Christ life.

"I cannot tell," said the humble shepherd's wife, "what sermon it was that led me into a life of victory. I cannot even explain the creed or the catechism, but I know that something has changed me entirely. Last summer John and I washed the sheep in yonder stream. I cannot tell you where the water went, but I can show you the clean white fleece of the sheep. And so I may forget the doctrine, but I have its blessed fruit in my heart and life."

Two of us were chatting with Sadhu Sundar Singh in my office one morning. The Sadhu had just arrived in London. We knew little concerning him, and my friend was anxious to find out if he knew the doctrine of that "perfect love" of which Saint John speaks.

"Does he understand?" asked my friend, turning to me.

The Sadhu smiled and quietly said: "When I throw a stone at the fruit tree, the fruit tree throws no stone back, but gives me fruit. Is it that?" Then he went on to ask: "Should not we, who love the Lord Jesus, be like sandalwood, which imparts its fragrance to the ax which cuts it?"

DAY 128

Be courageous; be strong.

1 CORINTHIANS 16:13

Never pray for an easier life—pray to be a stronger person! Never pray for tasks equal to your power—pray for power equal to your tasks. Then doing your work will be no miracle—you will be the miracle. PHILLIPS BROOKS

We must remember that Christ will not lead us to greatness through an easy or self-indulgent life. An easy life does not lift us up but only takes us down. Heaven is always above us, and we must continually be looking toward it.

Some people always avoid things that are costly, or things that require self-denial, self-restraint, and self-sacrifice. Yet it is hard work and difficulties that ultimately lead us to greatness, for greatness is not found by walking the moss-covered path laid out for us through the meadow. It is found by being sent to carve out our own path with our own hands.

Are you willing to sacrifice to reach the glorious mountain peaks of God's purpose for you?

Be strong!
We are not here to play, to dream, to drift;
We have hard work to do, and loads to lift.
Shun not the struggle; face it.
It's God's gift.
Be strong!
Say not the days are evil—Who's to blame?
Or fold your hands, as in defeat—O shame!
Stand up, speak out, and bravely,
In God's name.

Be strong!
It matters not how deep entrenched the wrong,
How hard the battle goes, the day how long,
Faint not, fight on!
Tomorrow comes the song.

MALTBIE D. BABCOCK

DAY 129

The LORD is good to those whose hope is in him, to the one who seeks him; it is good to wait quietly for the salvation of the LORD.

LAMENTATIONS 3:25–26

It is easier to work than to wait. It is often more important to wait than to work. We can trust God to do the needed working while we are waiting; but if we are not willing to wait, and insist upon working while He would have us be still, we may interfere with the effective and triumphant working that He would do in our behalf. Our waiting may be the most difficult thing we can do; it may be the severest test that God can give us.

Oswald Chambers has said truly: One of the greatest strains in life is the strain of waiting for God. God takes the saint like a bow which He stretches; we get to a certain point and say I cannot stand any more; but God goes on stretching. He is not aiming at our mark, but at His own, and the patience of the saints is that we hold on until He lets the arrow fly straight to His goal. If we are willing to remember God's call and assurance there need be no strain at all while we are waiting. The "stretched bow" time may be a time of unbroken rest for us as we are "still before the LORD and wait patiently for him" (Ps. 37:7).

Unless a violin string is stretched until it cries out when the bow is drawn over it, there is no music. A loose violin string with no strain upon it is of no use—it is dead, has no voice. But when stretched till it strains it is brought to the proper tone, and then only is it useful to the music-maker. A. B. SIMPSON

In God's eternal plan, a month, a year,
Is but an hour of some slow April day,
Holding the germs of what we hope or fear,
To blossom far away.

The Almighty is tedious, but He's sure!

DAY 130

Jesus looked up and said, "Father, I thank you that you have heard me."

JOHN 11:41

The sequence of events in this passage seems strange and unusual. Lazarus was still in his tomb, yet Jesus' thanksgiving preceded the miracle of raising him from the dead. It seems that thanks would only have been lifted up once the great miracle had been accomplished and Lazarus had been restored to life. But Jesus gave thanks for what He was about to receive. His gratitude sprang forth before the blessing had arrived, in an expression of assurance that it was certainly on its way. The song of victory was sung before the battle had been fought. It was the Sower singing the song of harvest—it was thanksgiving before the miracle!

Who ever thinks of announcing a victory song as the army is just heading out to the battlefield? And where do we ever hear a song of gratitude and thanksgiving for an answer that has not yet been received?

Yet in this Scripture passage, there is nothing strange, forced, or unreasonable to the Master's sequence of praise before the miracle. Praise is actually the most vital preparation to the working of miracles. Miracles are performed through spiritual power, and our spiritual power is always in proportion to our faith. JOHN HENRY JOWETT

PRAISE CHANGES THINGS

Nothing pleases God more than praise as part of our prayer life, and nothing blesses someone who prays as much as the praise that is offered. I once received a great blessing from this while in China. I had recently received bad news from home, and deep shadows of darkness seemed to cover my soul. I prayed but the darkness remained. I forced myself to endure but the shadows only deepened. Then suddenly one day, as I entered a missionary's home at an inland station, I saw these words on the wall: "Try giving thanks." So I did, and in a moment every shadow was gone, never to return. Yes, the psalmist was right: "It is good to praise the LORD" (Ps. 92:1). HENRY W. FROST

DAY 131

My God in His lovingkindness will meet me; God will let me look triumphantly upon my foes.

PSALM 59:10 NASB

It matters not how great the scheme if God draws it out; it matters not how insurmountable the difficulties appear if God undertakes the responsibility. If we, His children, when we get into tangled corners even by our own folly and sometimes wrongdoing, would only turn to God as a King and as a Father and cast ourselves upon Him, He would work for us and lead us out of our troubles safely and in a manner worthy of a King.

This morning, Lord, I pray
Safeguard us through the day,

Especially at corners of the way.
For when the way is straight,
We fear no sudden fate,
But see ahead the evening's open gate.
But few and far between
Are days when all is seen
Of what will come, or yet of what has been.
For unexpected things
Swoop down on sudden wings
And overthrow us with their buffetings.
And so, dear Lord, we pray,
Control and guard this day
Thy children at the corners of their way.

"CORNERS" M. G. L.

Dr. S. D. Gordon says in his writings: "It is a good thing for us to be put in a tight corner. To be pushed and hemmed in on every side until you are forced to stand with your back to the wall, facing a foe at every angle, with barely standing room—that is good. For one thing, you find out that no matter how close the fit of that corner may be, it still can hold another in addition to yourself. Its very tightness brings you and your Lord into the very closest quarters. And only at closest touch will you find out what a wondrous Friend He is."

"Tight corners are famous places for chamber concerts. The acoustics are wonderful. David's exile Psalms have rung out a strangely sweet melody down all the ages, and out through all the world, and into thousands of hearts."

DAY 132

God is in the midst of her, she will not be moved;
God will help her when morning dawns.

PSALM 46:5 NASB

"Will not be moved"—what an inspiring declaration! Is it possible for us who are so easily moved by earthly things to come to a point where nothing can upset us or disturb our peace? The answer is yes, and the apostle Paul knew it. When he was on his way to Jerusalem, the Holy Spirit warned him that "prison and hardships" (Acts 20:23) awaited him. Yet he could triumphantly say, "But none of these things move me" (Acts 20:24 KJV).

Everything in Paul's life and experience that could be disturbed had already been shaken, and he no longer considered his life or any of his possessions as having any earthly value. And if we will only let God have His way with us, we can come to the same point. Then, like Paul, neither the stress and strain of little things nor the great and heavy trials of life will have enough power to move us from "the peace of God, which transcends all understanding" (Phil. 4:7). God declares this peace to be the inheritance of those who have learned to rest only on Him.

"The one who is victorious I will make a pillar in the temple of my God. Never again will they leave it" (Rev. 3:12). Becoming as immovable as a pillar in the house of God is such a worthy objective that we would gladly endure all the necessary trials that take us there! HANNAH WHITALL SMITH

When God is the center of a kingdom or a city, He makes it strong "like Mount Zion, which cannot be shaken" (Ps. 125:1). And when God is the center of a soul, although disasters may crowd in on all sides and roar like the waves of the sea, there is a constant calm within. The world can neither give nor take away this kind of peace. What is it that causes people to shake like leaves today at the first hint of danger? It is simply the lack of God living in their soul, and having the world in their hearts instead. R. LEIGHTON

"Those who trust in the LORD are like Mount Zion, which cannot be shaken but endures forever" (Ps. 125:1). There is an old Scottish version of this psalm that strengthens our blood like iron:

Who clings to God in constant trust
As Zion's mount he stands full just,
And who moves not, nor yet does reel,
But stands forever strong as steel!

DAY 133

No purpose of yours can be thwarted.

JOB 42:2

We believe in the providence of God, but we do not believe half enough in it. Remember that Omnipotence has servants everywhere, set in their places at every point of the road. In the old days of the post horses, there were always swift horses ready to carry onward the king's mails.

It is wonderful how God has His relays of providential agents; how when He has done with one there is always another ready to take his place. Sometimes you have found one friend fail you—he is just dead and buried. "Ah!" you say, "what shall I do?" Well, well, God knows how to carry on the purposes of His providence; He will raise up another. How strikingly punctual providence is! You and I make appointments and miss them by half an hour; but God never missed an appointment yet! God never is before His time though we often wish He were; but He is never behind—no, not by one tick of the clock.

When the children of Israel were to go down out of Egypt, all the Pharaohs in the pyramids, if they had risen to life again, could not have kept them in bondage another half minute. "Thus saith the LORD . . . Let my people go!" It was time, and go they must! All the kings of the earth, and all the princes thereof, are in subjection to the kingdom of God's providence, and He can move them just as He pleases. And now, trembler, wherefore are you afraid? "Fear thou not; for I am with thee" (Isa. 41:10 KJV). All the mysterious arrangements of providence work for our good. CHARLES H. SPURGEON

May 14th

DAY 134

Awake, north wind, and come, south wind! Blow on my garden, that its fragrance may spread everywhere.

SONG OF SONGS 4:16

Let us examine the meaning of this prayer for a moment. It is rooted in the fact that in the same way beautiful fragrances may lie hidden in a spice plant, certain gifts may lie unused or undeveloped in a Christian's heart. Many seeds of a profession of faith may be planted, but from some the air is never filled with the aroma of holy desires or godly deeds. The same winds blow on the thistle and the spice plant, but only one of them emits a rich fragrance.

Sometimes God causes severe winds of trial to blow upon His children to develop their gifts. Just as a torch burns more brightly when waved back and forth, and just as a juniper plant smells sweetest when thrown into the flames, so the richest qualities of a Christian often arise under the strong winds of suffering and adversity. Bruised hearts often emit the fragrance that God loves to smell.

I had a tiny box, a precious box
Of human love—my perfume of great price;
I kept it close within my heart of hearts
And scarce would lift the lid lest it should waste

Its fragrance on the air. One day a strange
Deep sorrow came with crushing weight, and fell
Upon my costly treasure, sweet and rare,
And broke the box to pieces. All my heart
Rose in dismay and sorrow at this waste,
But as I mourned, behold a miracle
Of grace Divine. My human love was changed
To Heaven's own, and poured in healing streams
On other broken hearts, while soft and clear
A voice above me whispered, "Child of Mine,
With comfort wherewith you are comforted,
From this time forth, go comfort others,
And you will know blest fellowship with Me,
Whose broken heart of love has healed the world."

May 15th

DAY 135

I AM WHO I AM.

EXODUS 3:14

God is His own equivalent, and God needs nothing but Himself to achieve the great purposes on which He has set His heart.

God gave Moses a blank, and as life went forward for the next forty years, Moses kept filling in the blank with his special need. He filled in fearlessness before Pharaoh. He filled in guidance across the Red Sea. He filled in manna for the whole population. He filled in water from the rock. He filled in guidance through the wilderness. He filled in victory over Amalek. He filled in clear revelation at Sinai. And so Moses, for the rest of his life, had little else to do than to go quietly alone, and taking God's blank checkbook, signed by God's name, I AM WHO I AM, write in I AM GUIDANCE; I AM BREAD. He presented the check and God honored it.

And whenever you come to live upon God's plan as Moses from that moment did, you may absolutely trust God. And when you come down to the hoar-head you will say, "Not one of all the good promises the LORD your God gave you has failed" (Josh. 23:14). A. B. SIMPSON

Joshua had tried God forty years in the brick kilns, forty years in the desert, and thirty years in the Promised Land, and this was his dying testimony. D. L. MOODY

Whatever life may bring to you,
"God" will ring true to you:
Star in your sky—
Food in your store—
Staff in your hand—
Friend by your side—
Light on your path—
Joy in your heart—
In your ears music—
In your mouth songs.
Yes, rapid as your race may run,
And scorching as may shine your sun,
And bitter as may blow your blast,
And lonely as your lot be cast—
Whatever life may bring to you,
"God" will aye ring true to you.

CHARLES HERBERT

DAY 136

Go from your country . . . to the land I will show you.

GENESIS 12:1

It was one of the great moments of history when this primitive caravan set out for Haran. As we dimly picture them setting forth in the pale dawn of history, we seem to see the laden camels, pacing slowly, towering above the slow-footed sheep; we hear the drovers' cries and bleating of the flocks, broken by the wail of parting women.

With those who stay behind we strain wistful eyes across the broad flood of old Euphrates, till in the wilderness beyond, the caravan is lost in a faint dust-haze—a stain and no more on the southern horizon.

Who does not feel that the grandeur of that moment centers in the loyalty of one human soul to one word of God?

> *"There's no sense in going further—it's the edge of cultivation."*
> *So they said and I believed it—broke my land and sowed my crop—*
> *Built my barns and strung my fences in the little border station—*
> *Tucked away below the foothills where the trails run out*
> *and stop.*
> *Till a voice, as bad as conscience, rang interminable changes*
> *On one everlasting whisper, day and night repeated so:*
> *"Something hidden. Go and find it. Go and look behind the Ranges—*
> *Something lost behind the Ranges, lost and waiting for you. Go!"*
> *Anybody might have found it, but—His whisper came to me!*

KIPLING

There remaineth yet very much land to be possessed!

Like the western prairies, there is no limit; it extends beyond the power of the human mind. "'What no eye has seen, what no ear has heard, and what no human mind has conceived'—the things God has prepared for those who love him" (1 Cor. 2:9).

The Holy Ghost is looking for simple-hearted believers who will claim for Jesus Christ the great stretches of unoccupied places of darkness. Who will strike the Trail?

May 17th

DAY 137

It will be even more fruitful.

JOHN 15:2

Two years ago I set out a rosebush in the corner of my garden. It was to bear yellow roses. And it was to bear them profusely. Yet, during these two years, it has not produced a blossom!

I asked the florist from whom I bought the bush why it was so barren of flowers. I had cultivated it carefully; had watered it often; had made the soil around it as rich as possible. And it had grown well.

"That's just why," said the florist. "That kind of rose needs the poorest soil in the garden. Sandy soil would be best, and never a bit of fertilizer. Take away the rich soil and put gravelly earth in its place. Cut the bush back severely. Then it will bloom."

I did—and the bush blossomed forth in the most gorgeous yellow known to nature. Then I moralized: that yellow rose is just like many lives. Hardships develop beauty in the soul; the soul thrives on troubles; trials bring out all the best in them; ease and comfort and applause only leave them barren.

PASTOR JOYCE

The bark by tempest vainly tossed
May founder in the calm;

And he who braved the polar frost
Faint by the isles of balm.

WHITTIER

The finest of flowers bloom in the sandiest of deserts as well as in the hothouses. God is the same Gardener.

DAY 138

You are my King and my God, who decrees victories for Jacob.

PSALM 44:4

There are no enemies to your growth in grace, or to your Christian work, that were not included in your Savior's victory. Remember, "The LORD said to Joshua, 'Do not be afraid of them, because . . . I will hand all of them . . . over to [you]'" (Josh. 11:6). Also recall the fact that when you resist your enemies, they "will flee from you" (James 4:7). And remember what Joshua said to the people: "Do not be afraid; do not be discouraged. Be strong and courageous" (Josh. 10:25). The Lord is with you, "mighty men of valour" (Josh. 1:14 KJV), and you are mighty because you are one with the Mightiest. So claim victory!

Whenever your enemies are closing in on you, claim victory! Whenever your heart and your flesh fail you, look up and claim victory! Be sure you claim your share in the triumph that Jesus won, for He won it not for Himself alone but for us all. Remember that you were in Him when He won it—so claim victory!

Count Christ's victory as yours and gather the spoils of the war. Neither the giant "descendants of Anak" (Num. 13:33) nor fortified cities need intimidate or defeat you. You are a part of the conquering army. Claim your share in the Savior's victory. F. B. MEYER JOSHUA

We are children of the King. Therefore which of these most honors our divine Sovereign: failing to claim our rights and even doubting they belong to us, or asserting our privilege as children of the Royal Family and demanding the rights that accompany our inheritance?

May 19th

DAY 139

His praise will always be on my lips.

PSALM 34:1

I heard a joyous strain—
A lark on a leafless bough
Sat singing in the rain.

I heard him singing early in the morning. It was hardly light! I could not understand that song; it was fairly a lilt of joy. It had been a portentous night for me, full of dreams that did disturb me. Old things that I had hoped to forget, and new things that I had prayed could never come, trooped through my dreams like grinning little bare-faced imps. Certainly I was in no humor to sing. What could possess that fellow out yonder to be telling the whole township how joyous he was? He was perched on the rail fence by the spring run. He was drenched. It had rained in the night and evidently he had been poorly housed. I pitied him. What comfort could he have had through that night bathed in the storm? He never thought of comfort. His song was not bought by any such duplicity. It was in his heart. Then I shook myself: The shame that a lark has finer poise than a man! G. A. LEICHLITER

"Nothing can break you as long as you sing."

DAY 140

In the shadow of his hand he hid me; he made me into a polished arrow and concealed me in his quiver.

ISAIAH 49:2

"In the shadow"—each of us must go there sometimes. The glare of the sunlight is too bright, and our eyes become injured. Soon they are unable to discern the subtle shades of color or appreciate neutral tints, such as the shadowed sickroom, the shadowed house of grief, or the shadowed life where the sunlight has departed.

But fear not! It is the shadow of God's hand. He is leading you, and there are lessons that can be learned only where He leads.

The photograph of His face can only be developed in the dark room. But do not assume that He has pushed you aside.

You are still "in his quiver." He has not thrown you away as something worthless.

He is only keeping you nearby till the moment comes when He can send you quickly and confidently on some mission that will bring Him glory. O shadowed, isolated one, remember how closely the quiver is tied to the warrior. It is always within easy reach of his hand and jealously protected. F. B. MEYER

In some realms of nature, shadows or darkness are the places of greatest growth. The beautiful Indian corn never grows more rapidly than in the darkness of a warm summer night. The sun withers and curls the leaves in the scorching light of noon, but once a cloud hides the sun, they quickly unfold. The shadows provide a service that the sunlight does not. The starry beauty of the sky cannot be seen at its peak until the shadows of night slip over the sky. Lands with fog, clouds, and shade are lush with greenery. And there are beautiful flowers that bloom in the shade that will never bloom in the sun. Florists now have their evening primrose as well as their morning glory. The evening primrose will not open in the noonday sun but only reveals its beauty as the shadows of the evening grow longer.

If all of life were sunshine,
Our face would long to gain
And feel once more upon it
The cooling splash of rain.

HENRY JACKSON VAN DYKE

DAY 141

May 21st

But whatever were gains to me I now consider loss for the sake of Christ.

PHILIPPIANS 3:7

If God has called you to be really like Christ, He may draw you into a life of crucifixion and humility, and put on you such demands of obedience that He will not allow you to follow other Christians, and in many ways He will seem to let other good people do things which He will not let you do.

Other Christians, who seem very religious and useful, may push themselves, pull wires, and work schemes to carry out their plans, but you cannot do it; and if you attempt it you will meet with such failure and rebuke from the Lord as to make you sorely penitent.

Others may boast of themselves, of their work, of their success, of their writing, but the Holy Spirit will not allow you to do any such thing, and if you begin it He will lead you into some deep mortification, that will make you despise yourself and all your good works.

Others will be allowed to succeed in making money . . . but it is likely God will keep you poor, because He wants you to have something farbetter than gold, and that is a helpless dependence on Him, that He may have the privilege of supplying your needs day by day out of an unseen treasury.

The Lord will let others be honored and put forward, and keep you hid away in obscurity because He wants to produce some choice fragrant fruit for His coming glory.

He will let others be great, but keep you small. He will let others do a work for Him, and get the credit for it, but He will make you work and toil without knowing how much you are doing.

The Holy Spirit will put a strict watch over you . . . rebuking you for little words and feelings, or for wasting time.

God is an Infinite Sovereign: He has a right to do as He pleases with His own.

Settle it forever, then, that you are to deal directly with the Lord Jesus—that He is to have the privilege of tying your tongue, chaining your hand, or closing your eyes in ways that He does not deal with others.

Then, you will have found the vestibule of heaven.

"Others may. You cannot!"

DAY 142

So when he heard that Lazarus was sick, he stayed where he was two more days.

JOHN 11:6

This miraculous story begins with the following declaration: "Jesus loved Martha and her sister and Lazarus" (v. 5). It is as if God were teaching us that at the very heart and foundation of all His dealings with us, no matter how dark and mysterious they may be, we must dare to believe in and affirm His infinite, unmerited, and unchanging love. Yet love permits pain to occur.

Mary and Martha never doubted that Jesus would quickly avert every obstacle to keep their brother from death, but "when he heard that Lazarus was sick, he stayed where he was two more days."

What a startling word: "but"! Jesus refrained from going not because He did not love them but because He did love them. It was His love alone that kept Him from hurrying at once to their beloved yet grief-stricken home. Anything less than infinite love would have rushed instantly to the relief of those beloved and troubled hearts, in an effort to end their grief, to have the blessing of wiping and stopping the flow of their tears, and to cause their sorrow and pain to flee. Only the power of divine love could have held back the spontaneity of the Savior's tenderheartedness until the angel of pain had finished his work.

Who can estimate the great debt we owe to suffering and pain? If not for them, we would have little capacity for many of the great virtues of the Christian life. Where would our faith be if not for the trials that test it; or patience, without anything to endure or experience and without tribulations to develop it?

Loved! then the way will not be drear;
For One we know is ever near,
Proving it to our hearts so clear
That we are loved.
Loved when our sky is clouded o'er,
And days of sorrow press us sore;
Still we will trust Him evermore,
For we are loved.
Time, that affects all things below,
Can never change the love He'll show;
The heart of Christ with love will flow,
And we are loved.

DAY 143

And now, do not be distressed and do not be angry with yourselves for selling me here, because it was to save lives that God sent me ahead of you.

GENESIS 45:5

When you are disappointed or vexed or hedged in or thwarted; when you are seemingly abandoned, remember, son of God, heir of Heaven, that you are being prepared for the higher life. You need courage, patience, perseverance, and it is in the hard places that they are developed. You need faith, and you will never have it unless you are brought to circumstances in which you are compelled to act by the invisible rather than the visible. You need those Christian graces of which the Bible speaks, and of which the pulpit preaches; and practical life, with its various vicissitudes, is God's school in which you are to acquire these things. Do not be discouraged or cast down.

When you are bestead, remember that God is dealing with you as a good schoolmaster. You will thank Him for His severity by and by.

When God is dealing with you, do not accuse Him. Do not cry out, "Why hast thou forsaken me?" Remember, that to those who are exercised thereby God shows His love and His Fatherhood. Bow yourselves meekly to the chastisements of God, and study not how you can get away from the trouble, but how you can rise above it by being made better by it.

I knew I had been sold,
For circumstance
Dark as a desert pit
And dismal as the slaver's caravan
Surrounded me,
And seemed to crush me down;
I had been sold.
I also had been sent.

The circumstance
Shone with the light Divine,
And through the wrath of men
God put me in His own appointed place.
He set on high
And none could bow me down.
I Had Been Sent.

"JOSEPH," M. MANNINGTON DEXTER

Had we no tests, no great hedged-in experiences, we would never know what a wonderful Deliverer and triumphant Guide we have!

He never limits us, except to liberate us!

DAY 144

Though the fig tree does not bud and there are no grapes on the vines, though the olive crop fails and the fields produce no food, though there are no sheep in the pen and no cattle in the stalls, yet I will rejoice in the Lord, I will be joyful in God my Savior.

HABAKKUK 3:17–18

I ask you to observe what a disastrous situation is being described in this passage and to notice how courageous is the faith that is expressed. It is as if the writer were actually saying, "Even if I am forced to undergo the extreme condition of not knowing where to find my next meal, and although my house is empty and my fields yield no crops and I see the evidence of divine pestilence where I once saw the fruits of God's plentiful provision, 'yet I will rejoice in the Lord.'"

I believe that these words are worthy of being written forever in stone with a diamond tool. Oh, by God's grace, may they be deeply etched on the tablets of each of our hearts! Although the above verse is very concise, it nevertheless implies or expresses the following thoughts of the writer: that in his time of distress he would flee to God; that he would maintain his spiritual composure under the darkest of circumstances; and that in the midst of everything, he would delight himself with a sacred joy in God and have cheerful expectations of Him.

Heroic confidence! Glorious faith! Unconquerable love! PHILIP DODDRIDGE

Last night I heard a robin singing in the rain,
And the raindrop's patter made a sweet refrain,
Making all the sweeter the music of the strain.
So, I thought, when trouble comes, as trouble will,
Why should I stop singing? Just beyond the hill
It may be that sunshine floods the green world still.
He who faces the trouble with a heart of cheer
Makes the burden lighter. If there falls a tear,
Sweeter is the cadence in the song we hear.
I have learned your lesson, bird with spotted wing,
Listening to your music with its tune of spring—
When the storm cloud darkens, it's the time to sing.

EBEN EUGENE REXFORD

DAY 145

See how he loved him!

JOHN 11:36

He loved, yet lingered. We are so quick to think that delayed answer to prayer means that the prayer is not going to be answered. Dr. Stuart Holden has said truly: "Many a time we pray and are prone to interpret God's silence as a denial of our petitions; whereas, in truth, He only defers their fulfillment until such time as we ourselves are ready to cooperate to the full in His purposes." Prayer registered in heaven is prayer dealt with, although the vision still tarries.

Faith is trained to its supreme mission under the discipline of patience. The man who can wait God's time, knowing that He edits his prayer in wisdom and affection, will always discover that He never comes to man's aid one minute too soon or too late.

God's delay in answering the prayer of our longing heart is the most loving thing God can do. He may be waiting for us to come closer to Him, prostrate ourselves at His feet and abide there in trustful submission, that His granting of the longed-for answer may mean infinitely greater blessing than if we received it anywhere else than in the dust at His feet.

O wait, impatient heart!
As winter waits, her songbirds fed.
And every nestling blossom dead;
Beyond the purple seas they sing!
Beneath soft snows they sleep!
They only sleep. Sweet patience keep
And wait, as winter waits the spring.

Nothing can hold our ship down when the tide comes in!

The aloe blooms but once in a hundred years; but every hour of all that century is needed to produce the delicate texture and resplendent beauty of the flower.

Faith heard the sound of "the tread of rain," and yet God made Elijah wait!

God never hastens, and He never tarries!

DAY 146

He has given us his very great and precious promises.

2 PETER 1:4.

When a shipbuilder erects a boat, does he do so only to keep it on the scaffolding? No, he builds it to sail the seas and to weather the storms. In fact, if he does not think of strong winds and hurricanes as he builds it, he is a poor shipbuilder.

In the same way, when God made you a believer, He meant to test you. And when He gave you promises and asked you to trust them, He made His promises suitable for times of storms and high seas. Do you believe that some of His promises are counterfeit, similar to a life vest that looks good in the store but is of no use in the sea?

We have all seen swords that are beautiful but are useless in war, or shoes made for decoration but not for walking. Yet God's shoes are made of iron and brass, and we can walk all the way to heaven in them, without ever wearing them out. And we could swim the Atlantic a thousand times in His life vest, with no fear of ever sinking. His Word of promise is meant to be tried and tested.

There is nothing Christ dislikes more than for His people to publicly profess Him and then not use Him. He loves for us to make use of Him, for His covenant blessings are not simply meant to be looked at but should be appropriated. Our Lord Jesus has been given to us for our present use. Are you making use of Him as you should?

O beloved, I plead with you not to treat God's promises as something to be displayed in a museum but to use them as everyday sources of comfort. And whenever you have a time of need, trust the Lord. CHARLES H. SPURGEON

Go to the depths of God's promise,
And claim whatsoever you will;

The blessing of God will not fail you,
His Word He will surely fulfill.

How can God say no to something He has promised?

May 27th

DAY 147

He is able to save completely.

HEBREWS 7:25

What a magnificent prospect! Does it not take your breath away? It may well do so; but nevertheless it is true, gloriously and eternally true, for it is written in the Word of God. Grip that fact; grip it with your whole heart; take risks on it; stake your all on it; whisper it to yourself with clenched teeth when you are in the heat of the fight; shout it to the heavens when you see the enemy about to flee; triumph in it; exult in it!

Faith in this one thing can transfigure your whole life, and lift you to the heights of victory and glory that once seemed to you as far off and remote as the distant snows of some shining mountain summit seem to the traveler when, through a haze of sunshine, he lifts up his eyes to gaze as at some holy thing up in the blue air.

Remember, that the life of sanctification and spiritual power can never be had cheaply. To bestow it upon us the Lord Jesus paid the price of Calvary. To receive it we must be at least willing to pay the price of obedience to His simple conditions. Remember, too, it is the only life worth living. READER HARRIS

It costs to have a vision, but it costs too much to remember only the price.

DAY 148

If clouds are full of water, they pour rain upon the earth.

ECCLESIASTES 11:3

If we believe the message of this verse, then why do we dread the clouds that darken our sky? It is true that for a while the dark clouds hide the sun, but it is not extinguished and it will soon shine again. Meanwhile those clouds are filled with rain, and the darker they are, the more likely they are to bring plentiful showers.

How can we have rain without clouds? Our troubles have always brought us blessings, and they always will, for they are the dark chariots of God's bright and glorious grace. Before long the clouds will be emptied, and every tender plant will be happier due to the showers. Our God may drench us with grief, but He will refresh us with His mercy. Our Lord's love letters often come to us in dark envelopes. His wagons may rumble noisily across the sky, but they are loaded with benefits. And His rod blossoms with sweet flowers and nourishing fruits. So let us not worry about the clouds. Instead, let us sing because May flowers are brought to us through April clouds and showers.

O Lord, "clouds are the dust of [your] feet"! (Nah. 1:3). Help us remember how near You are during the dark and cloudy days! Love beholds You and is glad. Faith sees the clouds emptying themselves and thereby making the hills on every side rejoice. CHARLES H. SPURGEON

What seems so dark to your dim sight
May be a shadow, seen aright
Making some brightness doubly bright.
The flash that struck your tree—no more
To shelter thee—lets heaven's blue floor
Shine where it never shone before.

The cry wrung from your spirit's pain
May echo on some far-off plain,
And guide a wanderer home again.

The blue sky of heaven is much larger than the dark clouds.

DAY 149

If it dies, it produces many seeds.
JOHN 12:24

Infinite wisdom takes us in hand, and leads us through deep interior crucifixion to our fine parts, lofty reason, brightest hopes, cherished affections, our pious zeal, our spiritual impetuosity, our narrow culture, our creed and churchism, our success, our spiritual experience, our spiritual comforts.

The crucifixion goes on until we are dead and detached from all creatures, all saints, all thoughts, all hopes, all plans, all tender heart-yearnings, all preferences; dead to all trouble, all sorrow, all disappointments, all praise or blame, success or failure, comforts and annoyances, climates or nationalities; dead to all desires but Himself.

There is no field without a seed,
Life raised through death is life indeed.
The smallest, lowliest little flower
A secret is, of mighty power.
To die—it lives—buried to rise—
Abundant life through sacrifice.
Wouldst thou know sacrifice?
It is through loss;

Thou can'st not save but by the Cross.
A corn of wheat except it die,
Can never, never multiply.
The glorious fields of waving gold,
Through death are life a hundredfold.
Thou who for souls dost weep and pray,
Let not hell's legions thee dismay.
This is the way of ways for thee,
The way of certain victory.

THE SOUL WINNER'S SECRET

Let go of the old grain of wheat if you want a harvest.

May 30th

DAY 150

At once the Spirit sent him out into the wilderness.

MARK 1:12

This seemed a strange way for God to prove His favor. "At once"—after what? After heaven was opened and the Spirit descended "like a dove" (v. 10), and the Father voiced His blessing, "You are my Son, whom I love; with you I am well pleased" (v. 11). Yet it is not an abnormal experience.

You, my soul, have also experienced it. Aren't your times of deepest depression the moments that immediately follow your loftiest highs? Just yesterday you were soaring high in the heavens and singing in the radiance of the morning. Today, however, your wings are folded and your song is silent. At noon you were basking in the sunshine of the Father's smile, but by evening you were saying from the wilderness, "My way is hidden from the Lord" (Isa. 40:27).

No, my soul, the actual suddenness of the change is proof that it is not abnormal. Have you considered the comfort of the words "at once," and why the change comes so soon after the blessing? Simply to show that it is the sequel to the blessing. God shines His light on you to make you fit for life's wildernesses, Gethsemanes, and Calvaries. He lifts you to new heights to strengthen you so that you may go deeper still. He illuminates you so He may send you into the night, making you a help to the helpless.

You are not always worthy of the wilderness—you are only worthy of the wilderness after the splendor of the Jordan River experience. Nothing but the Son's vision can equip you to carry the Spirit's burden, and only the glory of baptism can withstand the hunger of the desert. GEORGE MATHESON

After blessings comes the battle.

The time of testing that distinguishes and greatly enriches a person's spiritual career is not an ordinary one but a period when it seems as if all hell were set loose. It is a time when we realize our soul is caught in a net, and we know God is allowing us to be gripped by the Devil's hand. Yet it is a period that always ends in certain triumph for those who have committed the keeping of their souls to God. And the testing "later on . . . produces a harvest of righteousness and peace" (Heb. 12:11) and paves the way for the thirtyfold to one hundredfold increase that is promised to follow (see Matt. 13:23). APHRA WHITE

DAY 151

May 31st

[Keep] no record of wrongs.

1 CORINTHIANS 13:5

"Let it rest!"

Ah! how many hearts on the brink of anxiety and disquietude, by this simple sentence have been made calm and happy!

Some proceeding has wounded us by its want of tact; let it rest; no one will think of it again.

A harsh or unjust sentence irritates us; let it rest; whoever may have given vent to it will be pleased to see it forgotten.

A painful scandal is about to estrange us from an old friend; let it rest, and thus preserve our charity and peace of mind.

A suspicious look is on the point of cooling our affection; let it rest; our look of trust will restore confidence.

Fancy we, who are so careful to remove the briars from our pathway for fear they should wound, yet take pleasure in collecting and piercing our hearts with thorns that meet us in our daily intercourse with one another! How childish and unreasonable we are! GOLD DUST

The rents made by Time will soon mend if you will let God have His way.

DAY 152

June 1st

I will cause you to ride in triumph on the heights of the land.

ISAIAH 58:14

One of the first rules of aerodynamics is that flying into the wind quickly increases altitude. The wings of the airplane create more lift by flying against the wind. How was this lesson learned? It was learned by watching birds fly. If a bird is simply flying for pleasure, it flies with the wind. But if it senses danger, it turns into the wind to gain altitude, and flies up toward the sun.

The sufferings of life are God's winds. Sometimes they blow against us and are very strong. They are His hurricanes, taking our lives to higher levels, toward His heavens.

Do you remember a summer day when the heat and humidity were so oppressive, you could hardly breathe? But a dark cloud appeared on the horizon, growing larger and larger, until it suddenly brought a rich blessing to your world. The storm raged, lightning flashed, and thunder rumbled. The storm covered your sky, the atmosphere was cleansed, new life was in the air, and your world was changed.

Human life works exactly on the same principle. When the storms of life appear, the atmosphere is changed, purified, filled with new life, and part of heaven is brought down to earth.

Facing obstacles should make us sing. The wind finds its voice not when rushing across an open sea but when it is hindered by the outstretched limbs of a pine tree or broken by the strings of an aeolian wind harp. Only then does the harp have songs of power and beauty. Send your soul, which has been set free, sweeping across the obstacles of life. Send it through the relentless forests of pain and against even the smallest hindrances and worries of life, and it too will find a voice with which to sing.

> Be like a bird that, halting in its flight,
> Rests on a limb too slight.
> And feeling it give way beneath him sings,
> Knowing he has wings.

DAY 153

Be still, and know that I am God.

PSALM 46:10

> *Let thy soul walk softly in thee*
> *Like a saint in heaven unshod,*
> *For to be alone with silence*
> *Is to be at home with God.*

Quiet hearts are as rare as radium. We need every day to be led by the Divine Shepherd into the green pastures and beside the still waters. We are losing the art of meditation. Inner preparation is necessary to outer service.

"Rest pauses" contribute to the finer music of life. "Jesus went out to a mountainside to pray" (Luke 6:12). "As he was praying, the appearance of his face changed" (9:29). Therein we have the example of our Lord.

We have yet to learn the power of silence. Not in the college or academy, but in the silence of the soul, do we learn the greater lessons of life and become rooted in spiritual inwardness.

The geologist says that certain crystals can only come to their perfect form in stillness. In the undistracted moment men are in touch with God and everlasting things.

The strenuousness of life and the increasing distractions of the world demand a zone of silence and the Quiet Hour.

"He said to them, 'Come with me by yourselves to a quiet place and get some rest.' So they went away by themselves in a boat to a solitary place" (Mark 6:31–32). Let us find that spot every day, and the fellowship of silence. On such moments infinite issues hinge!

In every life
There's a pause that is better than onward rush,
Better than hewing or mightiest doing;
'Tis the standing still at Sovereign will.
There's a hush that is better than ardent speech,
Better than sighing or wilderness crying;
'Tis the being still at Sovereign will.
The pause and the hush sing a double song
In unison low and for all time long.
O human soul, God's working plan
Goes on, nor needs the aid of man!
Stand still, and see!
Be still, and know!

DAY 154

I waited patiently for the LORD.

PSALM 40:1

Waiting is much more difficult than walking, for waiting requires patience, and patience is a rare virtue. We enjoy knowing that God builds hedges around His people, when we look at the hedge from the aspect of protection. But when we see it growing higher and higher until we can no longer see over it, we wonder if we will ever get out of our little sphere of influence and service, where we feel trapped. Sometimes it is hard for us to understand why we do not have a larger area of service, and it becomes difficult for us to "brighten the corner" where we are. But God has a purpose in all of His delays. "The steps of a good man are ordered by the LORD" (Ps. 37:23 KJV).

Next to this verse, in the margin of his Bible, George Mueller made this note: "And the stops too." It is a sad mistake for someone to break through God's hedges. It is a vital principle of the Lord's guidance for a Christian never to move from the spot where he is sure God has placed him, until the "pillar of cloud" (Ex. 13:21) moves. SUNDAY SCHOOL TIMES

Once we learn to wait for the Lord's leading in everything, we will know the strength that finds its highest point in an even and steady walk. Many of us are lacking the strength we so desire, but God gives complete power for every task He calls us to perform. Waiting—keeping yourself faithful to His leading—this is the secret of strength. And anything that does not align with obedience to Him is a waste of time and energy. Watch and wait for His leading. SAMUEL DICKEY GORDON

Must life be considered a failure for someone compelled to stand still, forced into inaction and required to watch the great, roaring tides of life from shore? No—victory is then to be won by standing still and quietly waiting. Yet this is a thousand times harder to do than in the past, when you rushed headlong into the busyness of life. It requires much more courage to stand and wait and still not lose heart or lose hope, to submit to the will of God, to give up opportunities for work and leave honors to others, and to be quiet, confident, and rejoicing while the busy multitude goes happily along their way.

The greatest life is: "after you have done everything, to stand" (Eph. 6:13). J. R. MILLER

DAY 155

I have never been eloquent.

EXODUS 4:10

Nothing is more dishonoring to God, or more dangerous for us, than a mock humility. When we refuse to occupy a position which the grace of God assigns us, because of our not possessing certain virtues and qualifications, this is not humility, for if we could but satisfy our own consciences in reference to such virtues and qualifications, we should then deem ourselves entitled to assume the position. If, for instance, Moses had possessed such a measure of eloquence as he deemed needful, we may suppose he would have been ready to go. Now the question is, how much eloquence would he have needed to furnish him for his mission? The answer is, without God no amount of human eloquence would have availed; but with God the merest stammerer would have proved an efficient minister. This is a great practical truth.

Unbelief is not humility, but thorough pride. It refuses to believe God because it does not find in self a reason for believing. This is the very height of presumption. C. H. M.

Move to the fore;
Say not another is fitter than thou.
Shame to thy shrinking! Up! Face thy task now.
Own thyself equal to all a soul may,

Cease thy evading—God needs thee today.
Move to the fore!
God Himself waits, and must wait till thou come;
Men are God's prophets though ages lie dumb.
Halts the Christ Kingdom with conquest so near?
Thou art the cause, thou soul in the rear.
Move to the fore!

Find your purpose and fling your life out into it; and the loftier your purpose is, the more sure you will be to make the world richer with every enrichment of yourself. PHILLIPS BROOKS

DAY 156

I have faith in God that it will happen just as he told me.

ACTS 27:25

A number of years ago I went to America with a steamship captain who was a very devoted Christian. When we were off the coast of Newfoundland, he said to me, "The last time I sailed here, which was five weeks ago, something happened that revolutionized my entire Christian life. I had been on the bridge for twenty-four straight hours when George Mueller of Bristol, England, who was a passenger on board, came to me and said, 'Captain, I need to tell you that I must be in Quebec on Saturday afternoon.' 'That is impossible,' I replied. 'Very well,' Mueller responded, 'if your ship cannot take me, God will find some other way, for I have never missed an engagement in fifty-seven years. Let's go down to the chartroom to pray.'

"I looked at this man of God and thought to myself, 'What lunatic asylum did he escape from?' I had never encountered someone like this. 'Mr. Mueller,' I said, 'do you realize how dense the fog is?' 'No,' he replied. 'My eye is not on the dense fog but on the living God, who controls every circumstance of my life.'

"He then knelt down and prayed one of the most simple prayers I've ever heard. When he had finished, I started to pray, but he put his hand on my shoulder and told me not to pray. He said, 'First, you do not believe God will answer, and second, I believe he has. Consequently, there is no need whatsoever for you to pray about it.'

"As I looked at him, he said, 'Captain, I have known my Lord for fifty-seven years, and there has never been even a single day that I have failed to get an audience with the King. Get up, Captain, and open the door, and you will see that the fog is gone.' I got up, and indeed the fog was gone. And on Saturday afternoon George Mueller was in Quebec for his meeting."

> If our love were just more simple,
> We would take Him at His word;
> And our lives would be all sunshine,
> In the sweetness of our Lord.

DAY 157

The angel of the L*ORD moved on ahead and stood in a narrow place where was no room to turn, either to the right or to the left.*

NUMBERS 22:26

"A narrow place!" You know that place; you have been there—you will very likely be there again before long—some of you may be there at this very moment; for it is not merely a defile away somewhere among the mountains to the east of Moab. It is a life passage in individual experience—a time when there we are brought face to face with some inevitable question. . . Temptation is such a "narrow place." In the serious crisis of the soul's history, it is alone. It is a path on which there is room only for itself, and before it there is God. Between these two always the matter has to be settled. Yes, or no, is the hinge on which everything turns. Shall I yield and dishonor God, or shall I resist and triumph in His might? There is no possible compromise; for compromise with sin is itself the most insidious form of sin. No man can pass through these crises, and be after them what he was before. He has met God face to face, and he must either be the better or the worse for that experience. Either, like Jacob at Peniel he can say, "My life is preserved," or like Saul after he had thrown off his allegiance to his God, "Jehovah has departed from me, and is become my enemy." WILLIAM M. TAYLOR

The harder the place the more He loves to show His power. If you wish to find Him real, come to Him in some great trouble. He has no chance to work until you get in a hard place. He led Israel out of the usual way till He got them to the Red Sea. Then there was room for His power to be manifested. God loves the hard places and the narrow places.

Rejoice if you are in such a place! Even if it is in the very heart of the foe, God is able to deliver you. Let not your faith in Him waver for a moment, and you will find His omnipotence is all upon your side for every difficulty in which you can be placed.

"When you get into a tight place," said Harriet Beecher Stowe, "and everything goes against you, till it seems as if you could not hold on a minute longer, never give up then, for that is just the place and the time that the tide will turn."

June 7th

DAY 158

[Hezekiah] went up to the temple of the LORD and spread it out before the LORD.

ISAIAH 37:14

Does it not often happen that you are in great difficulty how to act in some particular case? Your course is not plain; your way is not open: each side seems equally balanced, and you cannot tell which to choose. Your wishes, perhaps, point one way; your fears, another. You are afraid lest you should decide wrongly; lest you should take what, in the end, may prove hurtful to you.

It is very trying to be brought into this painful conflict. And it adds to our distress if we are forced to go forward at once, and take one course or the other. Shall I tell you how you may be sure to find unspeakable relief?

Go and lay your matter before the Lord, as Hezekiah did with the king of Assyria's letter. Do not, however, deceive yourself, as many do, and seek counsel of God, having determined to act according to your own will, and not according to His. But, simply and honestly, ask that He would guide you. Commit your case to your Father in heaven; surrender yourself as a little child to be led as He pleases. This is the way to be guided aright, and to realize the blessing of having a heavenly Counselor. A. OXENDEN

Surrendered—led alone by Thee, and wait Thy guidance still.

June 8th

DAY 159

Whatever you want me to do, I'll do for you.

1 SAMUEL 20:4

It is sometimes difficult to realize that the promises of God are to be taken at their face value. Too often they are regarded as a part of the general spiritual instruction of the Word, but not to be appropriated for our own need.

We fail to realize because we do not appropriate!

No matter what may be our requirements—guidance, spiritual refreshing, physical or temporal needs—God has given us some specific word on which to base our faith.

Then, since the promises are definite, should not our prayers be definite? Prayerfully search the Word to find the promise that will fit the case. Prove Him! Back of the word of the Lord is the person and character of God Himself; God, who cannot lie.

God honors the person who trusts Him implicitly.

It is not our worth, but Christ's, which has secured for us immediate access to the Throne, "For no matter how many promises God has made, they are 'Yes' in Christ. And so through him the 'Amen' is spoken" (2 Cor. 1:20).

With such a basis and assurance, why hesitate to claim the things the Lord has provided? Can you not trust the One who made the promise?

Whatever desire the Father permits to live in the heart of one of His saints, He will grant the fulfillment thereof. S. CHADWICK

Prove the immutable promises of God!

DAY 160

Everything is possible for one who believes.

MARK 9:23

Prayer takes the people to the Bank of Faith, and obtains the golden blessing. Mind how you pray! Pray! Make real business of it! Never let it be a dead formality! People pray a long time, but do not get what they are supposed to ask for, because they do not plead the promise in a truthful businesslike way. If you were to go into a bank and stand an hour talking to the clerk, and then come out again without your cash, what would be the good of it? CHARLES H. SPURGEON

Have you ever given God the chance to answer the Prayer of Faith?

Do not let us lose our last chance of believing by waiting till the dawn has broken into day! LILIAS TROTTER

If radio's slim finger can pluck a melody
From night, and toss it over a continent or sea;
If the petaled white notes of a violin
Are blown across a mountain or a city's din;
If songs, like crimson roses, are culled from thin blue air—
Why should mortals wonder if God hears prayer?

ETHEL ROMIG FULLER

When all things can be accomplished by prayer, why not yield to the test? Why not pray on? And through?

June 10th

DAY 161

Whoever wants to save their life will lose it.

MARK 8:35

The laying down of life is not only the foundation of a new life for ourselves, but also the foundation of a new life for others, just as the laying down of our Lord's life has brought forth its abundant harvest all through the years.

It is the laying down of life for the sake of the harvest; it is the grain of wheat falling into the ground to die in order that it may not abide alone.

John Coleridge Patterson's life was equipped with every gift to make it rich and happy in his own land; yet he laid it down to go to his hard and toilsome life in the South Seas. Had he been asked, "Are you regretful for what you have turned your back upon?" he would have answered, "The promise has been fulfilled to me."

An American Consul General in China once said to Matthew Culbertson, "You might have been a Major-General if you had stayed at home." He had been the best man in his class at West Point, but his mother's prayers had borne their fruitage and he became a missionary. "No," he said, "I do not regret it. The privilege of preaching the Gospel to four hundred millions of one's fellow creatures is the greatest privilege any man can have on earth." He had found his life!

Henry Martyn put his hand to the plow with these words, "Now, let me burn out for God!" No "looking back." No relinquishing the handles even for a holiday!

Think of James Gilmore in Mongolia in his uncompanioned life! Mongolia stretches from the Sea of Japan on the east to Turkestan on the west—a distance of three thousand miles; from the southern boundary of Asiatic Russia to the Great Wall of China—nine hundred miles. What a field! But what a plowman! He died in the furrow!

More than two thousand years ago our Lord lost His life and His fame. Or did He?

Speak, history! Who are life's victors? Unveil thy long annals and say, Are they those whom the world calls the victors, who won the success of a day? Thy martyrs, or Nero? The Spartans, who fell at Thermopylae's tryst, Or the Persians and Xerxes? His judges, or Socrates? Pilate or Christ? WILLIAM WETMORE STORY

June 11th

DAY 162

Jacob was left alone, and a man wrestled with him till daybreak.

GENESIS 32:24

In this passage, God is wrestling with Jacob more than Jacob is wrestling with God. The "man" referred to here is the Son of Man—the Angel of the Covenant. It was God in human form, pressing down on Jacob to press his old life from him. And by daybreak God had prevailed, for Jacob's "hip was wrenched" (v. 25). As Jacob "fell" from his old life, he fell into the arms of God, clinging to Him but also wrestling until his blessing came. His blessing was that of a new life, so he rose from the earthly to the heavenly, the human to the divine, and the natural to the supernatural. From that morning forward, he was a weak and broken man from a human perspective, but God was there. And the Lord's heavenly voice proclaimed, "Your name will no longer be Jacob, but Israel, because you have struggled with God and with humans and have overcome" (v. 28).

Beloved, this should be a typical scene in the life of everyone who has been transformed. If God has called us to His highest and best, each of us will have a time of crisis, when all our resources will fail and when we face either ruin or something better than we have ever dreamed. But before we can receive the blessing, we must rely on God's infinite help. We must be willing to let go, surrendering completely to Him, and cease from our own wisdom, strength, and righteousness. We must be "crucified with Christ" (Gal. 2:20) and yet alive in Him. God knows how to lead us to the point of crisis, and He knows how to lead us through it.

Is God leading you in this way? Is this the meaning of your mysterious trial, your difficult circumstances, your impossible situation, or that trying place you cannot seem to move past without Him? But do you have enough of Him to win the victory?

Then turn to Jacob's God! Throw yourself helplessly at His feet. Die in His loving arms to your own strength and wisdom, and rise like Jacob into His strength and sufficiency. There is no way out of your difficult and narrow situation except at the top. You must win deliverance by rising higher, coming into a new experience with God. And may it bring you into all that is meant by the revelation of "the Mighty One of Jacob" (Isa. 60:16)! There is no way out but God.

At Your feet I fall, Yield
You up my all,
To suffer, live, or die
For my Lord crucified.

DAY 163

He turned the sea into dry land, they passed through
the waters on foot—come, let us rejoice in him.

PSALM 66:6

It is a profound statement that "through the waters," the very place where we might have expected nothing but trembling, terror, anguish, and dismay, the children of Israel stopped to "rejoice in him"!

How many of us can relate to this experience? Who of us, right in the midst of our time of distress and sadness, have been able to triumph and rejoice, as the Israelites did?

How close God is to us through His promises, and how brightly those promises shine! Yet during times of prosperity, we lose sight of their brilliance. In the way the sun at noon hides the stars from sight, His promises become indiscernible. But when night falls—the deep, dark night of sorrow—a host of stars begin to shine, bringing forth God's blessed constellations of hope, and promises of comfort from His Word.

Just as Jacob experienced at Jabbok, it is only once the sun sets that the Angel of the Lord comes, wrestles with us, and we can overcome. It was at night, "at twilight" (Ex. 30:8), that Aaron lit the sanctuary lamps. And it is often during nights of trouble that the brightest lamps of believers are set ablaze.

It was during a dark time of loneliness and exile that John had the glorious vision of his Redeemer. Many of us today have our "Isle of Patmos," which produces the brightest memories of God's enduring presence, uplifting grace, and love in spite of solitude and sadness.

How many travelers today, still passing through their Red Seas and Jordan Rivers of earthly affliction, will be able to look back from eternity, filled with memories of God's great goodness, and say, "We 'passed through the waters on foot.' And yet, even in these dark experiences, with waves surging all around, we stopped and said, 'Let us rejoice in him'!" J. R. MACDUFF

There I will give her back her vineyards, and will make the Valley of Achor a door of hope. There she will [sing]. HOSEA 2:15

DAY 164

He brought me out into a spacious place; he rescued me because he delighted in me.

PSALM 18:19

What is this "spacious place"? What can it be but God Himself—the infinite Being through whom all other beings find their source and their end of life? God is indeed a "spacious place." And it was through humiliation, degradation, and a sense of worthlessness that David was taken to it.
MADAME GUYON

I carried you on eagles' wings and brought you to myself. Exodus 19:4

Fearing to launch on "full surrender's" tide,
I asked the Lord where would its waters glide
My little boat, "To troubled seas I dread?"
"Unto Myself," He said.
Weeping beside an open grave I stood,
In bitterness of soul I cried to God:
"Where leads this path of sorrow that I tread?"
"Unto Myself," He said.
Striving for souls, I loved the work too well;
Then disappointments came; I could not tell
The reason, till He said, "I am your all;
Unto Myself I call."
Watching my heroes—those I love the best—
I saw them fail; they could not stand the test,
Even by this the Lord, through tears not few,
Unto Himself me drew.
Unto Himself! No earthly tongue can tell
The bliss I find, since in His heart I dwell;

The things that charmed me once seem all as naught;
Unto Himself I'm brought.

June 14th

DAY 165

Then some Jews came [to Lystra] . . . and won the crowd over. They stoned Paul and dragged him outside the city, thinking he was dead. . . . The next day he . . . left for Derbe. They preached the gospel in that city. . . . Then they returned to Lystra.

ACTS 14:19–21

The cruel stones unerring fell upon him—
Until they deemed his bleeding form was dead;
His worth and work they knew not, and they cared not;
Enough, they madly hated what he said.
God touched him! and he rose, with new life given;
Nor in his bosom burned resentful pain;
And, by and by, when need and call both guided,
He to the stoning-place returned again.
Perchance thou, too, hast tasted cruel stoning—
And might'st be glad if call came ne'er again
To turn to scenes where surely there awaits thee
The cruel, cutting stones which make life vain.
Yet, if "back to the stones" the Finger pointeth,
Then thou shalt know there is no better way;
And there, just there, shall matchless grace await thee,
And God Himself shall be thy strength and stay.

J. DANSON SMITH

The most sublime moments lie very close to the most painful situations. Are we familiar with the road that leads back to the stones?

June 15th

DAY 166

The rest were to get there on planks or on other pieces of the ship. In this way everyone reached land safely.

ACTS 27:44

The miraculous story of Paul's voyage to Rome, with its trials and triumphs, is a wonderful example of the light and the darkness through the journey of faith of human life. And the most remarkable part of the journey is the difficult and narrow places that are interspersed with God's extraordinary providence and intervention.

It is a common misconception that the Christian's walk of faith is strewn with flowers and that when God intervenes in the lives of His people, He does so in such a wonderful way as to always lift us out of our difficult surroundings. In actual fact, however, the real experience is quite the opposite. And the message of the Bible is one of alternating trials and triumphs in the lives of "a great cloud of witnesses" (Heb. 12:1), everyone from Abel to the last martyr.

Paul, more than anyone else, is an example of how much a child of God can suffer without being defeated or broken in spirit. Because of his testimony given in Damascus, he was hunted down by persecutors and forced to flee for his life. Yet we see no heavenly chariot, amid lightning bolts of fire, coming to rescue the holy apostle from the hands of his enemies. God instead worked a simple way of escape for Paul: "His followers took him by night and lowered him in a basket through an opening in the wall" (Acts 9:25). Yes, he was in an old clothes basket, like a bundle of laundry or groceries. The servant of the Lord Jesus Christ was lowered from a window over the wall of Damascus, and in a humble way escaped the hatred of his foes.

Later we find him languishing for months in lonely dungeons, telling of his "sleepless nights and hunger" (2 Cor. 6:5), of being deserted by friends, and of his brutal, humiliating beatings. And even after God promised to deliver him, we see him left for days to toss upon a stormy sea and compelled to protect a treacherous sailor. And finally, once his deliverance comes, it is not by way of some heavenly ship sailing from the skies to rescue this illustrious prisoner. Nor is there an angel who comes walking on the water to still the raging sea. There is no supernatural sign at all of surpassing greatness being carried out, for one man is required to grab a piece of the mast to survive, another a floating timber, another a small fragment of the shipwreck, and yet another is forced to swim for his life.

In this account, we also find God's pattern for our own lives. It is meant to be good news to those who live in this everyday world in ordinary surroundings and who face thousands of ordinary situations, which must be met in completely ordinary ways.

God's promises and His providence do not lift us from the world of common sense and everyday trials, for it is through these very things that our faith is perfected. And it is in this world that God loves to interweave the golden threads of His love with the twists and turns of our common, everyday experiences. HARD PLACES IN THE WAY OF FAITH

DAY 167

I . . . brought you to myself.

EXODUS 19:4

How we have wondered at those events which stirred us up and set us loose from ties of home and friends; and how we have marveled at the ruthlessness of those providences which sent us headlong from our assured places into the uncertainties of what seemed empty space around and beneath us. But now we understand that every experience was in God's love and for the fulfillment of His high purposes toward us. No matter what happened, we soon saw His form and heard His heartening cry; and never did we grow weary but we immediately found that strong wings were beneath us. And oh, the wonder of it! when God brought us home to our resting-place beside Himself! HENRY W. FROST

Unto Myself, My dear child, I would bring thee!
Who like Myself thy sure solace can be?
Who can reach down, down so deeply within thee?
Give to thy heart such a full sympathy?
Mournest thou sore that thy loved ones have failed thee?
Failed, sadly failed thy true comfort to be?
"Why did they fail" dost thou ask? Let Me whisper—
"That thou should'st find thy heart's comfort in Me."
Unto Myself! Ah, no not unto others,
Dearest, or sweetest, or fairest, or best;
Only in Me lieth unchanging solace;
Only in Me is thy promise of rest!
Child of My love, to Myself I would bring thee!
Not to some place of most heavenly bliss:
Places, like people, may all disappoint thee,
Till thou hast learned to drink higher than this.
Unto Myself, My dear child, I would bring thee!
None like Myself thy full portion can be!
While, in My heart, there is hunger and longing
That I might find choicest treasure in thee.
Unto Myself! To Myself—not My service!
Then to most sweetly and certainly prove
That I can make thee My channel of blessing,
Use thee to shed forth the wealth of My love.

J. DANSON SMITH

DAY 168

By faith Abraham . . . obeyed and went, even though he did not know where he was going.

HEBREWS 11:8

This is faith without sight. Seeing is not faith but reasoning. When crossing the Atlantic by ship, I once observed this very principle of faith. I saw no path marked out on the sea, nor could I even see the shore. Yet each day, we marked our progress on a chart as if we had been following a giant chalk line across the water. And when we came within sight of land on the other side of the Atlantic, we knew exactly where we were, as if we had been able to see it from three thousand miles away.

How had our course been so precisely plotted? Every day, our captain had taken his instruments, looked to the sky, and determined his course by the sun. He was sailing using heavenly lights, not earthly ones.

Genuine faith also looks up and sails, by using God's great Son. It never travels by seeing the shoreline, earthly lighthouses, or paths along the way. And the steps of faith often lead to total uncertainty or even darkness and disaster, but the Lord will open the way and often makes the darkest of midnight hours as bright as the dawning of the day.

Let us move forth today, not knowing or seeing, but trusting. DAYS OF HEAVEN UPON EARTH

Too many of us want to see our way through a new endeavor before we will even start. Imagine if we could see our way from beginning to end. How would we ever develop our Christian gifts? Faith, hope, and love cannot be picked from trees, like ripe apples. Remember, after the words "In the beginning" (Gen. 1:1) comes the word "God." It is our first step of faith that turns the key in the lock of His powerhouse. It is true that God helps those who help themselves, but He also helps those who are helpless. So no matter your circumstance, you can depend on Him every time.

Waiting on God brings us to the end of our journey much faster than our feet.

Many an opportunity is lost while we deliberate after He has said, "Move!"

DAY 169

Gideon was threshing wheat. . . . When the angel of the LORD . . . said, "The LORD is with you."

JUDGES 6:11-12

More courage is required when coming to grips with the commonplace problems of the ordinary day than is required to face batteries of destruction on a field of military conflict.

It is much easier to follow on the track of the heroic than to remain true to Jesus in drab mean streets. Human nature unaided by God cannot do it.

The follower of Jesus is a laborer—but a laborer together with God. He is a man with a hoe—but one who has his part in the harvest whose reapers are the angels.

This is the place where Thou didst bid me stand;
And work and wait;
I thought it was a plot of fertile land,
To tend and cultivate:
Flowers and fruit, I said, are surely there,
In rich earth stored,
And I will make of it a garden fair,
For Thee, my Lord!
Lo! it is set where only bleak skies frown,
With rank weeds sown,
And over it the vagrant thistle-down
Like dust is blown;

Long have I labored, but the barren soil
No crop will yield:
This have I won for all my ceaseless toil—
A bare plowed field!
Nay, even here, where thou didst strive and weep,
Some sunny morn
Others shall come with joyous hearts and reap
The full-eared corn;
Yet is their harvest to thy labor due;
On Me 'twas spent—
Are not the furrows driven straight and true?
Be thou content!

"A TILLER OF THE SOIL"

June 19th

DAY 170

I have received full payment and even more.

PHILIPPIANS 4:18

In one of my garden books there is a chapter with a very interesting title: "Flowers That Grow in the Shade." It deals with those areas of a garden that never catch direct sunlight, and it lists the kinds of flowers that not only grow in the dark corners but actually seem to like them and to flourish in them.

There are similarities here to the spiritual world. There are Christians who seem to blossom when their material circumstances become the most harsh and severe. They grow in the darkness and shade. If this were not true, how could we otherwise explain some of the experiences of the apostle Paul?

When he wrote the above verse, he was a prisoner in Rome. The primary mission of his life appeared to have been broken. But it was in this persistent darkness that flowers began to show their faces in bright and fascinating glory. Paul may have seen them before, growing along the open road, but certainly never in the incomparable strength and beauty in which they now appeared. And words of promise opened their treasures to him in ways he had never before experienced.

Among those treasures were such wonderful things as Christ's grace, love, joy, and peace, and it seemed as though they had needed the circumstance of darkness to draw out their secret and inner glory. The dark and dingy prison had become the home of the revealed truth of God, and Paul began to realize as never before the width and the wealth of his spiritual inheritance.

Haven't we all known men and women who begin to wear strength and hopefulness like a regal robe as soon as they must endure a season of darkness and solitude? People like that may be put in prison by the world, but their treasure will be locked away with them, for true treasure cannot be locked out of their lives. Their material condition may look like a desert, but "the desert and the parched land will be glad; the wilderness will rejoice and blossom" (Isa. 35:1). JOHN HENRY JOWETT

Every flower, even the most beautiful, has its own shadow beneath it as it basks in the sunlight.

Where there is much light, there is also much shade.

DAY 171

June 20th

Just believe.

MARK 5:36

An old woman with a halo of silvered hair—the hot tears flowing down her furrowed cheeks—her worn hands busy over a washboard in a room of poverty—praying—for her son John—John who ran away from home in his teens to become a sailor—John, of whom it was now reported that he had become a very wicked man—praying, praying always, that her son might be of service to God.

What a marvelous subject for an artist's brush!

The mother believed in two things, the power of prayer and the reformation of her son. So while she scrubbed she continued to pray. God answered the prayer by working a miracle in the heart of John Newton. The black stains of sin were washed white in the blood of the Lamb. "Though your sins are like scarlet, they shall be as white as snow" (Isa. 1:18).

The washtub prayers were heard as are all prayers when asked in His name. John Newton, the drunken sailor, became John Newton, the sailor-preacher. Among the thousands of men and women he brought to Christ was Thomas Scott, cultured, selfish, and self-satisfied. Because of the washtub prayers another miracle was worked and Thomas Scott used both his pen and voice to lead thousands of unbelieving hearts to Christ—among them, a dyspeptic, melancholic young man, William Cowper by name.

He, too, was washed by the cleansing Blood and in a moment of inspiration wrote:

There is a fountain filled with blood
Drawn from Immanuel's veins,
And sinners, plunged beneath that flood,
Lose all their guilty stains.

And this song has brought countless thousands to the Man who died on Calvary. Among the thousands was William Wilberforce, who became a great Christian statesman, and helped to inspire many to unfasten the shackles from the feet of thousands of British slaves. Among those whom he led to the Lord was Leigh Richmond, a clergyman of the Established Church in one of the Channel Islands. He wrote a book, *The Dairyman's Daughter*, which was translated into forty languages and with the intensity of leaping flame burned the love of Christ into the hearts of thousands.

All this resulted because a mother took God at His Word and prayed that her son's heart might become as white as the soapsuds in the washtub.

June 21st

DAY 172

Before the coming of this faith, we were held in custody . . .
locked up until the faith that was to come would be revealed.

GALATIANS 3:23

God, in times past, caused people to be kept subject to His law so they would learn the more excellent way of faith. For it was through the law that they would see God's holy standard and thereby realize their own utter helplessness. Then they would gladly learn His way of faith.

God still causes us to be "locked up until the faith" is learned. Our own nature, circumstances, trials, and disappointments all serve to keep us submissive and "locked up" until we see that the only way out is His way of faith. Moses attempted the deliverance of his people by using self-effort, his personal influence, and even violence. So God "locked [him] up" for forty years in the wilderness before he was prepared for His work.

Paul and Silas were called of God to preach the gospel in Europe. In Philippi they were "severely flogged, they were thrown into prison, and the jailer . . . fastened their feet in the stocks" (Acts 16:23–24). They were "locked up" to faith. They trusted God and sang praises to Him in their darkest hour, and God brought deliverance and salvation.

The apostle John was also "locked up" to faith, when he was banished to the Isle of Patmos. And if he had never been sent there, he would never have seen such glorious visions of God.

Dear reader, are you in some terrible trouble? Have you experienced some distressing disappointment, sorrow, or inexpressible loss? Are you in a difficult situation? Cheer up! You have been "locked up" to faith. Accept your troubles in the proper way and commit them to God. Praise Him "that in all things God works for the good of those who love him" (Rom. 8:28) and that He "acts on behalf of those who wait for him" (Isa. 64:4). God will send you blessings and help, and will reveal truths to you that otherwise would never have come your way. And many others will also receive great insights and blessings because you were "locked up" to learn the way of faith. C. H. P.

Great things are done when man and mountains meet,
These are not done by walking down the street.

DAY 173

"He shall give you another Comforter, that
He may abide with you forever."
JOHN 14:16

Dear Heart, thou art not forsaken. Solitude and peace are 'round about thee, and God is over all. Like a pure white dove with folden wings His sweet messenger—Peace—is waiting near thee. Thou hearest a Voice speaking tenderly to thy soul. It is the whisper of the Eternal, bidding thee cast all thy cares upon Him. Through the long winter days may His peace abide with thee and thine!

GOD'S COMFORTING

"The world grows lonely, and, with many a tear,
I stretch out longing hands in vain, to clasp
The treasures of my life, and hold them here;
But 'all dear things seem slipping from my grasp.'
    "Oh, say not so, my heart! One stands beside
    Whose love, in all its fulness, is thine own;
    That love is changeless, and whate'er betide,
    He will not leave thee,—thou art not alone!
"God keeps my treasures, and some glad, bright day,
He'll give them to my longing sight again;
So Faith and Hope shall cheer me all the way,

And Love, their sweetest sister, soothe my pain.
"Thus, taking God's full cup of comforting,
Let me give thanks! and, pouring out most free
My life in loyal service, let me bring
To other lives the joy God giveth me."

DAY 174

Do not take revenge, my dear friends.

ROMANS 12:19

There are times when doing nothing demands much greater strength than taking action. Maintaining composure is often the best evidence of power. Even to the vilest and deadliest of charges, Jesus responded with deep, unbroken silence. His silence was so profound, it caused His accusers and spectators to wonder in awe. To the greatest insults, the most violent treatment, and to mockery that would bring righteous indignation to the feeblest of hearts, He responded with voiceless, confident calmness. Those who are unjustly accused, and mistreated without cause, know the tremendous strength that is necessary to keep silent and to leave revenge to God.

Men may misjudge your aim,
Think they have cause to blame,
Say, you are wrong;
Keep on your quiet way,
Christ is the Judge, not they,
Fear not, be strong.

The apostle Paul said, "None of these things move me" (Acts 20:24 KJV). He did not say, "None of these things hurt me." It is one thing to be hurt, and quite another to be moved. Paul had a very tender heart, for we do not read of any other apostle who cried as he did. It takes a strong man to cry. "Jesus wept" (John 11:35), and He was the strongest man that ever lived.

Therefore it does not say, "None of these things hurt me." The apostle Paul had determined not to move from what he believed was right. He did not value things as we are prone to do. He never looked for the easy way, and placed no value on his mortal life. He only cared about one thing, and that was his loyalty to Christ—to gain Christ's smile. To Paul, more than to any other man, doing Christ's work was his earthly pay, but gaining Christ's smile was heaven. MARGARET BOTTOME

DAY 175

Joseph said to them, ". . . You intended to harm me, but God intended it for good to accomplish what is now being done, the saving of many lives."

GENESIS 50:19–20

It had been a long road for Joseph; it had been a desperately rough road, too. There was the slimy pit, the brothers' treachery, the slave chains, the terrible palace temptation, and the prison cell. But what a different ending this story has: "So Pharaoh said to Joseph, 'I hereby put you in charge of the whole land of Egypt.' . . . 'Only with respect to the throne will I be greater than you'" (Gen. 41:41, 40). And can you not hear Joseph speaking to his brethren: "God intended it for good to accomplish . . . the saving of many lives."

A whole life committed to God in unswerving loyalty is held as a most sacred trust. The processes used in building a great soul are varied and consume much time. Many a long road seems to have no turning. Frequently "the night is dark and we seem to be far from home," but patience cries out, "Lead Thou me on," "Keep Thou my feet; I do not ask to see the distant scene—one step enough for me." Faith, courage, and patience are tremendous qualities in a great life, but the time element is the factor which is absolutely necessary to work all these out.

Blessed is that life which is so thoroughly rooted down into the life of God that it can feel and know that, though time moves slowly in long drawn-out tests and trials. God's tides move steadily on in accomplishing His glorious purposes. QUESTS AND CONQUESTS

O tarry thou His leisure,
Praise when He seems to pause,
Nor think that the Eternal One
Will set His clock by yours;
But wait His time, and trust His date,
It cannot be too soon, or late!
The turn on the long road comes at last!

DAY 176

You, LORD, are my lamp; the LORD turns my darkness into light.

2 SAMUEL 22:29

There are times when a Christian needs to lie still, when our only safety is doing nothing. The voice of our Savior-God is heard beside many a Red-Sea difficulty—"Stand still, and see the salvation of the LORD" (Ex. 14:13 KJV). It is a hard thing to "stand still" in the presence of opposing forces. Jehovah is the Living God. Cloud and storm are beneath His feet and His throne remains unmoved.

"Am I in the dark?" asks Charles H. Spurgeon. "Then Thou, O Lord, 'will lighten my darkness.' Before long things will change. Affairs may grow worse and more dreary, and cloud upon cloud may be piled upon cloud; but if it grows so dark that I cannot see my own hand, still I shall see the Hand of the Lord."

When I cannot find a light within me, or among my friends, or in the whole world, the Lord who said, "Let there be light" and there was light, can say the same thing again. He will speak me into the sunshine yet. The day is already breaking. This sweet text shines like a morning star: "You, LORD, are my lamp; the LORD turns my darkness into light."

Clouds pass; stars remain!

My lamp is shattered, I'm deprived of light; my lamp is shattered, and so dark the night. My lamp is shattered, yet to my glad sight—a star shines on.
My lamp is shattered, but a star shines bright, and by its glowing I can wend aright. My lamp is shattered, but I still can fight—for a star shines on.
My lamp is shattered, sad indeed my plight. My lamp is shattered, yet I'll reach the height—for a star shines on!

WILHELMINA STITCH

June 26th

DAY 177

Jesus loved Martha and her sister and Lazarus.

JOHN 11:5

Jesus does not want all His loved ones to be of one mold or color. He does not seek uniformity. He will not remove our individuality; He only seeks to glorify it. He loved "Martha and her sister and Lazarus."

"Jesus loved Martha." Martha is our biblical example of a practical woman; "Martha served" (John 12:2). In that place is enshrined her character.

"And her sister." Mary was contemplative, spending long hours in deep communion with the unseen. We need the Marys as well as the Marthas—the deep contemplative souls, whose spirits shed a fragrant restfulness over the hard and busy streets. We need the souls who sit at Jesus' feet and listen to His Word, and then interpret the sweet Gospels to a tired and weary world.

"And Lazarus." What do we know about him? Nothing! Lazarus seems to have been undistinguished and commonplace. Yet Jesus loved him. What a huge multitude come under the category of "nobodies"! Their names are on the register of births, and on the register of deaths, and the space between is a great obscurity. Thank God for the commonplace people! They turn our houses into homes; they make life restful and sweet. Jesus loves the commonplace. Here then is a great, comforting thought: we are all loved—the brilliant and the commonplace, the dreamy and the practical.

"Jesus loved Martha and her sister and Lazarus." J. H. JOWETT

"Does the wildflower bloom less carefully and are the tints less perfect because it rises beside the fallen tree in the thick woods where mankind never enters? Let us not bemoan the fact that we are not great, and that the eyes of the world are not upon us."

Loved! then the way will not be drear,
For One we know is ever near,
Proving it to our hearts so clear
That we are loved.
Loved when we sing the glad new song
To Christ, for whom we've waited long,
With all the happy ransomed throng—
Forever loved.

June 27th

DAY 178

There the LORD . . . put them to the test.

EXODUS 15:25

I once visited the testing room of a large steel mill. I was surrounded by instruments and equipment that tested pieces of steel to their limits and measured their breaking point. Some pieces had been twisted until they broke, and then were labeled with the level of pressure they could withstand. Some had been stretched to their breaking point, with their level of strength also noted. Others had been compressed to their crushing point and measured. Because of the testing, the manager of the mill knew exactly how much stress and strain each piece of steel could endure if it was used to build a ship, building, or bridge.

It is often much the same with God's children. He does not want us to be like fragile vases of glass or porcelain. He wants us to be like these toughened pieces of steel, able to endure twisting and crushing pressure to the utmost without collapse.

God does not want us to be like greenhouse plants, which are sheltered from rough weather, but like storm-beaten oaks; not like sand dunes that are driven back and forth by every gust of wind but like granite mountains that withstand the fiercest storms. Yet to accomplish this, He must take us into His testing room of suffering. And many of us need no other argument than our own experiences to prove that suffering is indeed God's testing room of faith. J. H. M.

It is quite easy for us to talk and to theorize about faith, but God often puts us into His crucible of affliction to test the purity of our gold and to separate the dross from the metal. How happy we are if the hurricanes that blow across life's raging sea have the effect of making Jesus more precious to us! It is better to weather the storm with Christ than to sail smooth waters without Him. J. R. MACDUFF

What if God could not manage to mature your life without suffering?

DAY 179

Isn't this the carpenter?

MARK 6:3

This is my Son, whom I love; with him I am well pleased.

MATTHEW 3:17

Yes, yes, a carpenter, same trade as mine!
How it warms my heart as I read that line.
I can stand the hard work, I can stand the poor pay,
For I'll see that Carpenter at no distant day.

MALTBIE D. BABCOCK

It suits our best sense that the One who spoke of "putting the hand to the plow," and "taking the yoke upon us," should have made plows and yokes, Himself, and people do not think His words less heavenly for not smelling of books and lamps. Let us not make the mistake of those Nazarenes: that Jesus was a carpenter was to them poor credentials of divinity, but it has been Divine credentials to the poor ever since. Let us not be deceived by social ratings and badges of the schools.

Carey was a cobbler, but he had a map of the world on his shop wall, and outdid Alexander the Great in dreaming and doing.

What thoughts were in the mind of Jesus at His workbench? One of them was that the kingdoms of this world should become the kingdoms of God—at any cost!

"What is that in your hand?" (Ex. 4:2)

Is it a hoe, a needle, a broom? A pen or a sword? A ledger or a schoolbook? A typewriter or a telegraph instrument? Is it an anvil or a printer's rule? Is it a carpenter's plane or a plasterer's trowel? Is it a throttle or a helm? Is it a scalpel or a yardstick? Is it a musical instrument or the gift of song?

Whatever it is, give it to God in loving service.

Many a tinker and weaver and stonecutter and hard worker has had open windows and a sky, and a mind with wings!

DAY 180

Carrying his own cross.

JOHN 19:17

The Changed Cross” is a poem that tells of a weary woman who thought that the cross she must bear surely was heavier than those of other people, so she wished she could choose another person’s instead. When she went to sleep, she dreamed she was taken to a place where there were many different crosses from which to choose. There were various shapes and sizes, but the most beautiful one was covered with jewels and gold. “This I could wear with comfort,” she said. So she picked it up, but her weak body staggered beneath its weight. The jewels and gold were beautiful, yet they were much too heavy for her to carry.

The next cross she noticed was quite lovely, with beautiful flowers entwined around its sculptured form. Surely this was the one for her. She lifted it, but beneath the flowers were large thorns that pierced and tore her skin.

Finally she came to a plain cross without jewels or any carvings and with only a few words of love inscribed on it. When she picked it up, it proved to be better than all the rest, and the easiest to carry. And as she looked at it, she noticed it was bathed in a radiance that fell from heaven. Then she recognized it as her own old cross. She had found it once again, and it was the best of all, and the lightest for her.

You see, God knows best what cross we need to bear, and we never know how heavy someone else’s cross may be. We envy someone who is rich, with a cross of gold adorned with jewels, but we do not know how heavy it is. We look at someone whose life seems so easy and who carries a cross covered with flowers. Yet if we could actually test all the crosses we think are lighter than ours, we would never find one better suited for us than our own. GLIMPSES THROUGH LIFE'S WINDOWS

If you, with impatience, give up your cross,
You will not find it in this world again;
Nor in another, but here and here alone
Is given for you to suffer for God's sake.
In the next world we may more perfectly
Love Him and serve Him, praise Him,
Grow nearer and nearer to Him with delight.
But then we will not anymore
Be called to suffer, which is our assignment here.
Can you not suffer, then, one hour or two?
If He should call you from your cross today,
Saying, "It is finished—that hard cross of yours
From which you pray for deliverance,"
Do you not think that some emotion of regret
Would overcome you? You would say,
"So soon? Let me go back and suffer yet awhile
More patiently. I have not yet praised God."
So whenever it comes, that summons we all look for,
It will seem soon, too soon. Let us take heed in life
That God may now be glorified in us.

UGO BASSI'S SERMON IN A HOSPITAL

DAY 181

I was not disobedient.

ACTS 26:19

Whither, O Christ? The vision did not say; nor did Paul ask, but started on the way.

If Paul had asked, and if the Lord had said; if Paul had known the long hard road ahead; if with the heavenly vision Paul had seen stark poverty with cold and hungry mien, black fetid prisons with their chains and stocks, fierce robbers lurking amid tumbled rocks, the raging of the mob, the crashing stones, the aching eyes, hot fever in the bones, perils of mountain passes wild and steep, perils of tempest in the angry deep, the drag of loneliness, the curse of lies, mad bigotry's suspicious peering eyes, the bitter foe, the weakly, blundering friend, the whirling sword of Caesar at the end—would Paul have turned his back with shuddering moan and settled down at Tarsus, had he known? No! and a thousand times the thundering No! Where Jesus went, there Paul rejoiced to go. Prisons were palaces where Jesus stayed; with Jesus near, he asked no other aid; the love of Jesus kept him glad and warm, bold before kings and safe in any storm. Whither, O Christ? The vision did not say. Paul did not care. He started on the way. AMOS R. WELLS

"A great must dominated the life of the Son of Man. That must will dominate ours if we follow in His footsteps. The Son of Man must, and so His followers must."

Lord, I would follow, but—
First I would see what means that wondrous call
That peals so sweetly through life's rainbow hall,
That thrills my heart with quivering golden chords,
And fills my soul with joys seraphical.
Lord, I would follow, but—

First I would leave things straight before I go—
Collect my dues, and pay the debts I owe:
Lest when I'm gone, and none is here to tend,
Time's ruthless hand my garnering o'erthrow.
Lord, I would follow, but—
First I would see the end of this high road
That stretches straight before me fair and broad;
So clear the way I cannot go astray,
It surely leads me equally to God.
Who answers Christ's insistent call
Must give himself, his life, his all,
Without one backward look.
Who sets his hand upon the plow,
And glances back with anxious brow,
His calling hath mistook;
Christ claims him wholly for His own;
He must be Christ's and Christ's alone.

The Spirit of God does not come with a voice like thunder (that may come ultimately) but as a gentle zephyr, yet it can only be described as an imperative compulsion—This thing must be done!

DAY 182

Some went out on the sea in ships; they were merchants on the mighty waters. They saw the works of the LORD, *his wonderful deeds in the deep.*

PSALM 107:23–24

The person who has not learned that every wind that blows can be used to guide us toward heaven has certainly not mastered the art of sailing and is nothing but an apprentice. In fact, the only thing that helps no one is a dead calm. Every wind, whether from the north, south, east, or west, may help us toward that blessed port. So seek only this: to stay well out to sea—and then have no fear of stormy winds. May our prayer be that of an old Englishman: "O Lord, send us into the deep water of the sea, for we are so close to shore that even a small breeze from the Devil could break our ship to pieces on the rocks. Again, Lord, send us into the deep water of the sea, where there will be plenty of room to win a glorious victory." MARK GUY PEARSE

Remember, our faith is always at its greatest point when we are in the middle of the trial, and confidence in the flesh will never endure testing. Fair-weather faith is not faith at all. CHARLES H. SPURGEON

DAY 183

Thou shalt be above only, and thou shalt not be beneath.

DEUTERONOMY 28:13 KJV

This verse came to me first as a very real message from God in a time of great pressure. We had fourteen guests in the Mission house and were almost without domestic help. I had, perforce, to lay aside correspondence and other duties and give my time and attention to cooking and housework, and was feeling the strain.

Then God's Word spoke to me with power: "Thou shalt be above only, and thou shalt not be beneath," and in a moment I saw there was no need to go under—no need to be overwhelmed by my circumstances. No need to trouble because it seemed as if I could not get through and my ordinary work was getting in arrears—somehow, I could be above it all! "Above only, and not beneath." How often I used to say as I went about my kitchen, "I refuse to go down," and how the lesson I learned in those difficult days has been an inspiration ever since. Do you wonder that Deuteronomy 28:13 is one of my favorite verses in the Bible?

I see in it the possibility of a life of constant victory—not up today in heights of blessedness, and down in the depths tomorrow. This is a steady life. It is the life that has been established and settled by the God of all grace.

"Above only" is a position of victory, too. It is that position which is ours in Christ Jesus. "Alive with Christ. . . . in heavenly realms in Christ Jesus" (Eph. 2:5–6). "Your life is now hidden with Christ in God" (Col. 3:3).

When we lived in Alexandria, Egypt, we used to see some fierce squalls of wind and rain, which lashed the sea into fury. The great buoys in the harbor would be covered with spray and foam, but when the wind died down again they were still there in their places, unmoved and steady. "Above only" for they had that within them which kept them on the top. And have we not power within us, too, which should insure our triumph?

Let us absolutely refuse to come down to live and work on a lower level.

A MISSIONARY'S TESTIMONY

"Far above all" (Eph. 1:21).

DAY 184

Blessed are those who have not seen and yet have believed.

JOHN 20:29

How important it is for God to keep us focused on things that are unseen, for we are so easily snared by the things we can see! If Peter was ever going to walk on the water, he had to walk, but if he was going to swim to Jesus, he had to swim. He could not do both. If a bird is going to fly, it must stay away from fences and trees, trusting the buoyancy of its wings. And if it tries to stay within easy reach of the ground, it will never fly very well.

God had to bring Abraham to the end of his own strength and let him see that with his own body he could do nothing. He had to consider his own body "as good as dead" (Heb. 11:12) and then trust God to do all the work. When he looked away from himself and trusted only God, he became "fully persuaded that God had power to do what he had promised" (Rom. 4:21).

This is what God is teaching us, and He has to keep results that are encouraging away from us until we learn to trust Him without them. Then He loves to make His Word as real to us in actuality as it is in our faith. A. B. SIMPSON

I do not ask that He must prove
His Word is true to me,
And that before I can believe
He first must let me see.
It is enough for me to know
It's true because He says it's so;
On His unchanging Word I'll stand
And trust till I can understand.

E. M. WINTER

July 4th

DAY 185

The Lord *makes firm the steps of the one who delights in him. The steps of a good man are ordered by the* Lord.

PSALM 37:23 NIV; KJV

We often make a great mistake thinking that God is not guiding us at all, because we cannot see far ahead. But He only undertakes that the steps of a good man should be ordered by the Lord; not next year, but tomorrow; not for the next mile, but the next yard: as you will acknowledge when you review it from the hilltops of Glory.

"The stops of a good man, as well as his steps, are ordered by the Lord," says George Müller. Naturally an opened door seems more like guidance to us than a closed one. Yet God may guide by the latter as definitely as by the former. His guidance of the children of Israel by the pillar of cloud and of fire is a clear case in point. When the cloud was lifted the Israelites took up their march: it was the guidance of God to move onward. But when the cloud tarried and abode upon the tabernacle, then the people rested in their tents. Both the tarrying and the journeying were guidance from the Lord—the one as much as the other.

I shall never be able to go too fast, if the Lord is in front of me; and I can never go too slowly, if I follow Him always, everywhere.

It is just as dark in advance of God's glorious leading as it is away behind Him.

You may be trying to go faster than He is moving. Wait till He comes up and then the way will no longer lie in darkness. He has left footprints for us to follow. Make no footprints of thine own!

Not so in haste, my heart!
Have faith in God and wait:
Although He linger long
He never comes too late.

Until He cometh, rest,
Nor grudge the hours that roll,
The feet that wait for God
Are soonest at the goal
Are soonest at the goal
That is not gained by speed.
Then hold thee still, my heart,
For I shall wait His lead.

BAYARD TAYLOR

Let the great Master's steps be thine!

DAY 186

I will build you with stones of turquoise.

ISAIAH 54:11

The stones in the wall said, "We have come from mountains far away—from the sides of rugged cliffs. Fire and water have worked on us for ages but have only produced crevices. Yet human hands like yours have made us into homes where children of your immortal race are born, suffer, rejoice, find rest and shelter, and learn the lessons that our Maker and yours is teaching. But to come to the point of being used for this purpose, we have endured much. Dynamite has torn at our very heart, and pickaxes have broken and split us into pieces. Often as we lay disfigured and broken in the quarry, everything seemed to be without design or meaning. But gradually we were cut into blocks, and some of us were chiseled with sharper instruments until we had a fine edge. Now we are complete, are in our proper places, and are of service.

"You, however, are still in your quarry. You are not complete, and because of that, as once was the case with us, there is much you do not understand. But you are destined for a higher building, and someday you will be placed in it by angelic hands, becoming a living stone in a heavenly temple."

In the still air the music lies unheard;
In the rough marble beauty hides unseen;
To make the music and the beauty needs
The master's touch, the sculptor's chisel keen.
Great Master, touch us with Your skillful hands;
Let not the music that is in us die!
Great Sculptor, hew and polish us; nor let,
Hidden and lost, Your form within us lie!

DAY 187

When you walk through the fire, you will not be burned.

ISAIAH 43:2

In giving a lecture on flame a scientist once made a most interesting experiment. He wanted to show that in the center of each flame there is a hollow—a place of entire stillness—around which its fire is a mere wall. To prove this he introduced into the midst of the flame a minute and carefully shielded charge of explosive powder. The protection was then carefully removed and no explosion followed. A second time the experiment was tried, and by a slight agitation of the hand the central security was lost and an immediate explosion was the result.

Our safety, then, is only in stillness of soul. If we are affrighted and exchange the principle of faith for that of fear, or if we are rebellious and restless, we shall be hurt by the flames and anguish and disappointment will be the result.

Moreover, God will be disappointed in us if we break down. Testing is the proof of His love and confidence, and who can tell what pleasure our steadfastness and stillness give to Him? If He allowed us to go without testing it would not be complementary to our spiritual experience. Much trial and suffering mean, therefore, that God has confidence in us; that He believes we are strong enough to endure; that we shall be true to Him even when He has left us without outward evidence of His care and seemingly at the mercy of His adversaries. If He increase the trials instead of diminishing them it is an expression of confidence in us up to the present, and a further proof that He is looking to us to glorify Him in yet hotter fires through which He is calling us to pass. Let us not be afraid! We shall be delivered from the transitory and the outward and drawn into closer fellowship with God Himself!

O God, make us children of quietness! AN ANCIENT LITURGY

July 7th

DAY 188

It has been granted to you . . . to suffer for him.

PHILIPPIANS 1:29

God runs a costly school, for many of His lessons are learned through tears. Richard Baxter, the seventeenth-century Puritan preacher, once said, "O God, I thank You for the discipline I have endured in this body for fifty-eight years." And he certainly is not the only person who has turned trouble into triumph.

Soon the school of our heavenly Father will close for us, for the end of the school term is closer every day. May we never run from a difficult lesson or flinch from the rod of discipline. Richer will be our crown, and sweeter will heaven be, if we cheerfully endure to the end. Then we will graduate in glory. THEODORE L. CUYLER

The world's finest china is fired in ovens at least three times, and some many more. Dresden china is always fired three times. Why is it forced to endure such intense heat? Shouldn't once or twice be enough? No, it is necessary to fire the china three times so the gold, crimson, and other colors are brighter, more beautiful, and permanently attached.

We are fashioned after the same principle. The human trials of life are burned into us numerous times, and through God's grace, beautiful colors are formed in us and made to shine forever. CORTLAND MYERS

Earth's fairest flowers grow not on sunny plain,
But where some vast upheaval tore in twain
The smiling land.
After the whirlwind's devastating blast,
And molten lava, fire, and ashes fall,
God's still small voice breathes healing over all.
From broken rocks and fern-clad chasms deep,
Flow living waters as from hearts that weep,
There in the afterglow soft dews distill
And angels tend God's plants when night falls still,
And the Beloved passing by the way
Will gather lilies at the break of day.

J. H. D.

DAY 189

They were employed in that work day and night.

1 CHRONICLES 9:33 KJV

There is a legend of a man who found the barn where Satan kept his seeds ready to be sown in the human heart, and on finding the seeds of discouragement more numerous than others, learned that those seeds could be made to grow almost anywhere. When Satan was questioned he reluctantly admitted that there was one place in which he could never get them to thrive.

"And where is that?" asked the man. Satan replied sadly, "In the heart of a grateful man."

The psalmist realized that gratitude plays an essential part in true worship. He sang praises to God at all times; often, in his darkest moments. When in his despair he called on God, his praises soon mingled with his cries of anguish, showing the victory accomplished by his habitual thankfulness.

Sometimes a light surprises the Christian while he sings.

Is it midnight in your experience? Is it an interminable time since the gold and crimson hope died out in the west—and a seemingly longer interval before the hoped-for dawning of day? Midnight! Still, dark, and eerie! It is time to pray! And it is time to sing! Strange how prayer and singing open prison doors—but they do!

Do you need doors to be opened? Try prayer and singing; they go together! They work wonders!

When the heaven is black with wind, the thunder crackling over our heads, then we may join in the paean of the Storm-spirits to Him whose pageant of power passes over the earth and harms us not in its march.

The choir of small birds, and night crickets, and all happy things, praise Him all the night long. Not somehow but triumphantly!

DAY 190

He saw the disciples straining at the oars.

MARK 6:48

Straining and striving does not accomplish the work God gives us to do. Only God Himself, who always works without stress and strain and who never overworks, can do the work He assigns to His children. When we restfully trust Him to do it, the work will be completed and will be done well. And the way to let Him do His work through us is to so fully abide in Christ by faith that He fills us to overflowing.

A man who learned this secret once said, "I came to Jesus and drank, and I believe I will never be thirsty again. My life's motto has become 'Not overwork but overflow,' and it has already made all the difference in my life."

There is no straining effort in an overflowing life, and it is quietly irresistible. It is the normal life of omnipotent and ceaseless accomplishment into which Christ invites each of us to enter—today and always. SUNDAY SCHOOL TIMES

Be all at rest, my soul, O blessed secret,
Of the true life that glorifies the Lord:
Not always does the busiest soul best serve Him,
But he that rests upon His faithful Word.
Be all at rest, let not your heart be rippled,
For tiny wavelets mar the image fair,
Which the still pool reflects of heaven's glory—
And thus the image He would have you bear.
Be all at rest, my soul, for rest is service,
To the still heart God does His secrets tell;
Thus will you learn to wait, and watch, and labor,
Strengthened to bear, since Christ in you does dwell.
For what is service but the life of Jesus,
Lived through a vessel of earth's fragile clay,
Loving and giving and poured forth for others,
A living sacrifice from day to day.
Be all at rest, so then you'll be an answer
To those who question, "Who is God and where?"
For God is rest, and where He dwells is stillness,
And they who dwell in Him, His rest will share.
And what will meet the deep unrest around you,
But the calm peace of God that filled His breast?

For still a living Voice calls to the weary,
From Him who said, "Come unto Me and rest."
FREDA HANBURY ALLEN

In Resurrection stillness there is Resurrection power.

DAY 191

They spring up like flowers.
JOB 14:2

The lotus flower is rooted in the mud. It is quite as much indebted to the mud and water for its beauty as to the air and sunshine in which it blooms.

We must not scorn the study of root culture, nor neglect it in enthusiasm for the beauties of the orchid; for though that exquisite flower is an air plant, it needs to attach itself to a sturdier growth that is rooted in the ground and draws its nourishment from the soil to feed both itself and its parasite. The tree will outlive many seasons of orchids!

"Some time ago in the late autumn," says a writer, "I was in the hothouse of one of our florists. We were in the cellar, and in the dimly lighted place one could see arranged in regular file long rows of flowerpots. The florist explained that in these pots had been planted the bulbs for their winter flowers. It was best for them, he said, that they be rooted in the dark." Not in the glaring sunlight, but in the subdued shadows their life-giving roots were putting forth. They would be ready for the open day a little later. Then their gay colors would cheer many hearts; then their sweet perfume would laden the winter air.

Rooted in the shadows to bloom in the light! Roots, then roses.

DAY 192

When you hear them sound a long blast on the trumpets, have the whole army give a loud shout; then the wall of the city will collapse and the army will go up, everyone straight in.

JOSHUA 6:5

The "loud shout" of steadfast faith is the exact opposite of the groans of wavering faith and the complaints of discouraged hearts. Of all "the secret[s] of the LORD" (Ps. 25:14 KJV), I do not believe there are any more valuable than the secret of this "loud shout" of faith. "The LORD said to Joshua, 'See, I have delivered Jericho into your hands, along with its king and its fighting men'" (Josh. 6:2). He did not say, "I will deliver" but "I have delivered." The victory already belonged to the children of Israel, and now they were called to take possession of it. But the big question still remaining was how. It looked impossible, but the Lord had a plan.

No one would normally believe that a shout could cause city walls to fall. Yet the secret of their victory lay precisely in just that shout, for it was the shout of faith. And it was a faith that dared to claim a promised victory solely on the basis of the authority of God's Word, even though there were no physical signs of fulfillment. God answered His promise in response to their faith, for when they shouted, He caused the walls to fall.

God had declared, "I have delivered Jericho into your hands," and faith believed this to be true. And many centuries later the Holy Spirit recorded this triumph of faith in the book of Hebrews as follows: "By faith the walls of Jericho fell, after the army had marched around them for seven days" (Heb. 11:30). HANNAH WHITALL SMITH

Faith can never reach its consummation,
Till the victor's thankful song we raise:
In the glorious city of salvation,
God has told us all the gates are praise.

July 17th

DAY 193

Then the fire of the LORD *fell and burned up the sacrifice, the wood, the stones and the soil, and also licked up the water in the trench.*

1 KINGS 18:38

Prayer is one of the most sacred and precious privileges vouchsafed to mortals. The following is a scene from the life of that mighty Elijah in prayer, Charles G. Finney.

The summer of 1853 was unusually hot and dry; pastures were scorched. There seemed likely to be a total crop failure. At the church in Oberlin the great congregation had gathered as usual. Though the sky was clear the burden of Finney's prayer was for rain.

"We do not presume, O Lord, to dictate to Thee what is best for us; yet Thou didst invite us to come to Thee as children to an earthly father and tell Thee all our wants. We want rain. Our pastures are dry. The earth is gaping open for rain. The cows are wandering about and lowing in search of water. Even the squirrels are suffering from thirst. Unless Thou givest us rain our cattle will die, and our harvest will come to naught. O Lord, send us rain, and send it now! This is an easy thing for Thee to do. Send it now, Lord, for Christ's sake."

In a few minutes he had to cease preaching; his voice could not be heard because of the roar and rattle of the rain! LIFE OF FINNEY

Life has outgrown
Faith's childish way,
The proud and scoffing
Folk insist;
And so they laugh
At all who say
God's miracles exist.
Well, let them laugh!

The trusting heart
Has joys which they
Know naught thereof.
And, daily, miracles are wrought
For us who hold
To faith and love!

"MIRACLES" BY JOHN RICHARD MORELAND

The world wants something that has God in it!

DAY 194

My Presence will go with you, and I will give you rest.

EXODUS 33:14

What is rest?

To step out of self-life into Christ-life; to lie still, and let Him lift you out of it; to fold your hands close, and hide your face on the hem of His garment; to let Him lay His cooling, soothing, healing hands upon your soul, and draw all the hurry and fever from its veins; to realize that you are not a mighty messenger, an important worker of His, full of care and responsibility, but only a little child, with a Father's gentle bidding to heed and fulfill; to lay your busy plans and ambitions confidently in His hands, as a child brings its broken toys at its mother's call; to serve Him by waiting; to praise Him by saying, "Holy, Holy, Holy"; to cease to hurry, so you may not lose sight of His face; to learn to follow Him, and not to run ahead of orders! To cease to live in self and for self, and to live in Him and for Him; to love His honor more than your own; to be a clear medium for His life-tide to shine and glow through. This is consecration, this is rest.

Thou sweet, beloved will of God,
My anchor ground, my fortress hill,
My spirit's silent, fair abode,
In Thee I hide me and am still.
Thy beautiful sweet will, my God,
Holds fast in its sublime embrace
My captive will, a gladsome bird,
Prison'd in such a realm of grace.
Upon God's will I lay me down,
As child upon its mother's breast,
No silken couch, nor softest bed,
Could ever give me such deep rest.

TERSTEEGEN

DAY 195

Christ in you.

COLOSSIANS 1:27

It is a great secret I tell you today, nay, I can give you—if you will take it from Him, not from me—a secret which has been to me, oh, so wonderful! Many years ago I came to Him burdened with guilt and fear; I took that simple secret, and it took away my fear and sin. Years passed on, and I found sin overcame me, and my temptations were too strong for me. I came to Him a second time, and He whispered to me, "Christ in you." And I have had victory, rest and sweet blessing ever since . . . I look back with unutterable gratitude to the lonely and sorrowful night, when, mistaken in many things, and imperfect in all, and not knowing but that it would be death in the most literal sense before the morning light, my heart's first full consecration was made, and, with unreserved surrender, I first could say,

Jesus, I my cross have taken,
All to leave and follow Thee:
Destitute, despised, forsaken,
Thou from hence my all shall be.

Never, perhaps, has my heart known such a thrill of joy as when, the following Sunday morning, I gave out these lines, and sang them with all my heart. And, if God has been pleased to use me in any fuller measure, it has been because of that hour. And it will be still, in the measure in which that hour is made the keynote of a consecrated, crucified, and Christ-devoted life. This experience of Christ our Sanctifier marks a definite and distinct crisis in the history of a soul. We do not grow into it, but we cross a definite line of demarcation, as clear as when the hosts of Joshua crossed the Jordan and were over in the Promised Land, and set up a great heap of stones, so that they never could forget that crisis hour. A. B. SIMPSON

DAY 196

You remain.

HEBREWS 1:11

There are so many people who sit by their fireplace all alone! They sit by another chair, once filled, and cannot restrain the tears that flow. They sit alone so much, but there is someone who is unseen and just within their reach. But for some reason, they don't realize His presence. Realizing it is blessed yet quite rare. It is dependent upon their mood, their feelings, their physical condition, and the weather. The rain or thick fog outside, the lack of sleep and the intense pain, seem to affect their mood and blur their vision so they do not realize His presence.

There is, however, something even better than realizing, and even more blessed. It is completely independent of these other conditions and is something that will abide with you. It is this: recognizing that unseen presence, which is so wonderful, quieting, soothing, calming, and warming. So recognize the presence of the Master. He is here, close to you, and His presence is real. Recognizing will also help your ability to realize but is never dependent upon it.

Yes, there is immeasurably more—the truth is a presence, not a thing, a fact, or a statement. Some One is present, and He is a warmhearted Friend and the all-powerful Lord. This is a joyful truth for weeping hearts everywhere, no matter the reason for the tears, or whatever stream their weeping willow is planted beside. SAMUEL DICKEY GORDON

When from my life the old-time joys have vanished,
Treasures once mine, I may no longer claim,
This truth may feed my hungry heart, and famished:
Lord, You remain here! You are still the same!
When streams have dried, those streams of glad refreshing—
Friendships so blest, so rich, so free;
When sun-kissed skies give place to clouds depressing,
Lord, You remain here! Still my heart has Thee.
When strength has failed, and feet, now worn and weary,
On happy errands may no longer go,
Why should I sigh, or let the days be dreary?
Lord, You remain here! Could You more bestow?
Thus through life's days—whoe'er or what may fail me,
Friends, friendships, joys, in small or great degree,
Songs may be mine, no sadness need assault me,
Lord, You remain here! Still my heart has Thee.

J. DANSON SMITH

DAY 197

The greatest of these is love.

1 CORINTHIANS 13:13

I'll master it!" said the ax; and his blows fell heavily on the iron. And every blow made his edge more blunt till he ceased to strike.

"Leave it to me!" said the saw; and with his relentless teeth he worked backward and forward on its surface till his teeth were worn down and broken, and he fell aside.

"Ha, ha!" said the hammer. "I knew you wouldn't succeed! I'll show you the way!" But at the first fierce stroke off flew his head, and the iron remained as before.

"Shall I try?" asked the still, small flame.

They all despised the flame, but he curled gently around the iron and embraced it, and never left it till it melted under his irresistible influence.

Hard indeed is the heart that can resist love.

"And now these three remain: faith, hope and love. But the greatest of these is love."

DAY 198

God is our refuge and strength, an ever-present help in trouble.

PSALM 46:1

Why didn't God help me sooner?" This is a question that is often asked, but it is not His will to act on your schedule. He desires to change you through the trouble and cause you to learn a lesson from it. He has promised, "I will be with him in trouble, I will deliver him and honor him" (Ps. 91:15). He will be with you in trouble all day and through the night. Afterward he will take you out of it, but not until you have stopped being restless and worried over it and have become calm and quiet. Then He will say, "It is enough."

God uses trouble to teach His children precious lessons. Difficulties are intended to educate us, and when their good work is done, a glorious reward will become ours through them. There is a sweet joy and a real value in difficulties, for He regards them not as difficulties but as opportunities.

Not always out of our troubled times,
And the struggles fierce and grim,
But in—deeper in—to our sure rest,
The place of our peace, in Him.

ANNIE JOHNSON FLINT

I once heard the following statement from a simple old man, and I have never forgotten it: "When God tests you, it is a good time to test Him by putting His promises to the test and then claiming from Him exactly what your trials have made necessary." There are two ways of getting out of a trial. One is simply to try to get rid of the trial, and then to be thankful when it is over. The other is to recognize the trial as a challenge from God to claim a larger blessing than we have ever before experienced, and to accept it with delight as an opportunity of receiving a greater measure of God's divine grace.

In this way, even the Adversary becomes a help to us, and all the things that seem to be against us turn out to assist us along our way. Surely this is what is meant by the words "In all these things we are more than conquerors through him who loved us" (Rom. 8:37). A. B. SIMPSON

DAY 199

The land which I do give to them, even to the children of Israel.

JOSHUA 1:2 KJV

God is speaking about something immediate in this verse. It is not something He is going to do but something He does do, at this very moment. As faith continues to speak, God continues to give. He meets you today in the present and tests your faith. As long as you are waiting, hoping, or looking, you are not believing. You may have hope or an earnest desire, but that is not faith, for "faith is confidence in what we hope for and assurance about what we do not see" (Heb. 11:1). The command regarding believing prayer is: "Whatever you ask for in prayer, believe that you have received it, and it will be yours" (Mark 11:24). We are to believe that we have received—this present moment. Have we come to the point where we have met God in His everlasting now? A. B. SIMPSON

True faith relies on God and believes before seeing. Naturally, we want some evidence that our petition is granted before we believe, but when we "live by faith" (2 Cor. 5:7), we need no evidence other than God's Word. He has spoken, and in harmony with our faith it will be done. We will see because we have believed, and true faith sustains us in the most trying of times, even when everything around us seems to contradict God's Word.

The psalmist said, "I remain confident of this: I will see the goodness of the LORD in the land of the living" (Ps. 27:13). He had not yet seen the Lord's answer to his prayers, but he was confident he would see, and his confidence sustained him.

Faith that believes it will see, will keep us from becoming discouraged. We will laugh at seemingly impossible situations while we watch with delight to see how God is going to open a path through our Red Sea. It is in these places of severe testing, with no human way out of our difficulty, that our faith grows and is strengthened.

Dear troubled one, have you been waiting for God to work during long nights and weary days, fearing you have been forgotten? Lift up your head and begin praising Him right now for the deliverance that is on its way to you. LIFE OF PRAISE

DAY 200

Thou hast enlarged me when I was in distress.

PSALM 4:1 KJV

This verse is one of the greatest testimonies ever written regarding the effectiveness of God's work on our behalf during times of crisis. It is a statement of thanksgiving for having been set free not from suffering but rather through suffering. In stating, "Thou hast enlarged me when I was in distress," the psalmist is declaring that the sorrows of life have themselves been the source of life's enlargement.

Haven't each of us experienced this a thousand times and found it to be true? Someone once said of Joseph that when he was in the dungeon, "iron entered his soul." And the strength of iron is exactly what he needed, for earlier he had only experienced the glitter of gold. He had been rejoicing in youthful dreams, and dreaming actually hardens the heart. Someone who sheds great tears over a simple romance will not be of much help in a real crisis, for true sorrow will be too deep for him. We all need the iron in life to enlarge our character. The gold is simply a passing vision, whereas the iron is the true experience of life. The chain that is the common bond uniting us to others must be one of iron. The common touch of humanity that gives the world true kinship is not joy but sorrow—gold is partial to only a few, but iron is universal.

Dear soul, if you want your sympathy for others to be enlarged, you must be willing to have your life narrowed to certain degrees of suffering. Joseph's dungeon was the very road to his throne, and he would have been unable to lift the iron load of his brothers had he not experienced the iron in his own life.

Your life will be enlarged in proportion to the amount of iron you have endured, for it is in the shadows of your life that you will find the actual fulfillment of your dreams of glory. So do not complain about the shadows of darkness—in reality, they are better than your dreams could ever be. Do not say that the darkness of the prison has shackled you, for your shackles are wings—wings of flight into the heart and soul of humanity. And the gate of your prison is the gate into the heart of the universe. God has enlarged you through the suffering of sorrow's chain. GEORGE MATHESON

If Joseph had never been Egypt's prisoner, he would have never been Egypt's governor. The iron chain that bound his feet brought about the golden chain around his neck.

DAY 201

I know whom I have believed.

2 TIMOTHY 1:12

God loves an uttermost confidence in Himself—to be wholly trusted. This is the sublimest of all the characteristics of a true Christian—the basis of all character.

Is there anything that pleases you more than to be trusted—to have even a little child look up into your face, and put out its hand to meet yours, and come to you confidingly? By so much as God is better than you are, by so much more does He love to be trusted.

There is a Hand stretched out to you; a Hand with a wound in the palm of it. Reach out the hand of your faith to clasp it, and cling to it, for "without faith it is impossible to please God" (Heb. 11:6). HENRY VAN DYKE

Reach up as far as you can, and God will reach down all the rest of the way. BISHOP VINCENT

Not what, but whom I do believe!
That, in my darkest hour of need,

Hath comfort that no mortal creed
To mortal man may give.
Not what, but whom!
For Christ is more than all the creeds,
And His full life of gentle deeds
Shall all the creeds outlive.
Not what I do believe, but whom!
who walks beside me in the gloom?
who shares the burden wearisome?
who all the dim way doth illume,
And bids me look beyond the tomb
The larger life to live?
Not what I do believe, but whom!
Not what,
But whom!

JOHN OXENHAM

DAY 202

Some [seed] fell on rocky places, where it did not have much soil. It sprang up quickly, because the soil was shallow.

MATTHEW 13:5

Shallow! From the context of the teaching of this parable, it seems that we must have something to do with the depth of the soil. The fruitful seed fell on "good soil" (v. 8), or good and honest hearts. I suppose the shallow people are those who "did not have much soil"—those who have no real purpose in life and are easily swayed by a tender appeal, a good sermon, or a simple melody. And at first it seems as if they will amount to something for God, but because they "[do] not have much soil," they have no depth or genuine purpose, and no earnest desire to know His will in order to do it. Therefore we should be careful to maintain the soil of our hearts.

When a Roman soldier was told by his guide that if he insisted on taking a certain journey, it would probably be fatal, he answered, "It is necessary for me to go—it is not necessary for me to live." That was true depth of conviction, and only when we are likewise convicted will our lives amount to something. But a shallow life lives on its impulses, impressions, intuitions, instincts, and largely on its circumstances. Those with profound character, however, look beyond all these and move steadily ahead, seeing the future, where sorrow, seeming defeat, and failure will be reversed. They sail right through storm clouds into the bright sunshine, which always awaits them on the other side.

Once God has deepened us, He can give us His deepest truths, His most profound secrets, and will trust us with greater power. Lord, lead us into the depths of Your life and save us from a shallow existence!

On to broader fields of holy vision;
On to loftier heights of faith and love;
Onward, upward, apprehending wholly,
All for which He calls you from above.

A. B. SIMPSON

DAY 203

Spread the sail.

ISAIAH 33:23 KJV

Picture a vessel lying becalmed on a glassy sea—not a breath of air stirs a sail. But, presently, the little pennant far up on the masthead begins to stir and lift! There is not a ripple on the water; not the slightest movement of the air on deck, but there is a current stirring in the upper air! At once the sails are spread to catch it!

"So in life," says Dr. Miller, "there are higher and lower currents. Too many of us use only the lower sails, and catch only the winds blowing along earthly levels. It would be an unspeakable gain to us all were we to let our life fall under the influence of these upper currents."

Far out to sea, at close of day,
A lonely albatross flew by.
We watched him as he soared away—
A speck against the glowing sky!
Thought I: This lordly feathered one
Is trusting in the faithfulness
Of wind and tide, of star and sun;
And shall I trust the Maker less?
O soul of mine, spread wide thy wings:
Mount up; push out with courage strong!
And—like a bird which, soaring, sings—
Let heaven vibrate with thy song!
Spread wide thy wings, o soul of mine,
For God will ever faithful be:
His love shall guide thee; winds Divine
Shall waft thee o'er this troubled sea.
Though dangers threaten in the night,
Though tides of death below thee roll,
Though storms attend thy homeward flight,
Spread wide thy pinions, o my soul!
Though shadows veil the verdant shore,
And distant seems the hallowed dawn,
Spread wide thy pinions—evermore
Spread wide thy pinions, and press on.

ROBERT CRUMLY

Spread your sails to catch the upper currents!

DAY 204

The Lord will vindicate me.

PSALM 138:8

There is a divine mystery in suffering, one that has a strange and supernatural power and has never been completely understood by human reason. No one has ever developed a deep level of spirituality or holiness without experiencing a great deal of suffering. When a person who suffers reaches a point where he can be calm and carefree, inwardly smiling at his own suffering, and no longer asking God to be delivered from it, then the suffering has accomplished its blessed ministry, perseverance has "finish[ed] its work" (James 1:4), and the pain of the Crucifixion has begun to weave itself into a crown.

It is in this experience of complete suffering that the Holy Spirit works many miraculous things deep within our soul. In this condition, our entire being lies perfectly still under the hand of God; every power and ability of the mind, will, and heart are at last submissive; a quietness of eternity settles into the entire soul; and finally, the mouth becomes quiet, having only a few words to say, and stops crying out the words Christ quoted on the cross: "My God, my God, why have you forsaken me?" (Ps. 22:1).

At this point the person stops imagining castles in the sky, and pursuing foolish ideas, and his reasoning becomes calm and relaxed, with all choices removed, because the only choice has now become the purpose of God. Also, his emotions are weaned away from other people and things, becoming deadened so that nothing can hurt, offend, hinder, or get in his way. He can now let the circumstances be what they may, and continue to seek only God and His will, with the calm assurance that He is causing everything in the universe, whether good or bad, past or present, to work "for the good of those who love him" (Rom. 8:28).

Oh, the blessings of absolute submission to Christ! What a blessing to lose our own strength, wisdom, plans, and desires and to be where every ounce of our being becomes like a peaceful Sea of Galilee under the omnipotent feet of Jesus! SOUL FOOD

The main thing is to suffer without becoming discouraged. FRANÇOIS FÉNELON

The heart that serves, and loves, and clings,
Hears everywhere the rush of angel wings.

July 24th

DAY 205

What has happened to me has actually served to advance the gospel.
PHILIPPIANS 1:12

We cannot expect to learn much of the life of trust without passing through hard places. When they come let us not say as Jacob did, "Everything is against me!" (Gen. 42:36).

Let us rather climb our Hills of Difficulty and say, "These are faith's opportunities!"

I would not lose the hard things from my life,
The rocks o'er which I stumbled long ago,
The griefs and fears, the failures and mistakes,
That tried and tested faith and patience so.
I need them now: they make the deep-laid wall,
The firm foundation-stones on which I raise—
To mount therein from stair to higher stair—
The lofty towers of my House of Praise.
Soft was the roadside turf to weary feet,
And cool the meadows where I fain had trod,

And sweet beneath the trees to lie at rest
And breathe the incense of the flower-starred sod;
But not on these might I securely build;
Nor sand nor sod withstand the earthquake shock;
I need the rough hard boulders of the hills,
To set my house on everlasting rock.

ANNIE JOHNSON FLINT

Crises reveal character: when we are put to the test we reveal exactly the hidden resources of our character.

July 25th

DAY 206

After waiting patiently, Abraham received what was promised.

HEBREWS 6:15

Abraham was tested for a very long time, but he was richly rewarded. The Lord tested him by delaying the fulfillment of His promise. Satan tested him through temptation, and people tested him through their jealousy, distrust, and opposition to him. Sarah tested him through her worrisome temperament. Yet he patiently endured, not questioning God's truthfulness and power or doubting God's faithfulness and love. Instead, Abraham submitted to God's divine sovereignty and infinite wisdom. And he was silent through many delays, willing to wait for the Lord's timing. Having patiently endured, he then obtained the fulfillment of the promise.

Beloved, God's promises can never fail to be accomplished, and those who patiently wait can never be disappointed, for believing faith leads to realization. Abraham's life condemns a spirit of hastiness, admonishes those who complain, commends those who are patient, and encourages quiet submission to God's will and way.

Remember, Abraham was tested but he patiently waited, ultimately received what was promised, and was satisfied. If you will imitate his example, you will share the same blessing.

DAY 207

As Jesus started on his way, a man ran up to him and. . . . asked, "what must I do to inherit eternal life? . . . Jesus looked at him and loved him. "One thing you lack," he said. "Go, sell everything you have . . . and you will have treasure in heaven. Then come, follow me." At this the man's face fell. He went away sad, because he had great wealth.

MARK 10:17, 21–22

Such was the preparation necessary before this admirable soul could become a disciple of Jesus Christ. To use the language of Dr. Donald Davidson:

"Strip yourself of every possession, cut away every affection, disengage yourself from all things, be as if you were a naked soul, alone in the world; be a mere man merely, and then be God's. "Sell everything you have and. . . . follow me"! Reduce yourself down, if I may say so, till nothing remains but your consciousness of yourself, and then cast the self-consciousness at the feet of God in Christ.

"The only way to Jesus is alone. Will you strip yourself and separate yourself and take that lonely road, or will you too 'go away sorrowful'?"

We are not told his name—this "rich young ruler"
Who sought the Lord that day;
We only know that he had great possessions
And that—he went away.
He went away; he kept his earthly treasure
But oh, at what a cost!

Afraid to take the cross and lose his riches—
And God and Heaven were lost.
So for the tinsel bonds that held and drew him
What honor he let slip—
Comrade of John and Paul and friend of Jesus—
What glorious fellowship!
For they who left their all to follow Jesus
Have found a deathless fame,
On his immortal scroll of saints and martyrs
God wrote each shining name.
We should have read his there—the rich young ruler—If he had stayed that day;
Nameless—though Jesus loved him—ever nameless because—he went away.

DAY 208

Who is this coming up from the wilderness leaning on her beloved?

SONG OF SONGS 8:5

I once learned a great lesson at a prayer meeting at a southern church. As one man prayed, he asked the Lord for various blessings, just as you or I would, and he thanked the Lord for many blessings already received, just as you or I would. But he closed his prayer with this unusual petition: "And, O Lord, support us! Yes, support us on every leaning side!"

Do you have any "leaning sides"? This humble man's prayer pictured them in a new way and illustrated the Great Supporter in a new light as well. He saw God as always walking alongside the Christian, ready to extend His mighty arm to steady the weak on "every leaning side."

Child of My love, lean hard,
And let Me feel the pressure of your care;
I know your burden, child. I shaped it;
Balanced it in Mine Own hand; made no proportion
In its weight to your unaided strength,
For even as I laid it on, I said,
"I will be near, and while she leans on Me,
This burden will be Mine, not hers;
So will I keep My child within the circling arms
Of My Own love." Here lay it down, nor fear
To impose it on a shoulder that upholds
The government of worlds. Yet closer come:
You are not near enough. I would embrace your care;
So I might feel My child reclining on My breast.
You love Me, I know. So then do not doubt;
But loving Me, lean hard.

DAY 209

How precious to me are your thoughts, God!
How vast is the sum of them!
PSALM 139:17

Nothing is more beautiful than our Lord's foresight!

There never was anyone so faithful or considerate or farseeing as Jesus. He had great commendation to give a woman, because she came "beforehand" with her ministry. It was His own manner to anticipate events. He was always thinking ahead of the disciples.

When He sent His disciples to prepare the Passover, there was found an upper room furnished and prepared. He had thought it all out. His plans were not made only for that day. He was always in advance of time. When the disciples came back from fishing, Jesus was on the seashore with a fire of coals and fish laid thereon. He thinks of the morning duties before you are astir; He is there before you. He is waiting long before you are awake. His anticipations are all along the way of life before you.

After the Resurrection, the disciples were bewildered, and the way looked black. But the angel said, "[He] is going ahead of you into Galilee" (Matt. 28:7). He is always ahead, thinking ahead, preparing ahead. Take this text with you into the future, take it into today's experience: "Do not let your hearts be troubled and do not be afraid. . . . I am going there to prepare a place for you" (John 14:27, 2). He is out in the world doing it. He will be there before you. He will bring you to your appointed place, and you will find your appointed resources. You will discover His insight, His oversight, and His foresight. You may not always see Him, but you can walk by faith in the dark if you know that He sees you, and you can sing as you journey, even through the night. JOHN MACBEATH

We mean a lot to Someone;
And 'tis everything to me
That to God His wayward children
Were worth a Calvary.
It's the meaning of my Sunday,
And to Saturday from Monday
It is my hope that one day
My Savior I shall see.
Though the day be dark and dreary,
Here's comfort for the weary—
We mean a lot to Someone
Who died for you and me.

"VALUE" AND OTHER POEMS

July 29th

DAY 210

Be still before the L*ORD* *and wait patiently for him.*

PSALM 37:7

Have you prayed and prayed, and waited and waited, and still you see no evidence of an answer? Are you tired of seeing no movement? Are you at the point of giving up? Then perhaps you have not waited in the right way, which removes you from the right place—the place where the Lord can meet you.

"Wait for it patiently" (Rom. 8:25). Patience eliminates worry. The Lord said He would come, and His promise is equal to His presence. Patience eliminates weeping. Why feel sad and discouraged? He knows your needs better than you do, and His purpose in waiting is to receive more glory through it. Patience eliminates self-works. "The work of God is this: to believe" (John 6:29), and once you believe, you may know all is well. Patience eliminates all want. Perhaps your desire to receive what you want is stronger than your desire for the will of God to be fulfilled.

Patience eliminates all weakness. Instead of thinking of waiting as being wasted time, realize that God is preparing His resources and strengthening you as well. Patience eliminates all wobbling. "He touched me and raised me to my feet" (Dan. 8:18). God's foundations are steady, and when we have His patience within, we are steady while we wait. Patience yields worship. Sometimes the best part of praiseful waiting is experiencing "great endurance and patience" joyfully (Col. 1:11). While you wait, "let [all these aspects of] patience have her perfect work" (James 1:4 KJV), and you will be greatly enriched. C. H. P.

Hold steady when the fires burn,
When inner lessons come to learn,
And from this path there seems no turn—
"Let patience have her perfect work."

L. S. P.

DAY 211

Surely he will save you from the fowler's snare.

PSALM 91:3

The noblest souls are the most tempted. The devil is a sportsman and likes big game. He makes the deadliest assaults on the richest natures, the finest minds, the noblest spirits. JOHN L. LAWRENCE

Lord!—the fowler lays his net
In Thine evening hour;
When our souls are full of sleep—
Void of full power . . .
Look! The wild fowl sees him not
As he lays it lower!
Creeping round the water's edge
In the dusk of day;
Drops his net, just out of sight,
Weighted lightly!—Stay!
You can see him at his work . . .
Fly to God!—And pray!
Like the wild birds; knowing not
Nets lie underneath!
Gliding near the water's edge—
Fowler's snare beneath—
Little feet, caught in the net:
Souls lie, near to death.
But the promise still rings clear: "He delivers thee,"
From the snare, however great
He will set thee free.
"Pluck my feet out of the net!" He delivers me.

When Thou dost deliver, Lord,
From the fowler's snare,
Then—the glory is all Thine,
Thou madest us aware,
And though it was stealthy-laid,
We saw it was there!

L. M. WARNER

Those who have the gale of Holy Spirit go forward even in sleep. BROTHER LAWRENCE

DAY 212

Whoever wants to be my disciple must deny themselves and take up their cross and follow me.

MARK 8:34

The cross that my Lord calls me to carry may assume many different shapes. I may have to be content with mundane tasks in a limited area of service, when I may believe my abilities are suited for much greater work. I may be required to continually cultivate the same field year after year, even though it yields no harvest whatsoever. I may be asked of God to nurture kind and loving thoughts about the very person who has wronged me and to speak gently to him, take his side when others oppose him, and bestow sympathy and comfort to him. I may have to openly testify of my Master before those who do not want to be reminded of Him or His claims. And I may be called to walk through this world with a bright, smiling face while my heart is breaking.

Yes, there are many crosses, and every one of them is heavy and painful. And it is unlikely that I would seek out even one of them on my own. Yet Jesus is never as near to me as when I lift my cross, lay it submissively on my shoulder, and welcome it with a patient and uncomplaining spirit.

He draws close to me in order to mature my wisdom, deepen my peace, increase my courage, and supplement my power. All this He does so that through the very experience that is so painful and distressing to me, I will be of greater use to others.

And then I will echo these words of one of the Scottish Covenantors of the seventeenth century, imprisoned for his faith by John Graham of Claverhouse—"I grow under the load." ALEXANDER SMELLIE

Use the cross you bear as a crutch to help you on your way,
not as a stumbling block that causes you to fall.
You may others from sadness to gladness beguile,
If you carry your cross with a smile.

Aug 1st

DAY 213

I consider everything a loss because of the surpassing worth of knowing Christ Jesus my Lord.

PHILIPPIANS 3:8

The Swedish Nightingale, Jennie Lind, won great success as an operatic singer, and money poured into her purse. Yet she left the stage while she was singing her best, and never returned to it. She must have missed the money, the fame, and the applause of thousands, but she was content to live in privacy.

Once an English friend found her sitting on the steps of a bathing machine on the sea sands with a Bible on her knee, looking out into the glory of a sunset. They talked, and the conversation drew near to the inevitable question: "Oh, Madame Goldschmidt, how is it that you came to abandon the stage at the very height of your success?"

"When every day," was the quiet answer, "it made me think less of this (laying a finger on the Bible) and nothing at all of that (pointing to the sunset), what else could I do?"

May I not covet the world's greatness! It will cost me the crown of life!

DAY 214

Awake, north wind, and come, south wind! Blow on my garden, that its fragrance may spread everywhere.

SONG OF SONGS 4:16

Some of the spices and plants mentioned in verse 14 of the above chapter are very descriptive and symbolic. The juice of the aloe plant has a bitter taste but is soothing when applied to the skin, so it tells us of the sweetness of bitter things, the bittersweet, having an important application that only those who have used it will understand. Myrrh is symbolic of death, having been used to embalm the dead. It represents the sweetness that comes to the heart after it has died to self-will, pride, and sin.

What inexpressible charm seems to encircle some Christians, simply because they carry upon their pure countenance and gentle spirit the imprint of the cross! It is the holy evidence of having died to something that was once proud and strong but is now forever surrendered at the feet of Jesus. And it is also the heavenly charm of a broken spirit and a contrite heart, the beautiful music that rises from a minor key, and the sweetness brought about by the touch of frost on ripened fruit.

Finally, frankincense was a fragrance that arose only after being touched with fire. The burning incense became clouds of sweetness arising from the heart of the flames. It symbolizes a person's heart whose sweetness has been brought forth by the flames of affliction until the holy, innermost part of the soul is filled with clouds of praise and prayer.

Beloved, are our lives yielding spices and perfumes—sweet fragrances of the heart? THE LOVE-LIFE OF OUR LORD

A Persian fable says: One day
A wanderer found a lump of clay
So savory of sweet perfume
Its odors scented all the room.
"What are you?" was his quick demand,
"Are you some gem from Samarkand,
Or pure nard in this plain disguise,
Or other costly merchandise?"
"No, I am but a lump of clay."
"Then whence this wondrous perfume—say!"
"Friend, if the secret I disclose,
I have been dwelling with the rose."
Sweet parable! and will not those
Who love to dwell with Sharon's rose,
Distill sweet odors all around,
Though low and poor themselves are found?
Dear Lord, abide with us that we
May draw our perfume fresh from Thee.

DAY 215

Aug 3rd

Having loved his own . . . he loved them to the end.

JOHN 13:1

Sadhu Sundar Singh passed a crowd of people putting out a jungle fire at the foot of the Himalayas. Several men, however, were standing gazing at a tree, the branches of which were already alight.

"What are you looking at?" he asked. They pointed to a nest of young birds in the tree. Above it a bird was flying wildly to and fro in great distress. The men said, "We wish we could save that tree, but the fire prevents us from getting near to it."

A few minutes later the nest caught fire. The Sadhu thought the mother bird would fly away. But no! she flew down, spread her wings over the young ones, and in a few minutes was burned to ashes with them.

Such love, such wondrous love,
Such love, such wondrous love,
That God should love a sinner such as I,
How wonderful is love like this!
Let us have love heated to the point of sacrifice.

Aug 4th

DAY 216

Hide in the Kerith Ravine.
1 KINGS 17:3

God's servants must be taught the value of the hidden side of life. The person who is to serve in a lofty place before others must also assume a lowly place before his God. We should not be surprised if God occasionally says to us, "Dear child, you have had enough of this hurried pace, excitement, and publicity. Now I want you to go and hide yourself—'hide in the Kerith Ravine' of sickness, the 'Kerith Ravine' of sorrow, or some place of total solitude, from which the crowds have turned away." And happy is the person who can reply to the Lord, "Your will is also mine. Therefore I run to hide myself in You. 'I long to dwell in your tent forever and take refuge in the shelter of your wings' [Ps. 61:4]."

Every saintly soul that desires to wield great influence over others must first win the power in some hidden "Kerith Ravine." Acquiring spiritual power is impossible unless we hide from others and ourselves in some deep ravine where we may absorb the power of the eternal God. May our lives be like the vegetation centuries ago that absorbed the power of the sunshine and now gives the energy back after having become coal.

Lancelot Andrews, a bishop of the Church of England and one of the translators of the King James Bible of 1611, experienced his "Kerith Ravine," in which he spent five hours of every day in prayer and devotion to God. John Welsh, a contemporary of Andrews, and a Presbyterian who was imprisoned for his faith by James VI of Scotland, also had his "ravine." He believed his day to be wasted if he did not spend eight to ten hours of isolated communion with God. David Brainerd's "ravine" was the forests of North America while he served as a pioneer missionary to the Native Americans during the eighteenth century. And Christmas Evans, a preacher of the late-eighteenth and early-nineteenth centuries, had his long and lonely journeys through the hills of Wales.

Looking back to the blessed age from which we date the centuries, there are many notable "ravines." The Isle of Patmos, the solitude of the Roman prisons, the Arabian Desert, and the hills and valleys of Palestine are all as enduringly memorable as those experienced by the people who have shaped our modern world.

Our Lord Himself lived through His "Kerith Ravine" in Nazareth, in the wilderness of Judea, amid the olive trees of Bethany, and in the solitude of the city of Gadara. So none of us is exempt from a "ravine" experience, where the sounds of human voices are exchanged for the waters of quietness that flow from the throne of God, and where we taste the sweetness and soak up the power of a life "hidden with Christ" (Col. 3:3). F. B. MEYER ELIJAH

DAY 217

Aug 5th

Forgive as the Lord forgave you.

COLOSSIANS 3:13

A North African custom is "Forgiveness Week." Fixed in the dry season, when the weather itself is smiling, this is a week when every man and woman pledges himself or herself to forgive any neighbor any wrong, real or fancied, that may be a cause for misunderstanding, coldness, or quarrel between the parties.

It is, of course, a part of our religion that a man should forgive his brother. But among recent converts, and even older brethren, this great tenet is, perhaps naturally, apt to be forgotten or overlooked in the heat and burden of work. "Forgiveness Week" brings it forcibly to mind. The week itself terminates with a festival of happiness and rejoicing among the native Christians.

Nothing between, Lord—nothing between;
Shine with unclouded ray,
Chasing each mist away,
O'er my whole heart hold sway—
Nothing between.

Let grudges die "like cloudspots in the dawn!"
When God forgives, He forgets!

DAY 218

Put your hope in God, for I will yet praise him.

PSALM 42:5

During a truce in the Civil War in America, when the hostile armies sat sullenly facing each other with a field between them, a little brown bird rose suddenly from the long grass and darted skyward. There, a mere speck in the blue, it poured forth its liquid music of which the lark alone has the secret. And steely eyes melted to tears, and hard hearts grew pitiful and tender. There was a God who cared. There was hope for men.

Hope is like the lark on the battlefield. It will not sing in a gilded cage. It cannot soar in an atmosphere of religious luxury. But brave souls, exposing themselves fearlessly for God and their fellow-men on the battlefield of life, hear its song and are made strong and glad. E. HERMAN

Persons who held on in hope, with seemingly little for which to hope, were known to say: *Then was our mouth filled with laughter. . . . We were like them that dream.*

The tide may turn, the wind may change. New eras have been heard of before now!

In "hope against hope," I wait, Lord,
Faced by some fast-barred gate, Lord,
Hope never says "Too late," Lord,
Therefore in Thee I hope!
Hope though the night be long, Lord,
Hope of a glowing dawn, Lord,
Morning must break in song, Lord,
For we are "saved by hope."

HYMNS OF CONSECRATION AND FAITH

"Hope thou in God!"

DAY 219

Later on, however.

HEBREWS 12:11

It is not a bit of good struggling for the premature unfolding of the Divine mystery. The revelation awaits our arrival at a certain place in the road, and when Time brings us to that place, and we enter into its experiences, we shall find, to our delighted surprise, that it has become luminous.

And so the only thing we need to be concerned about is to be on the King's high road, stepping out in accordance with His most holy will.

"Light is sown for the righteous" (Ps. 97:11 KJV).

It is the end which justifies all and explains all. It is to the ultimate goal that God's eye is ever turning. At the right moment the shining harvest will appear! What though the seed may seem to perish in the dark cold ground! What will that matter when the blade bursts forth, and the ear unfolds, and the full corn waves over the golden harvest field?

Luther was once in earnest prayer over some matter of great moment, desiring to know the mind of God in it; and it seemed as though he heard God say to him, "I am not to be traced."

If God is not to be traced, He is to be trusted.

"Afterward Jesus appeared again to his disciples" (John 21:1).

However dark the nows may be in your experience, the afters of God are worth waiting for!

As we think of God's dealings with His children we are impressed with His leisureliness. God's ways may be hidden, but wait for God's Afters!

DAY 220

Aug 8th

Where there is no vision, the people perish.

PROVERBS 29:18 KJV

Waiting upon God is vital in order to see Him and receive a vision from Him. And the amount of time spent before Him is also critical, for our hearts are like a photographer's film—the longer exposed, the deeper the impression. For God's vision to be impressed on our hearts, we must sit in stillness at His feet for quite a long time. Remember, the troubled surface of a lake will not reflect an image.

Yes, our lives must be quiet and peaceful if we expect to see God. And the vision we see from Him has the power to affect our lives in the same way a lovely sunset brings peace to a troubled heart. Seeing God always transforms human life.

Jacob "crossed the ford of the Jabbok" (Gen. 32:22), saw God, and became Israel. Seeing a vision of God transformed Gideon from a coward into a courageous soldier. And Thomas, after seeing Christ, was changed from a doubting follower into a loyal, devoted disciple.

People since Bible times have also had visions of God. William Carey, English pioneer missionary of the eighteenth century who is considered by some to be the Father of Modern Missions, saw God and left his shoemaker's bench to go to India. David Livingstone saw God and left everything in Britain behind to become a missionary and explorer, following the Lord's leading through the thickest jungles of Africa during the nineteenth century. And literally thousands more have since had visions of God and today are serving Him in the uttermost parts of the earth, seeking the timely evangelization of the lost. DR. PARDINGTON

It is very unusual for there to be complete quiet in the soul, for God almost continually whispers to us. And whenever the sounds of the world subside in our soul, we hear the whispering of God. Yes, He continues to whisper to us, but we often do not hear Him because of the noise and distractions caused by the hurried pace of our lives. FREDERICK WILLIAM FABER

Speak, Lord, in the stillness,
While I wait on Thee;
Hushing my heart to listen
In expectancy.
Speak, O blessed Master,
In this quiet hour;
Let me see Your face, Lord,
Feel Your touch of power.
For the words that You speak,
"They are life," indeed;
Living bread from Heaven,
Now my spirit feed!

Speak, Your servant hears You!
Be not silent, Lord;
My soul on You does wait
For Your life-giving word!

Aug 9th

DAY 221

Those who live quietly in the land.

PSALM 35:20

We are to enter into God's chamber, and hide there, and be still. Then God will call us "those who live quietly in the land." Have this stamp upon you. Be quiet outside—you will then be quiet inside. Be quiet in spirit. Beware of soul activities. The dross must be burned out to have the mountain vision. We must get back to God only, and cease to see the human instruments. Hide deeper in God. He must be real—more and more real!

Hide with Christ in God at the Throne; Be at the Spring of things!

"In quietness and in confidence shall be your strength" (Isa. 30:15 KJV). Set yourself to move everything through God, not man. Go direct to Him. Every step with God "in quietness and in confidence" gives you absolute Victory over everything!

Keep in step with God.

Get quiet, beloved soul; tell out thy sorrow and complaint to God. Let not the greatest pressure of business divert thee from God. When men rage about thee, go and tell Jesus. Hide thee in His secret place when storms are high.

Get into thy closet, shut thy door, and quiet thyself as a weaned babe. But if thy voice is quiet to man, let it never cease to speak loudly and mightily for man.

We need to be quiet to get the ear of God!

'Mid all the traffic of the ways,
Turmoils without, within,
Make in my heart a quiet place,
And come and dwell therein!
A little shrine of quietness,
All sacred to Thyself,
Where Thou shalt all my soul possess,
And I may find myself!

JOHN OXENHAM

Pascal said: "One-half of the ills of life come because men are unwilling to sit down quietly for thirty minutes to think through all the possible consequences of their acts."

DAY 222

Aug 10th

My Father is the gardener.

JOHN 15:1

It is a comforting thought that trouble, in whatever form it comes to us, is a heavenly messenger that brings us something from God. Outwardly it may appear painful or even destructive, but inwardly its spiritual work produces blessings. Many of the richest blessings we have inherited are the fruit of sorrow or pain. We should never forget that redemption, the world's greatest blessing, is the fruit of the world's greatest sorrow. And whenever a time of deep pruning comes and the knife cuts deeply and the pain is severe, what an inexpressible comfort it is to know: "My Father is the gardener."

John Vincent, a Methodist Episcopal bishop of the late-nineteenth and early-twentieth centuries and a leader of the Sunday school movement in America, once told of being in a large greenhouse where clusters of luscious grapes were hanging on each side. The owner of the greenhouse told him,

"When the new gardener came here, he said he would not work with the vines unless he could cut them completely down to the stalk. I allowed him to do so, and we had no grapes for two years, but this is now the result."

There is rich symbolism in this account of the pruning process when applied to the Christian life. Pruning seems to be destroying the vine, and the gardener appears to be cutting everything away. Yet he sees the future and knows that the final result will be the enrichment of the life of the vine, and a greater abundance of fruit.

There are many blessings we will never receive until we are ready to pay the price of pain, for the path of suffering is the only way to reach them. J. R. MILLER

I walked a mile with Pleasure,
She chattered all the way;
But left me none the wiser
For all she had to say.
I walked a mile with Sorrow,
And ne'er a word said she;
But oh, the things I learned from her
When Sorrow walked with me.

DAY 223

Shall what is formed say to the one who formed it, "Why did you make me like this?"
ROMANS 9:20

A piece of wood once bitterly complained because it was being cut and filled with rifts and holes; but he who held the wood and whose knife was cutting into it so remorselessly did not listen to the sore complaining. He was making a flute out of the wood he held, and was too wise to desist when entreated to do so. He said:

"Oh, thou foolish piece of wood, without these rifts and holes thou wouldst be only a mere stick forever—a bit of hard black ebony with no power to make music or to be of any use. These rifts that I am making, which seem to be destroying thee, will change thee into a flute, and thy sweet music then shall charm the souls of men. My cutting thee is the making of thee, for then thou shalt be precious and valuable, and a blessing in the world."

David could never have sung his sweetest songs had he not been sorely afflicted. His afflictions made his life an instrument on which God could breathe the music of His love to charm and soothe the hearts of men.

We are but organs mute till a Master touches the keys—
Verily, vessels of earth into which God poureth the wine;
Harps are we—silent harps that have hung in the willow trees,
Dumb till our heartstrings swell and break with a pulse
Divine.
Not till the life is broken is it ready for the Master's use.

DAY 224

And there came a lion.

1 SAMUEL 17:34 KJV

It is a source of inspiration and strength to us to remember how the youthful David trusted God. Through his faith in the Lord, he defeated a lion and a bear and later overthrew the mighty Goliath. When the lion came to destroy his flock, it came as a wonderful opportunity for David. If he had faltered and failed, he would have missed God's opportunity for him and probably would never have been the Lord's chosen king of Israel.

"And there came a lion." Normally we think of a lion not as a special blessing from the Lord but only as a reason for alarm. Yet the lion was God's opportunity in disguise. Every difficulty and every temptation that comes our way, if we receive it correctly, is God's opportunity.

When a "lion" comes to your life, recognize it as an opportunity from the Lord, no matter how fierce it may outwardly seem. Even the tabernacle of God was covered with badger skins and goat hair. No one would think there would be any glory there, yet the Shechinah glory of God was very evident underneath the covering. May the Lord open our eyes to see Him, even in temptations, trials, dangers, and misfortunes. C. H. P.

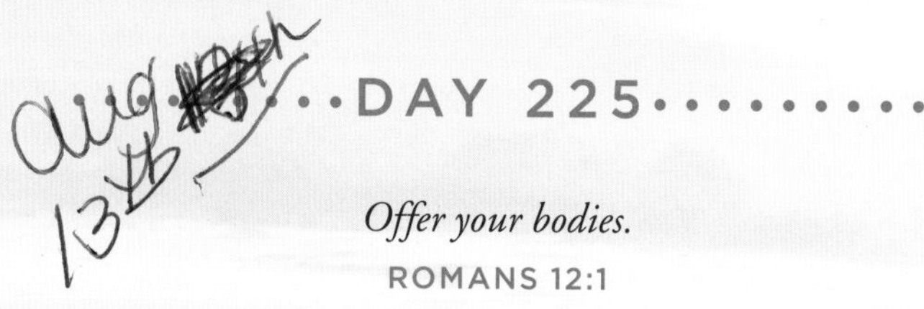

DAY 225

Offer your bodies.

ROMANS 12:1

Lend Me thy body, our Lord says. For a few brief years, in the body that was prepared for Me I delighted to do My Father's will. By means of that body I came into contact with the children of men—diseased, weary, sin-sick, heavy-laden ones. Those feet carried Me to the homes where sorrow and death had entered; those hands touched leprous bodies, palsied limbs, sightless eyes; those lips told of My Father's remedy for sin, His love for a prodigal world. In that body I bore the world's sin upon the tree, and through its offering once for all My followers are sanctified.

But I need a body still; wilt thou not lend Me thine? Millions of hearts are longing, with an indescribable hunger, for Me. On that far-off shore are men, women, and little children sitting in darkness and in the shadow of death—men who have never yet heard of My love. Wilt thou not lend Me thy body, that I may cross the ocean and tell them that the light after which they are groping has at last reached them; that the bread for which they have so often hungered is now at their very door?

I want a heart, that I may fill it with Divine compassion; and lips, purged from all uncleanness, wherewith to tell the story that brings hope to the despairing, freedom to the bound, healing to the diseased, and life to the dead. Wilt thou lend Me thine?

Wilt thou not lend Me thy body? J. GREGORY MANTLE

All that we own is Thine alone, a trust, O Lord, from Thee.

DAY 226

I consider everything a loss because of the surpassing worth of knowing Christ Jesus my Lord.

PHILIPPIANS 3:8

The autumn season we are now entering is one of cornfields ripe for harvest, of the cheerful song of those who reap the crops, and of gathered and securely stored grain. So allow me to draw your attention to the sermon of the fields. This is its solemn message: "You must die in order to live. You must refuse to consider your own comfort and well-being. You must be crucified, not only to your desires and habits that are obviously sinful, but also to many others that may appear to be innocent and right. If you desire to save others, you cannot save yourself, and if you desire to bear much fruit, you must be buried in darkness and solitude."

My heart fails me as I listen. But when the words are from Jesus, may I remind myself that it is my great privilege to enter into the "participation in his sufferings" (Phil. 3:10) and I am therefore in great company. May I also remind myself that all the suffering is designed to make me a vessel suitable for His use. And may I remember that His Calvary blossomed into abundant fruitfulness, and so will mine.

Pain leads to plenty, and death to life—it is the law of the kingdom! IN THE HOUR OF SILENCE

Do we call it dying when a bud blossoms into a flower?

Finding, following, keeping, struggling,
Is He sure to bless?
Saints, apostles, prophets, martyrs,
Answer, "Yes."

DAY 227

He took up our infirmities.

MATTHEW 8:17

I think perhaps the greatest of all hindrances in our getting hold of God for our bodies is the lack of knowing Him, for after all, in its deepest essence Divine healing is not a thing; it is not an experience; it is not an "it." It is the revelation of Jesus Christ as a living, almighty Person, and then the union of this living Christ with your body, so that there becomes a tie, a bond, a living link by which His life keeps flowing into yours, and because He lives you shall live also. This is so very real to me that I groan in spirit for those who do not know Him in this blessed union, and I wonder sometimes why He has let me know Him in this gracious manner. There is not an hour of the day or night that I am not conscious of Someone who is closer to me than my heart or my brain. I know that He is living in me, and it is the continual inflowing of the life of Another. If I had not that I could not live. My old constitutional strength gave out long, long ago, but Someone breathed in me gently, with no violence, no strange thrills, but just His wholesome life. A. B. SIMPSON

I remember how once I was taken suddenly and seriously ill alone in my study. I dropped upon my knees and cried to God for help. Instantly all pain left me and I was perfectly well. It seems as if God stood right there, and had put out His hand and touched me. The joy of healing was not so great as the joy of meeting God. R. A. TORREY

She only touched the hem of His garment,
As to His side she stole,
Amid the throng that had gathered around Him
And straightway she was whole.
Oh, touch the hem of His garment,
And thou, too, shall be free;
His healing power this very hour,
Will bring new life to thee.

"Jesus Christ . . . the same yesterday and today and forever" (Heb. 13:8).

DAY 228

Satan has asked to sift all of you as wheat. But I have prayed for you, Simon, that your faith may not fail.

LUKE 22:31–32

Our faith is the center of the target God aims at when He tests us, and if any gift escapes untested, it certainly will not be our faith. There is nothing that pierces faith to its very marrow—to find whether or not it is the faith of those who are immortal—like shooting the arrow of the feeling of being deserted into it. And only genuine faith will escape unharmed from the midst of the battle after having been stripped of its armor of earthly enjoyment and after having endured the circumstances coming against it that the powerful hand of God has allowed.

Faith must be tested, and the sense of feeling deserted is "the furnace heated seven times hotter than usual" (Dan. 3:19) into which it may be thrown. Blessed is the person who endures such an ordeal! CHARLES H. SPURGEON

Paul said, "I have kept the faith" (2 Tim. 4:7), but his head was removed! They cut it off, but they could not touch his faith. This great apostle to the

Gentiles rejoiced in three things: he had "fought the good fight," he had "finished the race," and he had "kept the faith." So what was the value of everything else? The apostle Paul had won the race and gained the ultimate prize—he had won not only the admiration of those on earth today but also the admiration of heaven. So why do we not live as if it pays to lose "all things . . . that [we] may gain Christ" (Phil. 3:8)? Why are we not as loyal to the truth as Paul was? It is because our math is different—he counted in a different way than we do. What we count as gain, he counted as loss. If we desire to ultimately wear the same crown, we must have his faith and live it.

DAY 229

Job. . . . blameless and upright; he feared God and shunned evil.

JOB 1:1

Such was Job's character as given by God. He asked Satan, "Have you considered my servant Job? There is no one on earth like him" (v. 8). Satan, in reply, says in effect, "Strip him, and he will curse Thee to Thy face." Satan sought Job's fall; God sought his blessing. Satan gets leave from God to strip Job. With malignant energy he sets to work, and in one day he brings the greatest man in all the East into abject poverty and visits him with sore bereavement. Blow after blow of such a crushing nature and with such rapidity falls upon Job, that one marvels at the testimony of the Holy Ghost that: "In all this, Job did not sin by charging God with wrongdoing" (v. 22). What a triumph for God! What a defeat for Satan!

"But these strange ashes, Lord? This nothingness,
This baffling sense of loss?"
"Son, was the anguish of My stripping less
Upon the torturing Cross?

"Was I not brought into the dust of death,
A worm, and no man I;
Yea, turned to ashes by the vehement breath
Of fire, on Calvary?
"O Son beloved, this is thy heart's desire:
This and no other thing
Follows the fall of the consuming fire
On the burnt offering.
"Go on and taste the joy set high afar,
No joy like that for thee;
See how it lights thy way like some great star!
Come now, and follow Me!"

A. W. C.

DAY 230

Whoever believes in me, as Scripture has said, rivers of living water will flow from within them.

JOHN 7:38

Some of us are troubled, wondering why the Holy Spirit doesn't fill us. The problem is that we have plenty coming in but we are not giving out to others. If you will give the blessing you have received, planning your life around greater service and being a blessing to those around you, then you will quickly find that the Holy Spirit is with you. He will bestow blessings to you for service, giving you all He can trust you to give away to others.

No music is as heavenly as that made by an aeolian harp. It is a beautiful occurrence of nature, but it has a spiritual parallel. The harp is nothing but a wooden box with strings arranged in harmony, waiting to be touched by the unseen fingers of the wandering wind. As the breath of heaven floats over the strings, notes that are nearly divine float upon the air, as if a choir of angels were wandering about and touching the strings.

In the same way, it is possible to keep our hearts so open to the touch of the Holy Spirit that He may play them as He chooses, while we quietly wait on the pathway of His service. DAYS OF HEAVEN UPON EARTH

When the apostles "were filled with the Holy Spirit" (Acts 2:4), they did not lease the Upper Room and stay there to hold holiness meetings. They went everywhere, preaching the gospel. WILL HUFF

"If I have eaten my morsel alone,"
The patriarch spoke with scorn;
What would he think of the Church were he shown
Heathendom—huge, forlorn, Godless,
Christless, with soul unfed,
While the Church's ailment is fullness of bread,
Eating her morsel alone?
"Freely you have received, so give,"
He says, who has given us all.
How will the soul in us longer live
Deaf to their starving call,
For whom the blood of the Lord was shed,
And His body broken to give them bread,
If we eat our morsel alone!

ARCHBISHOP WILLIAM ALEXANDER

"Where is your brother Abel?" (Gen. 4:9).

DAY 231

He cuts off every branch in me that bears no fruit, while every branch that does bear fruit he prunes so that it will be even more fruitful.

JOHN 15:2

Only a little more cutting." How strange the words sounded; and then I heard the ring of the gardener's ax as he cut away at the lilac bushes. They were very close to the windows and kept out the sunlight and air; more, they obstructed the view. We watched the process and as one bush after another fell, one remarked: "Only a little more cutting and we shall get it. These lilac bushes actually shut out the view of the White Mountains!"

I was glad the gardener did the cutting that day, for so much was brought out by the absence of the bushes and suggested by the exclamations that followed: "How lovely that little tree is! I did not see it before!" "What a beautiful evergreen that is! I never noticed it until now!" Have we not heard similar exclamations after severe cuttings and removals in our lives? Have we not said: "I never loved God so much as I have since He took my little one!" "I never saw the beauty of such and such a Scripture until now!"

Ah, He knows! Only trust Him. We shall see it all in the clear light sometime.

God is a zealous Pruner,
For He knows
Who, falsely tender, spares the knife
But spoils the rose.

"THE PRUNER," BY JOHN OXENHAM

Give me the courage to submit to the surgery of Thy Spirit. Give me the bravery to part with what I hold most dear if it separates me from Thee. Through Christ, I pray!

aug 20th

DAY 232

When they came to the border of Mysia, they tried to enter Bithynia, but the Spirit of Jesus would not allow them to.

ACTS 16:7

What a strange thing for the Lord to prohibit, for they were going into Bithynia to do Christ's work! And the door was shut before them by Christ's own Spirit.

There have been times when I have experienced the same thing. Sometimes I have been interrupted in what seemed to be quite productive work. And at times, opposition came and forced me to go back, or sickness came and forced me to rest in some isolated place.

During such times, it was difficult for me to leave my work unfinished when I believed it was service done in the power of His Spirit. But I finally remembered that the Spirit requires not only a service of work but also a service of waiting. I came to see that in the kingdom of Christ, there are not only times for action but times to refrain from action. And I also came to learn that a place of isolation is often the most useful place of all in this diverse world. Its harvest is more rich than the seasons when the corn and wine were the most abundant. So I have learned to thank the blessed Holy Spirit that many a beautiful Bithynia had to be left without a visit from me.

Dear Holy Spirit, my desire is still to be led by You. Nevertheless, my opportunities for usefulness seem to be disappointed, for today the door appears open into a life of service for You but tomorrow it closes before me just as I am about to enter. Teach me to see another door even in the midst of the inaction of this time. Help me to find, even in the area of service where You have closed a door, a new entrance into Your service. Inspire me with the knowledge that a person may sometimes be called to serve by doing nothing, by staying still, or by waiting. And when I remember the power of Your "gentle whisper" (1 Kings 19:12), I will not complain that sometimes the Spirit allows me not to go. GEORGE MATHESON

When I cannot understand my Father's leading,
And it seems to be but hard and cruel fate,
Still I hear that gentle whisper ever pleading,
God is working, God is faithful, only wait.

DAY 233

My glory was fresh in me, and my bow was renewed in my hand.

JOB 29:20 KJV

It was when Job's glory was fresh in him that his "bow was renewed" in his hand. Freshness and glory! And yet, the brilliant music of these words is brought down to a minor strain by the little touch "it was"—not it is.

"All my [fresh] springs are in thee" (Ps. 87:7 KJV).

If our glory is to be fresh in us, it all depends upon what the glory in us is! There is only one unfailing source—Christ Himself! He is "in you, the hope of glory" (Col. 1:27) if you have admitted Him; and He is your glory. Then you may sing, "My glory is fresh in me."

Jesus Christ is always fresh!

And so is the oil with which He anoints us. "I shall be anointed with fresh oil" (Ps. 92:10 KJV). Fresh oil of joy! Fresh oil of consecration! Fresh oil upon the sacrifice as we offer to God continually "the fruit of lips that openly profess his name" (Heb. 13:15).

My heart is parched by unbelief,
My spirit sere from inward strife;
The heavens above are turned to brass,
Arid and fruitless is my life.
Then falls Thy rain, O Holy One;
Fresh is the earth, and young once more;

Then falls Thy Spirit on my heart;
My life is green; the drought is o'er!
"DROUGHT," BY BETTY BRUECHERT

A desert road? when the Christian has ever at his command Fresh springs! Fresh oil! Fresh glory!

..........DAY 234..........

Jesus took with him Peter, James and John the brother of James, and led them up a high mountain by themselves. There he was transfigured before them. . . . Peter said to Jesus, "Lord, it is good for us to be here."

MATTHEW 17:1–2, 4

It is good to be the possessor of some mountaintop experience. Not to know life on the heights is to suffer an impoverishing incompleteness.

Those times when the Lord's presence is marvelously manifest to you—the moments of self-revelation—do not despise them. But beware of not acting upon what you see in your moments on the mount with God!

Horizons broaden when we stand on the heights. There is always, we find, the danger that we will make of life too much of a dead-level existence; a monotonous tread of beaten paths; a matter of absorbing, spiritless, deadening routine.

Do not drop your life into the passing current, to be steadily going you scarcely know where, or why.

Christian life, writes one, is not all a valley of humiliation. It has its heights of vision.

Abraham saw in the glorious depths of the starry firmament visions that no telescope could ever have revealed! Jacob's stony pillow led up to the ladder of vision!

Joseph's early dreams kept him in the hours of discouragement and despair that followed!

Moses, who spent one-third of his life in the desert, we find crying out: "I beseech thee, show me Thy glory!"

Job's vision showed him God and lifted him out of himself!

The mariner does not expect to see the sun and stars every day, but when he does, he takes his observations and sails by their light for many days to come.

God gives days of special illumination that we may be able to call to memory in the days of shadow, and say: "Therefore I will remember you from the land of the Jordan, the heights of Hermon—from Mount Mizar" (Ps. 42:6).

In the life of Paul, we find a few of these blessed interludes—when the Lord gave to him words of promise to remember in his days of trial that followed.

If these special experiences came too often they would lose their flavor! He walks in glory on the hills, and longs for men to join Him there.

DAY 235

The famine was still severe. . . . They had eaten all the grain. . . . "If we had not delayed, we could have gone and returned." . . . So the men took . . . double the amount of silver, and Benjamin also.

GENESIS 43:1–2, 10, 15

Praise God for the famine in our life, that drives us in utter helplessness back to Him!

Praise Him that what we have gets eaten up, and we must turn to Him for more! But how like unto the faltering, fearful family of Israel we act! We could find absolute relief, sufficiency, satisfaction in Jesus Christ; yet we delay, debate, wonder, waste time, and stay hungry. When finally in desperation we are driven to Him we think we must do some great thing to meet His terms, and we try to carry "double the . . . silver" in all sorts of ways, to make sure of what He is yearningly waiting to give us. He does ask us for one thing, and one only: and that is the dearest possession of our lives. With Israel's family the dearest possession was Benjamin. When we lay down our dearest possession, then the treasures of the kingdom are flung open to us and lavished into our life. MESSAGES FOR THE MORNING WATCH

A drying well will often lead the spirit to the river that flows from the throne of God.

DAY 236

Aug 24th

We live by faith, not by sight.

2 CORINTHIANS 5:7

As believers, "we live by faith, not by sight"—God never wants us to live by our feelings. Our inner self may want to live by feelings, and Satan may want us to, but God wants us to face the facts, not feelings. He wants us to face the facts of Christ and His finished and perfect work for us. And once we face these precious facts, and believe them simply because God says they are facts, He will take care of our feelings.

Yet God never gives us feelings to enable or encourage us to trust Him, and He never gives them to show us that we have already completely trusted Him. God only gives us feelings when He sees that we trust Him apart from our feelings, resting solely on His Word and His faithfulness to His promise. And these feelings that can only come from Him will be given at such a time and to such a degree as His love sees best for each individual circumstance.

Therefore we must choose between facing our feelings or facing the facts of God. Our feelings may be as uncertain and changing as the sea or shifting sand. God's facts, however, are as certain as the Rock of Ages Himself—"Jesus Christ . . . the same yesterday and today and forever" (Heb. 13:8).

When darkness veils His lovely face
I rest on His unchanging grace;
In every strong and stormy gale,
My anchor holds within the veil.

DAY 237

The Lord will give you as he promised.

EXODUS 12:25

God is to be trusted for what He is, and not for what He is not. We may confidently expect Him to act according to His nature, but never contrary to it. To dream that God will do this and that because we wish that He would is not faith, but fanaticism. Faith can only stand upon truth. We may be sure that God will so act as to honor His own justice, mercy, wisdom, power—in a word, so as to be Himself. Beyond all doubt He will fulfill His promises; and when faith grasps a promise she is on sure ground. To believe that God will give us what He has never promised to give is mere dreaming. Faith without a promise revealed or implied is folly. Yea, though our trust should cry itself hoarse in prayer, it should be nonetheless a vain absurdity if it had no word of God to warrant it. Happily, the promises and unveilings of Scripture are ample for every real emergency; but when unrestrained credence catches at every whim of its own imagination and thinks to see it realized, the disappointment is not to be wondered at.

It is ours to believe the sure things of God's revelation, but we are not to waste a grain of precious reliance upon anything outside of that circle.

CHARLES H. SPURGEON

"Faith does not mean that we are trying to believe something that is not so; it just means that we are taking God at His Word."

Faith is a thread
Slender and frail,
Easy to tear;
Yet it can lift
The weight of a soul
Up from despair.

MATTHEW BILLER

Aug 26th

..........DAY 238..........

So Jacob was left alone, and a man wrestled with him till daybreak.

GENESIS 32:24

"Left alone!" What different emotions these words bring to mind for each of us! To some they mean loneliness and grief, but to others they may mean rest and quiet. To be left alone without God would be too horrible for words, while being left alone with Him is a taste of heaven! And if His followers spent more time alone with Him, we would have spiritual giants again.

Our Master set an example for us. Remember how often He went to be alone with God? And there was a powerful purpose behind His command, "When you pray, go into your room, close the door and pray" (Matt. 6:6).

The greatest miracles of Elijah and Elisha took place when they were alone with God. Jacob was alone with God when he became a prince (see Gen. 32:28). In the same way, we too may become royalty and people who are "wondered at" (Zech. 3:8 KJV). Joshua was alone when the Lord came to him (see Josh. 1:1). Gideon and Jephthah were by themselves when commissioned to save Israel (see Judg. 6:11; 11:29). Moses was by himself at the burning bush (see Ex. 3:1–5). Cornelius was praying by himself when the Angel of God came to him (see Acts 10:1–4). No one was with Peter on the housetop when he was instructed to go to the Gentiles (see Acts 10:9–28). John the Baptist was alone in the wilderness (see Luke 1:80), and John the Beloved was alone on the island of Patmos when he was the closest to God (see Rev. 1:9).

Earnestly desire to get alone with God. If we neglect to do so, we not only rob ourselves of a blessing but rob others as well, since we will have no blessing to pass on to them. It may mean that we do less outward, visible work, but the work we do will have more depth and power. Another wonderful result will be that people will see "no one except Jesus" (Matt. 17:8) in our lives.

The impact of being alone with God in prayer cannot be overemphasized.

> If chosen men had never been alone,
> In deepest silence open-doored to God,
> No greatness would ever have been dreamed or done.

DAY 239

Keep yourself pure.

1 TIMOTHY 5:22

Does the judge know the story of the spotless fur that lines his robes of State? Does the society leader realize the sacrifice which makes possible the lovely ermine wrap which lies so gracefully about her shoulders? Do they know that the little animal whose coat they now wear, as he roamed the forest of Asia was as proud as they—aye, inordinately proud of his beautiful snowy coat? And we do not wonder, for it is the most beautiful fur to be found in all the markets of the world!

Such pride does the little carnivore take in his spotless coat, that nothing is permitted to soil it in the slightest degree. Hunters are well acquainted with this fact and take very unsportsmanlike advantage of this knowledge. No traps are set for him. No, indeed! Instead, they seek out his home—a tree stump, or rocky cleft, and then—be it said to their everlasting shame, they daub filth within and around the entrance. As the dogs are loosed and the chase begins the little animal naturally turns to his one place of refuge.

Reaching it, rather than enter such a place of uncleanness, he turns to face the yelping dogs.

Better to be stained by blood than sully his white coat!

Only a white coat, little ermine, but how your act condemns us! "Made in the image and likeness of God," with minds and immortal spirits; and yet, how often in order to obtain something we desire, our character is sacrificed on the altars of worldly pleasure, greed, selfishness!

Everything is lost when purity is gone—purity, which has been called the soul of character. Keep thyself pure: every thought, every word, every deed, even the motive behind the deed—all, ermine-pure.

> I ask this gift of thee—
> A life all lily fair,
> And fragrant as the garden be
> Where seraphs are.

DAY 240

In me . . . peace.

JOHN 16:33

There is a vast difference between pleasure and blessedness. Paul experienced imprisonment, pain, sacrifice, and suffering to their very limits, yet through it all he was blessed. All the beatitudes became real in his heart and life, in the midst of his difficult circumstances.

Paganini, the great Italian violinist, once stepped onstage only to discover there was something wrong with his violin, just as the audience was ending their applause. He looked at the instrument for a moment and suddenly realized it was not his best and most valuable one. In fact, the violin was not his at all. Momentarily he felt paralyzed, but he quickly turned to his audience, telling them there had been some mistake and he did not have his own violin. He stepped back behind the curtain, thinking he must have left it backstage, but discovered that someone had stolen his and left the inferior one in its place.

After remaining behind the curtain for a moment, Paganini stepped onstage again to speak to the audience. He said, "Ladies and Gentlemen, I will now demonstrate to you that the music is not in the instrument but in the soul." Then he played as never before, and beautiful music flowed from that inferior instrument until the audience was so enraptured that their enthusiastic applause nearly lifted the ceiling of the concert hall. He had indeed revealed to them that the music was not in his instrument but in his own soul!

Dear tested and tried believer, it is your mission to walk onto the stage of this world in order to reveal to all of heaven and earth that the music of life lies not in your circumstances or external things but in your own soul.

If peace be in your heart,
The wildest winter storm is full of solemn beauty,
The midnight flash but shows your path of duty,
Each living creature tells some new and joyous story,
The very trees and stones all catch a ray of glory,
If peace be in your heart.

CHARLES FRANCIS RICHARDSON

DAY 241

On the day when I act . . . they will be my treasured possession. And they shall be mine . . . in that day when I make up my jewels.

MALACHI 3:17 NIV; KJV

Christ died that He might make us a "peculiar people" (1 Pet. 2:9 KJV). A great many Christians are afraid that they will be peculiar. A few weeks before Enoch was translated his acquaintances would probably have said that he was a little peculiar; they would have told you that when they had a Bridge

Party and the whole countryside were invited, you would not find Enoch or one of his family present. He was very peculiar, very.

We are not told that he was a great warrior or a great scientist or a great scholar. In fact, we are not told that he was anything that the world would call great, but he walked with God three hundred and sixty-five years, and he is the brightest star that shone in that dispensation.

If he could walk with God, cannot you and I? He took a long walk one day, and has not come back as yet. The Lord liked his company so well that He said, "Enoch, come up higher."

I suppose that if we asked the men in Elijah's time what kind of a man he was, they would have said, "He is very peculiar." The King would have said, "I hate him." Jezebel did not like him; the whole royal court did not like him and a great number of the nominal Christians did not like him; he was too radical.

I am glad that the Lord had seven thousand that had not bowed the knee to Baal; but I would rather have Elijah's little finger than the whole seven thousand. I would not give much for seven thousand Christians in hiding. They will just barely get into heaven; they will not have crowns.

See that "no one will take your crown" (Rev. 3:11). Be willing to be one of Christ's peculiar people, no matter what men may say of you! D. L. MOODY

DAY 242

I am a man of prayer.

PSALM 109:4

All too often we are in a "holy" hurry in our devotional time. How much actual time do we spend in quiet devotion on a daily basis? Can it be easily measured in minutes? Can you think of even one person of great spiritual stature who did not spend much of his time in prayer? Has anyone ever exhibited much of the spirit of prayer who did not devote a great deal of time to prayer?

George Whitefield, the English preacher who was one of the leading figures in the eighteenth-century American revival known as the Great Awakening, once said, "I have spent entire days and weeks lying prostrate on the ground, engaged in silent or spoken prayer." And the words of another person, whose life confirmed his own assertion, were these: "Fall to your knees and grow there."

It has been said that no great work of literature or science has ever been produced by someone who did not love solitude. It is also a fundamental principle of faith that no tremendous growth in holiness has ever been achieved by anyone who has not taken the time frequently, and for long periods, to be alone with God. THE STILL HOUR

"Come, come," He calls you, "O soul oppressed and weary,
Come to the shadows of My desert rest;
Come walk with Me far from life's noisy discords,
And peace will breathe like music in your breast."

Aug 31st

DAY 243

Why, my soul, are you downcast?

PSALM 43:5

The other evening I found myself staggering alone under a load that was heavy enough to crush half a dozen strong men. Out of sheer exhaustion I put it down and had a good look at it. I found that it was all borrowed; part of it belonged to the following day; part of it belonged to the following week—and here was I borrowing it that it might crush me now! It is a very stupid, but a very ancient blunder. F. W. BOREHAM

You and I are to take our trials, our black Fridays, our lone and long nights, and we are to come to Him and say, "Manage these, Thou Wondrous Friend who canst turn the very night into the morning; manage these for me!"

Sparrow, He guardeth thee;
Never a flight but thy wings He upholdeth;
Never a night but thy nest He enfoldeth;
Safely He guardeth thee.
Lily, He robeth thee;
Though thou must fade, by the Summer bemoaned,
Thou art arrayed fair as monarch enthroned;
Spotless He robeth thee.
Hear, thou of little faith;
Sparrow and lily are soulless and dying;
Deathless art thou; will He slight thy faint crying?
Trust, thou of little faith!

R. G. W.

DAY 244

That is why, for Christ's sake, I delight in weaknesses, in insults, in hardships, in persecutions, in difficulties. For when I am weak, then I am strong.

2 CORINTHIANS 12:10

The literal translation of this verse adds a startling emphasis to it, allowing it to speak for itself with power we have probably never realized. It is as follows: "Therefore I take pleasure in being without strength, being insulted, experiencing emergencies, and being chased and forced into a corner for Christ's sake; for when I am without strength, I am *dynamite*."

The secret of knowing God's complete sufficiency is in coming to the end of everything in ourselves and our circumstances. Once we reach this point, we will stop seeking sympathy for our difficult situation or ill treatment, because we will recognize these things as the necessary conditions for blessings. We will then turn from our circumstances to God, realizing they are the evidence of Him working in our lives. A. B. SIMPSON

George Matheson, the well-known blind preacher of Scotland, once said, "My dear God, I have never thanked You for my thorns. I have thanked You a thousand times for my roses but not once for my thorns. I have always looked forward to the place where I will be rewarded for my cross, but I have never thought of my cross as a present glory itself.

"Teach me, O Lord, to glory in my cross. Teach me the value of my thorns. Show me how I have climbed to You through the path of pain. Show me it is through my tears I have seen my rainbows."

Alas for him who never sees
The stars shine through the cypress trees.

DAY 245

Has not the Lord gone ahead of you?

JUDGES 4:14

God has guided the heroes and saints of all ages to do things which the common sense of the community has regarded as ridiculous and mad. Have you ever taken any risks for Christ? CHARLES E. COWMAN

"Am I not sending you?" (Judg. 6:14).

God knows, and you know, what He has sent you to do. God sent Moses to Egypt to bring three million bondmen out of the house of bondage into the Promised Land. Did he fail? It looked at first as if he were going to. But did he? God sent Elijah to stand before Ahab, and it was a bold thing for him to say that there should be neither dew nor rain: but did he not lock up the heavens for three years and six months? Did he fail?

And you cannot find any place in Scripture where a man was ever sent by God to do a work in which he ever failed. D. L. MOODY

Had Moses failed to go, had God
Granted his prayer, there would have been
For him no leadership to win;
No pillared fire; no magic rod;
No wonders in the land of Zin;
No smiting of the sea; no tears
Ecstatic, shed on Sinai's steep;
No Nebo with a God to keep
His burial; only forty years
Of desert, watching with his sheep.

J. R. MILLER

Our might is His Almightiness.

DAY 246

Sept 3rd

In order to keep me from becoming conceited,
I was given a thorn in my flesh.

2 CORINTHIANS 12:7

Flowers there are all along life's way; but the thorns are rife also. "When the thorns of life have pierced us till we bleed," where but to heaven shall we look? To whom shall we go but to Him—the Christ who cures? He was crowned with thorns. He alone can transform our testing, torturing thorns into triumphal experiences of grace and glory. B. MCCALL BARBOUR

Your path is thorny and rough? Tramp it! You will find wherever you set your foot upon a thorn, Another Foot has been there before and taken off the sharpness. THE MORNING MESSAGE

Strange gift indeed!—a thorn to prick,
To pierce into the very quick;
To cause perpetual sense of pain;
Strange gift!—and yet, 'twas given for gain.
Unwelcome, yet it came to stay;
Nor could it e'en be prayed away.
It came to fill its God-planned place,
A life-enriching means of grace.
God's grace-thorns—ah, what forms they take;
What piercing, smarting pain they make!
And yet, each one in love is sent,
And always just for blessing meant.
And so, whate'er thy thorn may be,
From God accept it willingly;
But reckon Christ—His life—the power
To keep, in thy most trying hour.
And sure—thy life will richer grow;
He grace sufficient will bestow;
And in Heav'n's morn thy joy 'twill be
That, by His thorn, He strengthened thee.

J. DANSON SMITH

DAY 247

It was good for me to be afflicted.

PSALM 119:71

It is a remarkable occurrence of nature that the most brilliant colors of plants are found on the highest mountains, in places that are the most exposed to the fiercest weather. The brightest lichens and mosses, as well as the most beautiful wildflowers, abound high upon the windswept, storm-ravaged peaks.

One of the finest arrays of living color I have ever seen was just above the great Saint Bernard Hospice near the ten-thousand-foot summit of Mont Cenis in the French Alps. The entire face of one expansive rock was covered with a strikingly vivid yellow lichen, which shone in the sunshine like a golden wall protecting an enchanted castle. Amid the loneliness and barrenness of that high altitude and exposed to the fiercest winds of the sky, this lichen exhibited glorious color it has never displayed in the shelter of the valley.

As I write these words, I have two specimens of the same type of lichen before me. One is from this Saint Bernard area, and the other is from the wall of a Scottish castle, which is surrounded by sycamore trees. The difference in their form and coloring is quite striking. The one grown amid the fierce storms of the mountain peak has a lovely yellow color of a primrose, a smooth texture, and a definite form and shape. But the one cultivated amid the warm air and the soft showers of the lowland valley has a dull, rusty color, a rough texture, and an indistinct and broken shape.

Isn't it the same with a Christian who is afflicted, storm-tossed, and without comfort? Until the storms and difficulties allowed by God's providence beat upon a believer again and again, his character appears flawed and blurred. Yet the trials actually clear away the clouds and shadows, perfect the form of his character, and bestow brightness and blessing to his life.

Amidst my list of blessings infinite
Stands this the foremost, that my heart has bled;
For all I bless You, most for the severe.

HUGH MACMILLAN

DAY 248

Those who hope in me will not be disappointed.
They shall not be ashamed that wait for me.

ISAIAH 49:23 NIV; KJV

"They shall not be ashamed that wait for me." Such is the veritable record of the living God—a record made good in the experience of all those who have been enabled, through grace, to exercise a living faith. We must remember how much is involved in these three words—"Wait for me." The waiting must be a real thing. It will not do to say we are waiting on God, when in reality, our eye is askance upon some human prop. We must absolutely be "shut up" to God. We must be brought to the end of self and to the bottom of circumstance, in order fully to prove what God's resources are. "My soul, wait thou only upon God" (Ps. 62:5 KJV).

Thus it was with Jehoshaphat, in that scene recorded in 2 Chronicles 20. He was wholly wrecked upon God; it was either God or nothing. "We have no power" (v. 12). But what then? "Our eyes are on you" (v. 12). This was enough. Jehoshaphat was in the very best attitude and condition to prove what God was. To have been possessed of creature strength or creature wisdom would only have proved a hindrance to him in leaning exclusively upon the arm and the counsel of the Almighty God. THINGS NEW AND OLD

When you feel at the end of your tether, remember God is at the other end!

DAY 249

He took them with him and they withdrew by themselves.

LUKE 9:10

In order to grow in grace, we must spend a great deal of time in quiet solitude. Contact with others in society is not what causes the soul to grow most vigorously. In fact, one quiet hour of prayer will often yield greater results than many days spent in the company of others. It is in the desert that the dew is freshest and the air is the most pure. ANDREW BONAR

Come with Me by yourselves and rest awhile,
I know you're weary of the stress and throng,
Wipe from your brow the sweat and dust of toil,
And in My quiet strength again be strong.
Come now aside from all the world holds dear,
For fellowship the world has never known,
Alone with Me, and with My Father here,
With Me and with My Father, not alone.
Come, tell Me all that you have said and done,
Your victories and failures, hopes and fears.
I know how hardened hearts are wooed and won;
My choicest wreaths are always wet with tears.
Come now and rest; the journey is too great,
And you will faint beside the way and sink;
The bread of life is here for you to eat,
And here for you the wine of love to drink.
Then from fellowship with your Lord return,
And work till daylight softens into even:
Those brief hours are not lost in which you learn
More of your Master and His rest in Heaven.

DAY 250

And we know that in all things God works for the good of those who love him, who have been called according to his purpose.

ROMANS 8:28

The poet Cowper was subject to fits of depression. One day he ordered a cab, and told the driver to take him to London Bridge. Soon a dense fog settled down upon the city. The cabby wandered about for two hours, and then admitted he was lost. Cowper asked him if he thought he could find the way home. The cabby thought that he could, and in another hour landed him at his door. When Cowper asked what the fare would be the driver felt that he should not take anything since he had not gotten his fare to his destination. Cowper insisted, saying, "Never mind that, you have saved my life. I was on my way to throw myself off London Bridge." He then went into the house and wrote:

God moves in a mysterious way
His wonders to perform;
He plants His footsteps on the sea,
And rides upon the storm.

The plans at the chapel went wrong; the minister was snowed up. The plans of the boy under the gallery went wrong; the snowstorm shut him off from the church of his choice. Those two wrongs together made a tremendous right, for out of those shattered plans and programs came an event that has incalculably enriched mankind—Spurgeon's conversion.

A very old Chinese man named Sai had only one son and one horse. Once the horse ran away and Sai was very worried. Only one horse and lost! Someone said, "Don't suffer, wait a little." The horse came back. Not long after this the only son went out to the field riding the horse. Returning home he fell from the horse and broke his leg. What a sorrow had poor Sai then! He could not eat; he could not sleep; he could not even attend well to the wants of his son. Only one son and injured! But someone said, "More patience, Sai!" Soon after the accident a war broke out. All the young men went to the war; none of them returned. Only Sai's son stayed at home, and remained to live long to his father's joy.

Sept 8th

DAY 251

Where there is no vision, the people perish.

PROVERBS 29:18 KJV

We must see something before we make our ventures! Faith must first have visions: faith sees a light, if you will, an imaginary light, and leaps! Faith is always born of vision and hope! We must have the gleam of the thing hoped for shining across the waste before we can have an energetic and energizing faith.

Are we not safe in saying that the majority of people have no fine hopes, are devoid of the vision splendid, and therefore, have no spiritual audacity in spiritual adventure and enterprise? Our hopes are petty and peddling, and they don't give birth to crusades. There are no shining towers and minarets on our horizon, no new Jerusalem, and therefore we do not set out in chivalrous explorations.

We need a transformation in the "things hoped for" (Heb. 11:1 KJV). We need to be renewed in mind, and renewed in mind daily. We need to have the far-off towering summits of vast and noble possibilities enthroned in our imaginations. Our gray and uninviting horizons must glow with the unfading colors of immortal hopes.

So few men venture out beyond the blazed trail,
'Tis he who has the courage to go past this sign

That cannot in his mission fail.
He will have left at least some mark behind
To guide some other brave exploring mind.

No man is of any use until he has dared everything. ROBERT LOUIS STEVENSON

DAY 252

God chose the weak things of the world. . . . to nullify the things that are, so that no one may boast before him.

1 CORINTHIANS 1:27–29

Only a blast of rams' horns and a shout—and God made the walls of proud Jericho crumble to their foundations, and the key of all Canaan was in the hand of Israel! (Josh. 6)

Only two women—one, Deborah, inspired courage in the fainting hearts of Israel's men—the other, Jael, with a hammer and nail laid Israel's master low; thus the end came to twenty years of mighty oppression! (Judg. 4–5)

Only an ox goad—but with it six hundred Philistines were slain, and Israel delivered by Shamgar's God! (Judg. 3:31)

Only a trumpet blast, the smash of a lighted pitcher, a shout—but by these, and Gideon, God delivered Israel from the seven-year yoke of the Midianites! (Judg. 6–8)

Only the jawbone of an ass—yet heaps of Philistines fell before it, because God strengthened the arm that wielded it! (Judg. 15)

Only a sling, and a stone sent with unerring precision and directed by Almighty God—and that day Israel's mighty men were put to shame: the giant Philistine was slain, and God's honor was vindicated! (1 Sam. 17)

Only a few ignorant, yet wholehearted and consecrated men and women; but by the power of God they were to put men in possession of that Eternal

Salvation which would transform its possessors into the likeness of the Son Himself, and ultimately land them in Eternal Glory!

If you are one of the base, foolish, weak ciphers of this world, then the very same power, from the very same Lord, for the very same purpose, will be yours!

Under the control of God ordinary instruments become extraordinary.

Sept. 10th DAY 253

The Lord *blessed the latter part of Job's life more than the former part.*

JOB 42:12

Job found his legacy through the grief he experienced. He was tried that his godliness might be confirmed and validated. In the same way, my troubles are intended to deepen my character and to clothe me in gifts I had little of prior to my difficulties, for my ripest fruit grows against the roughest wall. I come to a place of glory only through my own humility, tears, and death, just as Job's afflictions left him with a higher view of God and more humble thoughts of himself. At last he cried, "Now my eyes have seen you" (v. 5).

If I experience the presence of God in His majesty through my pain and loss, so that I bow before Him and pray, "Your will be done" (Matt. 6:10), then I have gained much indeed. God gave Job glimpses of his future glory, for in those weary and difficult days and nights, he was allowed to penetrate God's veil and could honestly say, "I know that my redeemer lives" (Job 19:25). So truly: "The Lord blessed the latter part of Job's life more than the former part." IN THE HOUR OF SILENCE

Trouble never comes to someone unless it brings a nugget of gold in its hand.

Apparent adversity will ultimately become an advantage for those of us doing what is right, if we are willing to keep serving and to wait patiently. Think of the great victorious souls of the past who worked with steadfast faith and who were invincible and courageous! There are many blessings we will never obtain if we are unwilling to accept and endure suffering. There are certain joys that can come to us only through sorrow. There are revelations of God's divine truth that we will receive only when the lights of earth have been extinguished. And there are harvests that will grow only once the plow has done its work.

It is from suffering that the strongest souls ever known have emerged; the world's greatest display of character is seen in those who exhibit the scars of sorrow; the martyrs of the ages have worn their coronation robes that have glistened with fire, yet through their tears and sorrow have seen the gates of heaven. CHAPIN

I will know by the gleam and glitter
Of the golden chain you wear,
By your heart's calm strength in loving,
Of the fire you have had to bear.
Beat on, true heart, forever;
Shine bright, strong golden chain;
And bless the cleansing fire
And the furnace of living pain!

ADELAIDE PROCTOR

DAY 254

Sept 17

Not hidden from the Almighty.

JOB 24:1 KJV

Thy Savior is near thee, suffering, lonely, tempted friend! Thou art not the plaything of wild chance. There is a purpose in thy life which Jesus is working out. Let thy spirit flee for rest to Christ, and to His pierced hand which opens the book of thy life! Rest thee there! Be patient and trustful! All will work out right. Someday thou wilt understand. In the meantime, trust Him "though sun and moon fail, and the stars drop into the dark."

What though the way may be lonely,
And dark the shadows fall;
I know where'er it leadeth,
My Father planned it all.
The sun may shine tomorrow,
The shadows break and flee;
'Twill be the way He chooses,
The Father's plan for me.
He guides my halting footsteps
Along the weary way,
For well He knows the pathway
Will lead to endless day.
A day of light and gladness,
On which no shade will fall,
'Tis this at last awaits me—
My Father planned it all.
I sing through shade and sunshine,
And trust what'er befall;
His way is best—it leads to rest;
My Father planned it all.

"God is working out His purpose."

DAY 255

Some time later the brook dried up.

1 KINGS 17:7

The education of our faith is incomplete if we have yet to learn that God's providence works through loss, that there is a ministry to us through failure and the fading of things, and that He gives the gift of emptiness. It is, in fact, the material insecurities of life that cause our lives to be spiritually established. The dwindling brook at the Kerith Ravine, where Elijah sat deep in thought, is a true picture of each of our lives. "Some time later the brook dried up"—this is the history of our yesterdays, and a prophecy of our tomorrows.

One way or the other, we must all learn the difference between trusting in the gift and trusting in the Giver. The gift may last for a season, but the Giver is the only eternal love.

The Kerith Ravine was a difficult problem for Elijah until he arrived at Zarephath, and suddenly everything became as clear as daylight to him. God's hard instructions are never His last words to us, for the woe, the waste, and the tears of life belong to its interlude, not its finale.

If the Lord had led Elijah directly to Zarephath, he would have missed something that helped to make him a wiser prophet and a better man—living by faith at Kerith. And whenever our earthly stream or any other outer resource has dried up, it has been allowed so we may learn that our hope and help are in God, who made heaven and earth. F. B. MEYER

Perhaps you, too, have camped by such sweet waters,
And quenched with joy your weary, parched soul's thirst;
To find, as time goes on, your streamlet alters
From what it was at first.
Hearts that have cheered, or soothed, or blest, or strengthened;
Loves that have lavished unreservedly;

Joys, treasured joys—have passed, as time has lengthened,
Into obscurity.
If then, O soul, the brook your heart has cherished
Does fail you now—no more your thirst assuage—
If its once glad refreshing streams have perished,
Let Him your heart engage.
He will not fail, nor mock, nor disappoint you;
His comfort and care change not with the years;
With oil of joy He surely will anoint you,
And wipe away your tears.

J. DANSON SMITH

DAY 256

Whoever loses their life for my sake will find it.

MATTHEW 10:39

In my early life I entered into a partnership with a friend in the wholesale ice business. For two seasons in succession our ice was swept away by winter freshets. In the winter of which I speak, things had come to a serious pass and it seemed very necessary that we should have ice. The weather became very cold; the ice formed and grew thicker and thicker until it was fit to gather. Then there came an order for thousands of tons of ice which would lift us entirely from our financial stress. Not long before this, God had showed me that it was His will that I should commit my business to Him and trust Him with it absolutely. I never dreamed what testing was coming. At midnight there came an ominous sound—that of rain. By noon the storm was raging in all its violence; by afternoon I had come into a great spiritual crisis in my life.

I have learned this: a matter may be seemingly trivial, but the crisis that turns upon a small matter may be a profound and far-reaching one in our lives.

By midafternoon of that day I had come face to face with the tremendous fact that down deep in my heart was a spirit of rebellion against God. And that rebelliousness seemed to develop in a suggestion to my heart like this: "You gave all to God. This is the way He requites you." Then another voice: "My child, did you mean it when you said you would trust Me? Would I suffer anything to come into your life which will not work out for good for you?" And then the other voice: "But it is hard! Why should He take your business when it is clean and honest?"

At the end of two hours (during which waged one of the greatest spiritual battles of my life) by the grace of God I was able to cry out, "Take the business; take the ice; take everything; only give me the supreme blessing of a will absolutely submitted to Thee."

And then came peace!

By midnight there came another sound—that of wind. By morning the mercury had fallen to zero, and in a few days we were harvesting the finest ice we ever had. He gave back the ice; He blessed the business; and He led me on and out, until He guided me from it entirely into the place He had for me from the beginning—that of a teacher of His Word. JAMES H. MCCONKEY

Give your life to God, and God will give you back your life!

Sept 14th

DAY 257

He did not open his mouth.

ISAIAH 53:7

What grace it requires when we are misunderstood yet handle it correctly, or when we are judged unkindly yet receive it in holy sweetness! Nothing tests our character as a Christian more than having something evil said about us. This kind of grinding test is what exposes whether we are solid gold or simply gold-plated metal. If we could only see the blessings that lie hidden in our trials, we would say like David, when Shimei cursed him, "Let him curse. . . . It may be that the LORD will . . . restore to me his covenant blessing instead of his curse today" (2 Sam. 16:11–12).

Some Christians are easily turned away from the greatness of their life's calling by pursuing instead their own grievances and enemies. They ultimately turn their lives into one petty whirlwind of warfare. It reminds me of trying to deal with a hornet's nest. You may be able to disperse the hornets, but you will probably be terribly stung and receive nothing for your pain, for even their honey has no value.

May God grant us more of the Spirit of Christ, who, "when they hurled their insults at him, . . . did not retaliate. . . . Instead, he entrusted himself to him who judges justly" (1 Pet. 2:23). "Consider him who endured such opposition from sinners, so that you will not grow weary and lose heart" (Heb. 12:3). A. B. SIMPSON

For you He walked along the path of woe,
He was sharply struck with His head bent low.
He knew the deepest sorrow, pain, and grief,
He knew long endurance with no relief,
He took all the bitter from death's deep cup,
He kept no blood drops but gave them all up.
Yes, for you, and for me, He won the fight
To take us to glory and realms of light.

L. S. P.

DAY 258

The Lord is my shepherd.

PSALM 23:1

The great Father above is a Shepherd Chief. I am His and with Him. I want not. He throws out to me a rope, and the name of the rope is love, and He draws me to where the grass is green and the water is not dangerous.

Sometimes my heart is very weak, and falls down, but He lifts it up again and draws me into a good road.

Sometime, it may be very soon, it may be longer, it may be a long, long time, He will draw me into a place between mountains. It is dark there, but I'll draw back not. I'll be afraid not, for it is in there between the mountains that the Shepherd Chief will meet me, and the hunger I have felt in my heart all through this life will be satisfied. Sometimes He makes the love rope into a whip, but afterwards He gives me a staff to lean on.

He spreads a table before me with all kinds of food. He puts His hands upon my head, and all the "tired" is gone.

My cup He fills, till it runs over.

What I tell you is true, I lie not. The roads that are "away ahead" will stay with me through this life, and afterwards I will go to live in the "Big Tepee" and sit down with the Shepherd Chief forever. A NATIVE AMERICAN'S VERSION OF THE TWENTY-THIRD PSALM

Fear not, little flock, He goeth ahead,
Your Shepherd selecteth the path you must tread;
The water of Marah He'll sweeten for thee,
He drank all the bitter in Gethsemane.
Fear not, little flock, whatever your lot,
He enters all rooms, "The doors being shut";

He never forsakes; He never is gone,
So count on His presence in darkness and dawn.

PAUL RADER

DAY 259

Who among you fears the Lord and obeys the word of his servant? Let the one who walks in the dark, who has no light, trust in the name of the Lord and rely on their God.

ISAIAH 50:10

What is a believer to do in times of darkness—a darkness of perplexities and confusion—a darkness not of the heart but of the mind? These times of darkness come to a faithful and believing disciple who is walking obediently in the will of God. They come as seasons when he does not know what to do or which way to turn. His sky becomes overcast with clouds, and the clear light of heaven does not shine on his path, so that he feels as if he were groping his way through complete darkness.

Dear believer, does this describe you? What should you do in times of darkness? Listen to God's Word: "Let the one . . . trust in the name of the Lord and rely on their God." Actually, the first thing to do is nothing. This is a difficult thing for our lowly human nature to do. There is a saying, "When you're rattled, don't rush." In other words, "When you are confused and do not know what to do, do nothing." When you find yourself in a spiritual fog, do not run ahead, but slow the pace of your life. And if necessary, keep your life's ship anchored or tied to the dock.

The right thing is simply to trust God, for while we trust, He can work. Worrying, however, prevents Him from doing anything for us. If the darkness covering us strikes terror in our hearts and we run back and forth, seeking in vain to find a way of escape from the dark trial where God's providence has placed us, then the Lord cannot work on our behalf.

Only the peace of God will quiet our minds and put our hearts at rest. We must place our hand in His as a little child and allow Him to lead us into the bright sunshine of His love. He knows the way out of the dense, dark forest, so may we climb into His arms, trusting Him to rescue us by showing us the shortest and most reliable road. DR. PARDINGTON

Remember, we are never without a pilot—even when we do not know which way to steer.

Hold on, my heart, in your believing—
Only the steadfast wins the crown;
He who, when stormy winds are heaving,
Parts with his anchor, will go down;
But he who Jesus holds through all,
Will stand, though Heaven and earth should fall.
Hold on! An end will come to sorrow;
Hope from the dust will conquering rise;
The storm foretells a summer's morrow;
The Cross points on to Paradise;
The Father reigns! So cease all doubt;
Hold on, my heart. Hold on, hold out.

DAY 260

Restore that person gently. But watch yourselves,
or you also may be tempted.

GALATIANS 6:1

From the converts in Uganda
Comes to us a story grander,

In the lesson that it teaches,
Than a sermon often preaches.
For they tell what sore temptations
Come to them; what need of patience,
And a need, all else outweighing,
Of a place for private praying.
So each convert chose a corner
Far away from eye of scorner,
In the jungle, where he could
Pray to God in solitude.
And so often went he thither,
That the grass would fade and wither
Where he trod and you could trace
By the paths, each prayer place.
If they hear the evil tiding That a brother is backsliding,
And that some are even saying, "He no longer cares for praying," Then they say to one another, Very soft and gently, "Brother, You'll forgive us now for showing, On your path the grass is growing." And the erring one, relenting, Soon is bitterly repenting:
"Ah, how sad I am at knowing
On my path the grass is growing.
But it shall be so no longer; Prayer
I need to make me stronger; On my
path so oft I'm going,
Soon no grass will there be growing."

"GRASS ON THE PRAYER PATH"

Have a trysting place with God! And keep a little path open!

Sept 18th

DAY 261

Do not be anxious about anything.

PHILIPPIANS 4:6

Quite a few Christians live in a terrible state of anxiety, constantly fretting over the concerns of life. The secret of living in perfect peace amid the hectic pace of daily life is one well worth knowing. What good has worrying ever accomplished? It has never made anyone stronger, helped anyone do God's will, or provided for anyone a way of escape out of their anxiety or confusion. Worry only destroys the effectiveness of lives that would otherwise be useful and beautiful. Being restless and having worries and cares are absolutely forbidden by our Lord, who said, "So do not worry, saying, 'What shall we eat?' or 'What shall we drink?' or 'What shall we wear?'" (Matt. 6:31). He does not mean that we are not to think ahead or that our life should never have a plan or pattern to it. He simply means that we are not to worry about these things.

People will know that you live in a constant state of anxiety by the lines on your face, the tone of your voice, your negative attitude, and the lack of joy in your spirit. So scale the heights of a life abandoned to God, and your perspective will change to the point that you will look down on the clouds beneath your feet. DARLOW SARGEANT

It is a sign of weakness to always worry and fret, question everything, and mistrust everyone. Can anything be gained by it? Don't we only make ourselves unfit for action, and separate our minds from the ability to make wise decisions? We simply sink in our struggles when we could float by faith.

Oh, for the grace to be silent! Oh, to "be still, and know that [Jehovah is] God" (Ps. 46:10)! "The Holy One of Israel" (Ps. 89:18) will defend and deliver His own. We can be sure that His every word will stand forever, even though the mountains may fall into the sea. He deserves our total confidence. So come, my soul, return to your place of peace, and rest within the sweet embrace of the Lord Jesus.

Peace your inmost soul will fill
When you're still!

Sept 19th

DAY 262

Abraham built an altar there. . . . and took the knife to slay his son. But the angel of the L*ORD called out to him. . . . "Do not lay a hand on the boy."*

GENESIS 22:9–12

Our hardest sacrifices are never so hard as we thought they were going to be, if we go on with them to the uttermost that God asks. A sacrifice of self to God's will made halfway, or even nine-tenths, is a grinding, cruel experience. When it is made the whole way, with the altar built and self laid upon the altar, God always comes with an unexpected blessing that so overwhelms us with love and joy that the hardship of the sacrifice sinks out of sight. "Now I know that you fear God, because you have not withheld" (v. 12). Can He say that to us today? No one ever knows the full joy of hearing the word from God until the altar has been built, and the knife is laid to the sacrifice. MESSAGES FOR THE MORNING WATCH

Is your all on the altar of sacrifice laid?
Your heart, does the Spirit control?
You can only be blest and have peace and sweet rest
As you yield Him your body and soul.

Sept 20th

DAY 263

The Lord *longs to be gracious to you; therefore he will rise up to show you compassion.*

ISAIAH 30:18

The greenest grass is found wherever the most rain falls. So I suppose it is the fog and mist of Ireland that makes it "the Emerald Isle." And wherever you find the widespread fog of trouble and the mist of sorrow, you always find emerald green hearts that are full of the beautiful foliage of the comfort and love of God.

Dear Christian, do not say, "Where are all the swallows? They are all gone—they are dead." No, they are not dead. They have simply skimmed across the deep, blue sea, flying to a faraway land; but they will be back again soon.

Child of God, do not say, "All the flowers are dead—the winter has killed them, so they are gone." No! Although the winter has covered them with a white coat of snow, they will push up their heads again and will be alive very soon.

O believer, do not say that the sun has burned out, just because a cloud has hidden it. No, it is still there, planning a summer for you; for when it shines again, it will have caused those clouds to have dropped their April showers, each of them a mother to a sweet mayflower.

Above all, remember—when God hides His face from you, do not say that He has forgotten you. He is simply waiting for a little while to make you love Him more. And once He comes, you will rejoice with the inexpressible "joy of the Lord" (Neh. 8:10). Waiting on Him exercises your gift of grace and tests your faith. Therefore continue to wait in hope, for although the promise may linger, it will never come too late. CHARLES H. SPURGEON

Oh, every year has its winter,
And every year has its rain—

But a day is always coming
When the birds go north again.
When new leaves sprout in the forest,
And grass springs green on the plain,
And tulips boast their blossoms—
And the birds go north again.
Oh, every heart has its sorrow,
And every heart has its pain—
But a day is always coming
When the birds go north again.
It's the sweetest thing to remember,
If your courage starts to wane,
When the cold, dark days are over—
That the birds go north again.

DAY 264

They did not love their lives so much.

REVELATION 12:11

The persecution of the Christians during the reign of Marcus Aurelius was very bitter. The Emperor himself decreed the punishment of forty of the men who had refused to bow down to his image.

"Strip to the skin!" he commanded. They did so. "Now, go and stand on that frozen lake," he commanded, "until you are prepared to abandon your Nazarene-God!"

And forty naked men marched out into that howling storm on a winter's night. As they took their places on the ice they lifted up their voices and sang:

"Christ, forty wrestlers have come out to wrestle for Thee; to win for Thee the victory; to win from Thee the crown."

After a while, those standing by and watching noticed a disturbance among the men. One man had edged away, broken into a run, entered the temple and prostrated himself before the image of the Emperor.

The Captain of the Guard, who had witnessed the bravery of the men and whose heart had been touched by their teaching, tore off his helmet, threw down his spear, and disrobing himself, took up the cry as he took the place of the man who had weakened. The compensation was not slow in coming, for as the dawn broke there were forty corpses on the ice.

Who shall dream of shrinking, by our Captain led?

At least a thousand of God's saints served as living torches to illuminate the darkness of Nero's gardens, wrapped in garments steeped in pitch. "Every finger was a candle."

"Who follows in their train?"

I'm standing, Lord.
There is a mist that blinds my sight.
Steep jagged rocks, front, left, and right,
Lower, dim, gigantic, in the night.
Where is the way?
I'm standing, Lord.
The black rock hems me in behind.
Above my head a moaning wind
Chills and oppresses heart and mind.
I am afraid!
I'm standing, Lord.
The rock is hard beneath my feet.
I nearly slipped, Lord, on the sleet.
So weary, Lord, and where a seat?
Still must I stand?
He answered me, and on His face
A look ineffable of grace,
Of perfect, understanding love,

Which all my murmuring did remove.
I'm standing, Lord.
Since Thou hast spoken, Lord, I see
Thou hast beset; these rocks are Thee;
And since Thy love encloses me,
I stand and sing!

BETTY STAM

DAY 265

Do not fret.

PSALM 37:1

I believe that this verse is as much a divine command as "You shall not steal" (Ex. 20:15). But what does it mean to fret? One person once defined it as that which makes a person rough on the surface, causing him to rub and wear himself and others away. Isn't it true that an irritable, irrational, and critical person not only wears himself out but is also very draining and tiring to others? When we worry and fret, we are a constant annoyance. This psalm not only says, "Do not fret because of those who are evil" but leaves no room for fretting whatsoever. It is very harmful, and God does not want us to hurt ourselves or others.

A disposition of continual fretting is not conducive to a healthy body. The next step down from fretting is being quick-tempered, and that amounts to anger. May we set it aside once and for all and simply be obedient to the command "Do not fret." MARGARET BOTTOME

OVERHEARD IN AN ORCHARD

Said the Robin to the Sparrow:
"I should really like to know

Why these anxious human beings
Rush about and worry so."
Said the Sparrow to the Robin:
"Friend, I think that it must be
That they have no Heavenly Father
Such as cares for you and me."

ELIZABETH CHENEY

DAY 266

Until he to whom it rightfully belongs shall come.

EZEKIEL 21:27

Years ago in Cincinnati Handel's Messiah was rendered by perhaps the greatest chorus on earth: Patti, then in her prime, was the leading soprano; Whitney, the bass; Theodore Toedt, the tenor; Carey, the alto; and this quartet was supported by more than four thousand voices.

Just before the "Hallelujah Chorus," a deathlike stillness brooded over that vast assemblage. Suddenly the bass sang, "For He shall reign for ever and ever," the alto lifted it a little higher—"For ever and ever," and the tenor lifted it still higher—"For ever and ever," then Patti broke in as though inspired—"King of Kings, and Lord of Lords." As she broke off, paused, and lifted her eyes, a voice seemed to float down from above as the voice of an Angel flinging out through the great hall the question, "How long shall He reign?"—and the thousand sopranos in unison responded, "For ever and ever." Then the four thousand of the chorus broke forth like the shout of an angelic host, "Hallelujah! Hallelujah! Hallelujah!"

What a day for this poor sin-ruined, storm-torn, heartbroken, groping-in-the-blind world, when He shall take His rightful throne and reign in all hearts and over all lives forever and ever! ELMER ELLSWORTH HELMS

Hail, universal Lord!
Messiah—David's Son!
Take Thou the scepter of the world,
And reign supreme, alone!

Oh, it seems to me like a prophecy of the glad day when every knee shall bow, and all the nations of the earth shall confess that Jesus Christ is Lord, to the glory of God the Father. And from the teeming millions of Asia shall sound the anthem, "King of Kings, and Lord of Lords"; the shout from Europe will give it power; and the deep undertone of Africa will lend it volume; and America, and faraway Australia, and the islands of the sea will join the refrain and pour their matchless music into the ear of Christ; and together, from the uttermost parts of the earth, breaking out in triumphant voice, the whole world shall sing, "King of Kings, and Lord of Lords; the Lord God Omnipotent reigneth!"

Come back! Come back! Take the scepter of our lives! Mount the throne of our hearts! All hail the King! My King! And thine?

Sept 24th

DAY 267

Dying, and yet we live on.

2 CORINTHIANS 6:9

Last summer I had a flower bed of asters that nearly covered my garden in the country. They were planted late in the season, but how beautiful they were! While the outer portion of the plants were still producing fresh flowers, the tops had gone to seed, and when an early frost came, I found that the radiant beauty of the blossoms had withered. All I could say at this point was, "Oh well, I guess the season has been too much for them, and they have died." So I wished them a fond farewell.

After this I no longer enjoyed looking at the flower bed, for it seemed to be only a graveyard of flowers. Yet several weeks ago one of the gardeners called my attention to the fact that across the entire garden, asters were now sprouting up in great abundance. It appeared that every plant I thought the winter had destroyed had replanted fifty to take its place. What had the frost and the fierce winter wind done?

They had taken my flowers and destroyed them, casting them to the ground. They had walked across them with their snowy feet and, once finished with their work, said, "This is the end of you." And yet in the spring, for every one destroyed, fifty witnesses arose and said, "It is through 'dying . . . we live on.'"

As it is in the plant world, so it is in God's kingdom. Through death came everlasting life. Through crucifixion and the tomb came the throne and the palace of the eternal God. Through apparent defeat came victory.

So do not be afraid of suffering or defeat. It is through being "struck down, but not destroyed" (2 Cor. 4:9) and through being broken to pieces, and those pieces being torn to shreds, that we become people of strength. And it is the endurance of one believer that produces a multitude.

Others may yield to the appearance of things and follow the world. They may blossom quickly and find momentary prosperity, but their end will be one of eternal death. HENRY WARD BEECHER

Measure your life by loss and not by gain,
Not by the wine drunk but by the wine poured forth.
For love's strength is found in love's sacrifice,
And he who suffers most has most to give.

Sept 25th

DAY 268

May my meditation be pleasing to him.

PSALM 104:34

Isaac went into the fields to meditate. Jacob lingered on the eastern bank of the brook Jabbok after all his company had passed over; there he wrestled with the angel and prevailed. Moses, hidden in the clefts of Horeb, beheld the vanishing glory which marked the way by which Jehovah had gone. Elijah sent Ahab down to eat and drink while he himself withdrew to the lonely crest of Carmel. Daniel spent weeks in ecstasy of intercession on the banks of Hiddekel, which once had watered Paradise. And Paul, no doubt in order that he might have an opportunity for undisturbed meditation and prayer, was minded to go afoot from Troas to Assos.

Have you learned to understand the truths of these great paradoxes: the blessing of a curse, the voice of silence, the companionship of solitude?

I walk down the Valley of Silence,
Down the dim voiceless valley alone,
And I hear not the sound of a footstep
Around me, but God's and my own;
And the hush of my heart is as holy
As the bowers whence angels have flown.
In the hush of the Valley of Silence
I hear all the songs that I sing,
And the notes float down the dim Valley
Till each finds a word for a wing,
That to men, like the dove of the deluge
The message of peace they may bring.
But far on the deep there are billows
That never shall break on the beach;

And I have heard songs in the silence
That never shall float into speech;
And I have had dreams in the Valley
Too lofty for language to reach.
Do you ask me the place of the Valley?
To hearts that are harrowed by care
It lieth afar, between mountains,
And God and His angels are there—
One is the dark mountain of sorrow,
And one the bright mountain of prayer.

"THE SONG OF A MYSTIC"

DAY 269

Sept 26th

. . . and gave him success in whatever he did.

GENESIS 39:23

A little bird I am,
Shut from the fields of air,
And in my cage I sit and sing
To Him who placed me there;
Well pleased a prisoner to be,
Because, My God, it pleases Thee.
My cage confines me round,
Freely I cannot fly,
But though my wings are closely bound,
My soul is at liberty;
For prison walls cannot control
The flight or freedom of the soul.

I have learned to love the darkness of sorrow, for it is there I see the brightness of God's face. MADAME GUYON

DAY 270

Joseph's master took him and put him in prison. . . . But . . . the Lord was with him . . . and gave him success in whatever he did.

GENESIS 39:20–21

When God allows us to go to prison because of our service to Him, it is nearly the most blessed place in the world that we could be, because He goes with us. Joseph seems to have known this truth. He did not sulk, become discouraged and rebellious, or engage in self-pity by thinking "everything was against him." If he had done so, the prison warden would never have trusted him.

May we remember that if self-pity is allowed to set in, we will never be used by God again until it is totally removed. Joseph simply placed everything in joyful trust upon the Lord, and as a result, the prison warden placed everything into Joseph's care.

Lord Jesus, when the prison door closes behind me, keep me trusting in You with complete and overflowing joy. Give Your work through me great success, and even in prison make me "free indeed" (John 8:36).

DAY 271

You may ask . . . and I will do it.

JOHN 14:14

Who is it here who offers to do for us if we will only ask? It is God Himself! It is the mightiest doer in the universe who says, "I will do, if you ask."

Think a moment who it is that promises: the God who holds the sea in the hollow of His hand; the God who swings this ponderous globe of earth in its orbit; the God who marshals the stars and guides the planets in their blazing paths with undeviating accuracy; the heaven-creating, devil-conquering, dead-raising God. It is this very God who says: "You may ask . . . and I will do it"!

Unrivaled wisdom, boundless skill, limitless power, infinite resources are His.

Wouldst thou not rather call forth Mine omnipotent doing by thine asking, if to this I have called thee, than even to be busy with thine own doing?
JAMES H. MCCONKEY

"I will do marvels!"

DAY 272

Sept 29th

Do not be anxious about anything.

PHILIPPIANS 4:6

Anxiety should never be found in a believer. In spite of the magnitude, quantity, and diversity of our trials, afflictions, and difficulties, anxiety should not exist under any circumstances. This is because we have a Father in heaven who is almighty, who loves His children as He loves His "one and only Son" (John 3:16), and whose complete joy and delight it is to continually assist them under all circumstances. We should heed His Word, which says, "Do not be anxious about anything, but in every situation, by prayer and petition, with thanksgiving, present your requests to God."

"In every situation"—not simply when our house is on fire or when our beloved spouse and children are gravely ill, but even in the smallest matters of life. We are to take everything to God—little things, very little things, even what the world calls trivial things. Yes, we are to take everything, living all day long in holy fellowship with our heavenly Father and our precious Lord Jesus. We should develop something of a spiritual instinct, causing us to immediately turn to God when a concern keeps us awake at night. During those sleepless nights, we should speak to Him, bringing our various concerns before Him, no matter how small they may be. Also speak to the Lord about any trial you are facing or any difficulties you may have in your family or professional life.

"By prayer and petition"—earnestly pleading, persevering and enduring, and waiting, waiting, waiting on God.

"With thanksgiving"—always laying a good foundation. Even if we have no possessions, there is one thing for which we can always be thankful—that He has saved us from hell. We can also give thanks that He has given us His Holy Word, His Holy Spirit, and the most precious gift of all—His Son. Therefore when we consider all this, we have abundant reasons for thanksgiving. May this be our goal!

"And the peace of God, which transcends all understanding, will guard your hearts and your minds in Christ Jesus" (Phil. 4:7). This is such a wonderful, genuine, and precious blessing that to truly know it, you must experience it, for it "transcends all understanding."

May we take these truths to heart, instinctively walking in them, so the result will be lives that glorify God more abundantly than ever before.

GEORGE MUELLER LIFE OF TRUST

Search your heart several times a day, and if you find something that is disturbing your peace, remember to take the proper steps to restore the calm.

FRANCIS DE SALES

DAY 273

When he heard that Lazarus was sick, he stayed where he was two more days.

JOHN 11:6

And so the silence of God was itself an answer. It is not merely said that there was no audible response to the cry from Bethany; it is distinctly stated that the absence of an audible response was itself the answer to the cry—it was when the Lord heard that Lazarus was sick that therefore He abode two days still in the same place which He was. I have often heard the outward silence. A hundred times have I sent up aspirations whose only answer has seemed to be the echo of my own voice, and I have cried out in the night of my despair, "Why art Thou so far from helping me?" But I never thought that the seeming farness was itself the nearness of God—that the very silence was an answer.

It was a very grand answer to the household of Bethany. They had asked not too much, but too little. They had asked only the life of Lazarus. They were to get the life of Lazarus and a revelation of eternal life as well.

There are some prayers that are followed by a Divine silence because we are not yet ripe for all we have asked; there are others which are so followed because we are ripe for more. We do not always know the full strength of our own capacity; we have to be prepared for receiving greater blessings than we have ever dreamed of. We come to the door of the sepulcher and beg with tears the dead body of Jesus; we are answered by silence because we are to get something better—a living Lord.

My soul, be not afraid of God's silence; it is another form of His voice. God's silence is more than man's speech. God's negative is better than the world's affirmative. Have thy prayers been followed by a calm stillness? Well! Is not that God's voice—a voice that will suffice thee in the meantime till the full disclosure comes? Has He moved not from His place to help thee? Well, but His stillness makes thee still, and He has something better than help to give thee.

Wait for Him in the silence, and ere long it shall become vocal; death shall be swallowed up in victory! GEORGE MATHESON

All God's dealings are slow!

Think not that God's silence is coldness or indifference. When birds are on the nest preparing to bring forth life, they never sing. God's stillness is full of brooding. Be not impatient of God!

When the Lord is to lead a soul to great faith, He for a time leaves his prayer unanswered.

Oct 1st

DAY 274

Suddenly an angel of the Lord appeared and a light shone in the cell. He struck Peter on the side and woke him up. "Quick, get up!" he said, and the chains fell off Peter's wrists. . . . About midnight Paul and Silas were praying and singing hymns to God. . . . Suddenly there was such a violent earthquake that the foundations of the prison were shaken. At once all the prison doors flew open, and everybody's chains came loose.

ACTS 12:7; 16:25–26

This is the way God works. In our darkest hour, He walks to us across the waves, just as an angel came to Peter's cell when the day of Peter's execution dawned. And when the scaffold was completed for Mordecai's execution, the king's sleeplessness ultimately led to his action favoring God's favored race. (See Est. 6.)

Dear soul, you may have to experience the very worst before you are delivered, but you will be delivered! God may keep you waiting, but He will always remember His promise and will appear in time to fulfill His sacred Word that cannot be broken. F. B. MEYER

God has a simplicity about Him in working out His plans, and yet He possesses a resourcefulness equal to any difficulty. His faithfulness to His trusting children is unwavering, and He is steadfast in holding to His purpose. In Joseph's life, we see God work through a fellow prisoner, later through a dream, and finally through lifting Joseph from a prison to the position of governor. And the length of Joseph's prison stay gave him the strength and steadiness he needed as governor.

It is always safe to trust God's methods and to live by His clock. SAMUEL DICKEY GORDON

God in His providence has a thousand keys to open a thousand different doors in order to deliver His own, no matter how desperate the situation may have become. May we be faithful to do our part, which is simply to suffer for Him, and to place Christ's part on Him and then leave it there. GEORGE MACDONALD

Difficulty is actually the atmosphere surrounding a miracle, or a miracle in its initial stage. Yet if it is to be a great miracle, the surrounding condition will be not simply a difficulty but an utter impossibility. And it is the clinging hand of His child that makes a desperate situation a delight to God.

DAY 275

This is the confidence we have in approaching God: that if we ask anything according to his will, he hears us. And if we know that he hears us—whatever we ask—we know that we have what we asked of him.

1 JOHN 5:14–15

Prayer can obtain everything: it can open the windows of heaven, and shut the gates of hell; it can put a holy constraint upon God, and detain an angel until he leave a blessing; it can open the treasures of rain, and soften the iron ribs of rocks till they melt into tears and a flowing river; prayer can unclasp the girdles of the north—saying to a mountain of ice, "Be thou removed hence, and cast into the bottom of the sea"; it can arrest the sun in the midst of his course, and send the swift-winged winds upon our errands; and to all these strange things and secret decrees, add unrevealed transactions which are above the stars.

When Hudson Taylor was asked if he ever prayed without any consciousness of joy, he replied: "Often: sometimes I pray on with my heart feeling like wood; often, too, the most wonderful answers have come when prayer has been a real effort of faith without any joy whatever."

I never prayed sincerely and earnestly for anything but it came; at some time—no matter how distant the day—somehow, in some shape, probably the last I should have devised, it came. ADONIRAM JUDSON

For years I've prayed, and yet I see no change.
The mountain stands exactly where it stood;
The shadows that it casts are just as deep;
The pathway to its summit e'en more steep.
Shall I pray on?
Shall I pray on with ne'er a hopeful sign?
Not only does the mountain still remain,
But, while I watch to see it disappear,
Becomes the more appalling year by year.
Shall I pray on?
I shall pray on. Though distant as it seems
The answer may be almost at my door,
Or just around the corner on its way,
But, whether near or far, yes, I shall pray—
I shall pray on.

EDITH MAPES

If thou wilt keep the incense burning there, His glory thou shalt see—sometime, somewhere!

DAY 276

The spirit shrieked, convulsed him violently and came out.

MARK 9:26

Evil never surrenders its grasp without a tremendous fight. We never arrive at any spiritual inheritance through the enjoyment of a picnic but always through the fierce conflicts of the battlefield. And it is the same in the deep recesses of the soul. Every human capacity that wins its spiritual freedom does so at the cost of blood. Satan is not put to flight by our courteous request. He completely blocks our way, and our progress must be recorded in blood and tears. We need to remember this, or else we will be held responsible for the arrogance of misinterpretation. When we are born again, it is not into a soft and protected nursery but into the open countryside, where we actually draw our strength from the distress of the storm. "We must go through many hardships to enter the kingdom of God" (Acts 14:22). JOHN HENRY JOWETT

Faith of our Fathers! living still,
In spite of dungeon, fire and sword:
Oh, how our hearts beat high with joy
Whene'er we hear that glorious word.
Faith of our Fathers! Holy Faith!
We will be true to Thee till death!
Our fathers, chained in prisons dark,
Were still in heart of conscience free;
How sweet would be their children's fate,
If they, like them, could die for Thee!

Oct 4th

DAY 277

If . . . God so commands, you will be able.

EXODUS 18:23

Charles G. Finney once said: "When God commands you to do a thing, it is the highest possible evidence, equal to an oath, that we can do it."

The thing that taxes Almightiness is the very thing that you as a disciple of Jesus Christ ought to believe He would do. Sometimes we must be shipwrecked upon the supernatural; we must be thrown upon God; we must lose the temporal—that we may find the Eternal.

"It is God who works" (Phil. 2:13). Men work like men and nothing more is expected of man than what man can do. But God worketh like a God, and with Him nothing is impossible.

There is for us a source of heightened power. A most suggestive translation (James Moffatt) of 1 Samuel 2:1 reads: My heart thrills to the Eternal; my powers are heightened by my God.

Amos was just a herdsman from Tekoa, but his powers were heightened by his God. It happened to Peter. It happened to Paul. Abraham Lincoln faced ending slavery.

We are all in need of more power, more courage, more wisdom than we actually possess. This "plus extra" comes to him whose heart thrills over the Eternal; who daily waits for Divine resources.

"Difficulty" is a relative term. It all depends upon the power you have available. Difficulty diminishes as the power increases; and altogether vanishes when the power rises to Omnipotence. "Our sufficiency is of God" (2 Cor. 3:5 KJV) All God's biddings are enablings. Always provided that we are on the line of God's written Word, in the current of His revealed purpose, there is nothing you may not trust Him for.

As one of a thousand you may just fail; but as "one, plus God," you are bound to win.

DAY 278

[God] will hear.

PSALM 55:19

I was standing at a bank counter in Liverpool waiting for a clerk to come. I picked up a pen and began to print on a blotter in large letters two words which had gripped me like a vise: "Pray through." I kept talking to a friend and printing until I had the desk blotter filled from top to bottom with a column. I transacted my business and went away. The next day my friend came to see me, and said he had a striking story to tell.

A businessman came into the bank soon after we had gone. He had grown discouraged with business troubles. He started to transact some business with the same clerk, over that blotter, when his eye caught the long column of "Pray through." He asked who wrote those words and when he was told exclaimed, "That is the very message I needed. I will pray through. I have tried in my own strength to worry through, and have merely mentioned my troubles to God; now I am going to pray the situation through until I get light." CHARLES M. ALEXANDER

Don't stop praying, but have more trust;
Don't stop praying! for pray we must;
Faith will banish a mount of care;
Don't stop praying! God answers prayer.

C. M. A.

All I have seen teaches me to trust the Creator for what I have not seen!

Oct 6th DAY 279

For he spoke and stirred up a tempest that lifted high the waves.

PSALM 107:25

Stormy wind fulfilling His word. By the time the wind blows upon us it is His wind for us. We have nothing to do with what first of all stirred up that wind. It could not ruffle a leaf on the smallest tree in the forest had He not opened the way for it to blow through the fields of air. He commandeth even the winds, and they obey Him. To the winds as to His servants He saith to one, "Go," and it goeth; and to another, "Come," and it cometh; and to another, "Do this," and it doeth it. So, whatever wind blows on us it is His wind for us, His wind fulfilling His word.

God's winds do effectual work. They shake loose from us the things that can be shaken, that those things which cannot be shaken may remain, those eternal things which belong to the Kingdom which cannot be moved. They have their part to play in stripping us and strengthening us so that we may be the more ready for the uses of Eternal Love. Then can we refuse to welcome them?

Art thou indeed willing for any wind at any time? GOLD BY MOONLIGHT

Be like the pine on the hilltop, alone in the wind for God.

There is a curious comfort in remembering that the Father depends upon His child not to give way. It is inspiring to be trusted with a hard thing. You never asked for summer breezes to blow upon your tree. It is enough that you are not alone upon the hill.

And let the storm that does Thy work deal with me as it may.

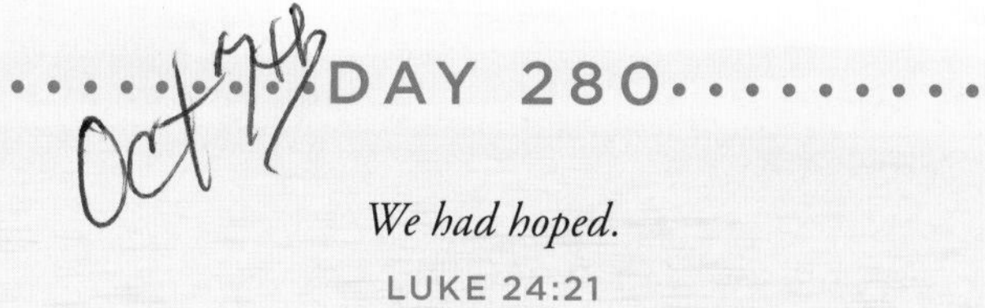

DAY 280

We had hoped.

LUKE 24:21

I have always been so sorry that the two disciples walking with Jesus on the road to Emmaus did not say to Him, "We still hope" instead of "We had hoped." The situation is very sad, because in their minds it is over.

Oh, if only they had said, "Everything has come against our hope, and it looks as if our trust were in vain. Yet we will not give up, because we believe we will see Him again." Instead, they walked by His side, declaring their shattered faith. Jesus had to say to them, "How foolish you are, and how slow to believe!" (Luke 24:25).

Are we not in danger of having these same words said to us? We can afford to lose every possession we have, except our faith in the God of truth and love. May we never express our faith, as these disciples did, in the past tense—"We had hoped." Yet may we always say, "I have hope." CRUMBS

The soft, sweet summer was warm and glowing,
Bright were the blossoms on every bough:
I trusted Him when the roses were blooming;
I trust Him now. . . .
Small was my faith should it weakly falter
Now that the roses have ceased to blow;
Frail was the trust that now should alter,
Doubting His love when storm clouds grow.

THE SONG OF A BIRD IN A WINTER STORM

DAY 281

Oct 8/4

You will be like a well-watered garden, like
a spring whose waters never fail.

ISAIAH 58:11

Holiness appeared to me to be of a sweet, pleasant . . . calm nature. It seemed to me . . . that it made the soul like a field or garden of God, with all manner of pleasant flowers— all pleasant, delightful and undisturbed; enjoying a sweet calm, and the gently vivifying beams of the sun.

The soul of a true Christian appeared like such a little white flower as we see in the spring of the year—low and humble on the ground—opening its bosom to receive the pleasant beams of the sun's glory—rejoicing, as it were, in a calm rapture—diffusing around a sweet fragrancy.

Once I rode out into the woods for my health. Having alighted from my horse in a retired place as my manner commonly had been, to walk for Divine contemplation and prayer, I had a view—that was for me extraordinary—of the glory of the Son of God. As near as I can judge, this continued about an hour; and kept me the greater part of the time in a flood of tears and weeping aloud. I felt an ardency of soul to be—what I know not otherwise how to express—emptied and annihilated; to love Him with a holy and pure love; to serve and follow Him; to be perfectly sanctified, and made pure with a Divine and heavenly purity. JONATHAN EDWARDS

> I never thought it could be thus, month after month to know
> The river of Thy peace without one ripple in its flow;
> Without one quiver in the trust, one flicker in the glow.

Oct 9th

DAY 282

Know for certain that for four hundred years your descendants will be strangers in a country not their own and that they will be . . . mistreated there. But . . . afterward they will come out with great possessions.

GENESIS 15:13–14

I can be sure that part of God's promised blessing to me is delay and suffering. The delay in Abraham's lifetime that seemed to put God's promise well beyond fulfillment was then followed by the seemingly unending delay experienced by Abraham's descendants. But it was indeed only a delay—the promise was fulfilled, for ultimately they did "come out with great possessions."

God is going to test me with delays, and along with the delays will come suffering. Yet through it all God's promise stands. I have His new covenant in Christ, and His sacred promise of every smaller blessing that I need. The delays and the suffering are actually part of the promised blessings, so may I praise Him for them today. May I "be strong and take heart and wait for the LORD" (Ps. 27:14). CHARLES GALLAUDET TRUMBULL

Unanswered yet the prayer your lips have pleaded
In agony of heart these many years?
Does faith begin to fail? Is hope departing?
And think you all in vain your falling tears?
Say not the Father has not heard your prayer;
You will have your desire sometime, somewhere.
Unanswered yet? No, do not say ungranted;
Perhaps your work is not yet wholly done.
The work began when first your prayer was uttered,
And God will finish what He has begun.
If you will keep the incense burning there,
His glory you will see sometime, somewhere.
Unanswered yet? Faith cannot be unanswered,
Its feet are firmly planted on the Rock;
Amid the wildest storms it stands undaunted,
Nor shakes before the loudest thunder shock.
It knows Omnipotence has heard its prayer,
And cries, "It will be done"—sometime, somewhere.

OPHELIA G. BROWNING

Oct 10th

DAY 283

Unless a kernel of wheat falls to the ground and dies, it remains only a single seed.

JOHN 12:24

A peasant once came to Tauler to confess; but in place of the peasant confessing to Tauler, Tauler confessed to the peasant. The great preacher said, "I am not satisfied." The peasant replied, "Tauler has to die before he can be satisfied."

That great man, who had thousands listening to him, withdrew to a place of quiet and asked God to work out that death in him.

After he had been there for two years, he came out and assembled his congregation. A great multitude came to hear him, for he had been a wonderful preacher. He began to preach, but he broke down and wept. The audience dispersed saying, "What is the matter with Tauler? He can't preach as he once did. He failed today!"

The next time he preached only a little handful came together—those who had caught a glimpse of something—and he preached to them in a brokenhearted way; but the power of God came down. God, by the power of the Spirit, had put John Tauler to death!

Beloved, are you willing to be crucified with Christ?

> Higher than the highest heavens,
> Deeper than the deepest sea,
> Lord, Thy love at last hath conquered:
> Grant me now my supplication,
> None of self, and all of Thee.

Oct. 11th DAY 284

The ark of the covenant of the Lord *went before them.*

NUMBERS 10:33

God sometimes does influence us with a simple touch or feeling, but not so we would act on the feeling. If the touch is from Him, He will then provide sufficient evidence to confirm it beyond the slightest doubt.

Consider the beautiful story of Jeremiah, when he felt God leading him to purchase the field at Anathoth. He did not act on his initial feeling but waited for God to completely fulfill His words to him before taking action. Then once his cousin came to him, bringing the external evidence of God's direction by making a proposal for the purchase, he responded and said, "I knew that this was the word of the Lord" (Jer. 32:8).

Jeremiah waited until God confirmed his feeling through a providential act, and then he worked with a clear view of the facts, which God could also use to bring conviction to others. God wants us to act only once we have His mind on a certain situation. We are not to ignore the Shepherd's personal voice to us, but like "Paul and his companions" (Acts 16:6) at Troas, we are to listen and also examine His providential work in our circumstances, in order to glean the full mind of the Lord. A. B. SIMPSON

Wherever God's finger points, His hand will clear a way.

Never say in your heart what you will or will not do but wait until God reveals His way to you. As long as that way is hidden, it is clear that there is no need of action and that He holds Himself accountable for all the results of keeping you exactly where you are.

> For God through ways we have not known,
> Will lead His own.

DAY 285

They reached the place God had told him about.

GENESIS 22:9

There the Lord bestows his blessing.

PSALM 133:3

Up, up the hill, to the whiter than snow-shine,
Help me to climb, and dwell in pardon's light.
I must be pure as Thou, or ever less
Than Thy design of me—therefore incline
My heart to take men's wrongs as Thou tak'st mine.

Have you come to the place God told you of? Have you gone through the sacrifice of death? Are you willing to make the moral decision that the thing die out in you which never was in Jesus?

Up to that whiter than snow-shine; up to that place that is as strong and firm as the Throne of God. Do not say, "That pure, white, holy life is never for me!" Let God lift you; let Him take the shrouds away; let Him lift up; up to the hill, to the whiter than snow-shine. And when you get to the top what do you find? A great, strong tableland, where your feet are on a rock; your steps enlarged under you; your goings established. OSWALD CHAMBERS

Jesus offers you "life more abundantly." Grasp the offer! Quit the boggy and dark low ground, and let Him lead you up higher! MOUNTAIN TOPS WITH JESUS

Take the supreme climb!
Jesus lead me up the mountain,
Where the whitest robes are seen,
Where the saints can see the fountain,
Where the pure are keeping clean.
Higher up, where light increases,
Rich above all earthly good,
Where the life of sinning ceases,
Where the Spirit comes in floods.
Lead me higher, nothing dreading,
In the race to never stop;
In Thy footsteps keep me treading,
Give me grace to reach the top.

Courage, my soul, and let us journey on!

Oct 13th

DAY 286

The peace of God, which transcends all understanding, will guard your hearts and your minds in Christ Jesus.

PHILIPPIANS 4:7

There is a part of the sea known as "the cushion of the sea." It lies beneath the surface that is agitated by storms and churned by the wind. It is so deep that it is a part of the sea that is never stirred. When the ocean floor in these deep places is dredged of the remains of plant or animal life, it reveals evidence of having remained completely undisturbed for hundreds, if not thousands, of years.

The peace of God is an eternal calm like the cushion of the sea. It lies so deeply within the human heart that no external difficulty or disturbance can reach it. And anyone who enters the presence of God becomes a partaker of that undisturbed and undisturbable calm. ARTHUR TAPPAN PIERSON

When winds are raging o'er the upper ocean,
And waves are tossed wild with an angry roar,
It's said, far down beneath the wild commotion,
That peaceful stillness reigns forevermore.
Far, far beneath, noise of tempests falls silent,
And silver waves lie ever peacefully,
And no storm, however fierce or violent,
Disturbs the Sabbath of that deeper sea.
So to the heart that knows Your love, O Father,
There is a temple sacred evermore,
And all life's angry voices causing bother
Die in hushed silence at its peaceful door.
Far, far away, the roars of strife fall silent,
And loving thoughts rise ever peacefully,

And no storm, however fierce or violent,
Disturbs the soul that dwells, O Lord, in Thee.
HARRIET BEECHER STOWE

Pilgrim was taken to a large upper room that faced the sunrise. And the name of the room was Peace. PILGRIM'S PROGRESS

DAY 287

Let perseverance finish its work so that you may be mature and complete, not lacking anything.
JAMES 1:4

Michelangelo went to Rome to carve statues, and found that other artists had taken over all the Carrara marble—all but one crooked and misshapen piece. He sat down before this and studied with infinite patience its very limitations, until he found that by bending the head of a statue here, and lifting its arms there, he could create a masterpiece: thus The Boy David was produced.

Let us sit down in front of our very limitations, and with the aid of patience dare to produce, with God's help, a masterpiece!

"I see the stubborn heights,
The bruising rocks, the straining soul."
"I see the goal!"
"I see the tearing plow,
The crushing drag, the beating rain."
"I see the grain!"
"I see compressing walls,
And seething flux, and heats untold."

"I see the gold!"
"I see the cruel blows,
The chisel sharp, the hammer's mace."
"I see My face!"

"OUR VIEW AND HIS" PHILIP WENDELL CRANNELL

Oct 15th

DAY 288

Doth the plowman plow all day to sow?

ISAIAH 28:24 KJV

Is not the plowing merely a preparation for the seed-sowing to follow, and after that for the wheat which is to feed many? When the plowshare goes through human hearts, surely it is for something! Someday we shall see when the ripe ears of corn appear, that the plowshare had to come for a season. We thought it would kill us! And no plowshare goes through the earth but some life is destroyed, but only that something better than that life may come.

Be still, poor heart! God is effectual in working. "Let him do what is good in his eyes" (1 Sam. 3:18).

God will not let my field lie fallow.
The plowshare is sharp, the feet of the oxen are heavy.
They hurt.
But I cannot stay God from His plowing.
He will not let my field lie fallow.

KARLE WILSON BAKER

I have seen a farmer drive his plowshare through the velvet greensward, and it looked like a harsh and cruel process; but the farmer's eye foresaw the springing blades of wheat, and knew that within a few months that torn soil would laugh with a golden harvest.

Deep soul-plowing brings rich fruits of the Spirit. There are bitter mercies as well as sweet mercies; but they are all mercies, whether given in honey or given in wormwood. T. L. CUYLER

The iron plowshare goes over the field of the heart until the nighttime . . . down the deep furrows the angels come and sow.

DAY 289

Understand what the Lord's will is.

EPHESIANS 5:17

It may seem a very terrible thing for the soul to yield itself wholly and unreservedly to the will of Christ. "What is going to happen? What about tomorrow? Will He not put a very heavy burden upon me if I yield; if I take the yoke?" Ah, you have not known my Master; you have not looked into His face; you have not realized His infinite love for you. Why, God's will for you means your fullest happiness! Christ's will and your deepest happiness are synonymous terms. How can you doubt that your Lord has planned for you the very best thing?

The admiral that goes out with his fleet under sealed orders does not know what is in the packet; but he goes out prepared to do the will of the Government of his country. And although it seems to you that you take from Christ the sealed packet of His will and know not what is in it, yet knowing who He is that has planned your future you can step out without realizing all that it means, just as you take His promises. The value of any promise depends upon the promiser; and so it is with His will. Whose will is it? Whose yoke is it?

"My yoke," says the gentle, loving Jesus; "Take My yoke upon you" (Matt. 11:29 NIV). To take His yoke is cheerfully to accept His will for us, not only in the present moment, but for the whole future that He has mapped out.

Surrender your will to God. He will never take advantage of you. EVAN H. HOPKINS

"I dare not promise, Lord," I cried,
"For future years close-sealed.
Surrender is a fearful thing—
I long—but dare not yield."
How clear and swift the answer came:
"I only ask of thee
A present of thyself for time
And for eternity."
An easy thing to make a gift!
My fears found swift release.
I gave myself to Him, and found
Past understanding, peace.

BERTHA GERNEAUX WOODS

Oct 17th

DAY 290

Now Moses was tending the flock of Jethro his father-in-law, the priest of Midian, and he led the flock to the far side of the wilderness and came to Horeb, the mountain of God. There the angel of the LORD *appeared to him in flames of fire from within a bush.*

EXODUS 3:1–2

The vision of the Angel of the Lord came to Moses while he was involved in his everyday work. That is exactly where the Lord delights in giving His revelations. He seeks a man traveling an ordinary road, and "suddenly a light from heaven" (Acts 9:3) shines on him. And a "stairway resting on the earth" (Gen. 28:12) can reach from the marketplace to heaven, transforming a life from one of drudgery to one of grace.

Beloved Father, help me to expect you as I travel the ordinary road of life. I am not asking for sensational experiences. Fellowship with me through my everyday work and service, and be my companion when I take an ordinary journey. And let my humble life be transformed by Your presence.

Some Christians think they must always be on the mountaintop of extraordinary joy and revelation, but this is not God's way. Those high spiritual times and wonderful communication with the unseen world are not promised to us, but a daily life of communion with Him is. And it is enough for us, for He will give us those times of exceptional revelation if it is the right thing for us.

There were only three disciples allowed to see the Transfiguration, and the same three also experienced the darkness of Gethsemane. No one can stay on the mountaintop of favor forever, for there are responsibilities in the valley. Christ fulfilled His life's work not in the glory but in the valley, and it was there He was truly and completely the Messiah.

The value of the vision and the accompanying glory is its gift of equipping us for service and endurance.

DAY 291

They were . . . preparing their nets. Jesus called them.

MATTHEW 4:21

Salome! Had you been with me in the boat,
    You would not chide and moan because our boys
Have gone with the Beloved from this our home.
    Let me, Salome, tell you how it came.
The night was still—the tide was running strong,
    Heavy our nets—the strain reached breaking point,
And while 'twas dark we docked, and as we worked
    I felt as though new strength and steady joy
Surged through my being, so I sang a Psalm—
    As David sang—a song to greet the morn;

And then my heart was filled with quiet calm.
The boat was soon in order, and we turned
To dry and mend our nets. Then Jesus came—
He called the boys, first John, then James, by name,
And they arose and went to follow Him.
I turned and gazed on Jesus standing there—
He seemed to me all clothed in shining light
As He stood in the pathway with the night
Behind Him and the dawn breaking around,
His form so radiant and glad and free.
And when He climbed the hill our sons went too—
James was behind, and John was by His side;
And when they talked, John scarcely seemed our John—
I felt that he had caught a marvelous light.
And all my being seemed to overflow;
I knew that night had passed—the dawn had come,
And then I knew that we must let them go.

"ZEBEDEE'S SONS"

"The share of the man who stayed with the supplies is to be the same as that of him who went down to the battle. All will share alike" (1 Sam. 30:24).

To some Christ calls: "Leave boat and bay,
And white-haired Zebedee";
To some the call is harder: "Stay
And mend the nets for Me."

DAY 292

Dear friends, do not be surprised at the fiery ordeal that has come to test you. . . . But rejoice inasmuch as you participate in the sufferings of Christ.

1 PETER 4:12–13

Many hours of waiting were necessary to enrich David's harp with song. And hours of waiting in the wilderness will provide us with psalms of "thanksgiving and the sound of singing" (Isa. 51:3). The hearts of the discouraged here below will be lifted, and joy will be brought to our Father's heavenly home.

What was the preparation for Jesse's son, David, to compose songs unlike any others ever heard before on earth? It was the sinful persecution he endured at the hands of the wicked that brought forth his cries for God's help. Then David's faint hope in God's goodness blossomed into full songs of rejoicing, declaring the Lord's mighty deliverances and multiplied mercies. Every sorrow was yet another note from his harp, and every deliverance another theme of praise.

One stinging sorrow spared would have been one blessing missed and unclaimed. One difficulty or danger escaped—how great would have been our loss! The thrilling psalms where God's people today find expression for their grief or praise might never have been known.

Waiting on God and abiding in His will is to know Him in "the power of his resurrection and participation in his sufferings" (Phil. 3:10) and "to be conformed to the likeness of his Son" (Rom. 8:29). Therefore if God's desire is to enlarge your capacity for spiritual understanding, do not be frightened by the greater realm of suffering that awaits you. The Lord's capacity for sympathy is greater still, for the breath of the Holy Spirit into His new creation never makes a heart hard and insensitive, but affectionate, tender, and true. ANNA SHIPTON

"I thank Christ Jesus our Lord, who has given me strength, that he considered me trustworthy, appointing me to his service" (1 Tim. 1:12).

DAY 293

Return to thy place, and abide with the king.

2 SAMUEL 15:19 KJV

There is a little fable which says that a primrose growing by itself in a shady corner of the garden became discontented as it saw the other flowers in their beds in the sunshine, and begged to be removed to a more conspicuous place. Its prayer was granted. The gardener transplanted it to a more showy and sunny spot. It was greatly pleased, but there came a change over it immediately. Its blossoms lost much of their beauty, and became pale and sickly. The hot sun caused them to faint and wither. So it prayed again to be taken back to its old place in the shade. The wise gardener knew best where to plant each flower.

So God, the Divine Husbandman, knows where His children will best grow into what He would have them to be. Some require the fierce storms; some will only thrive spiritually in the shadow of worldly adversity; and some come to ripeness more sweetly under the soft and gentle influences of prosperity, whose beauty rough experiences would mar.

Humbolt, the great naturalist and traveler, said that the most wonderful sight he had ever seen was a primrose flourishing on the bosom of a glacier.

> The brightest souls which glory ever knew
> Were rocked in storms and nursed when tempests blew.

DAY 294

I will make you into a threshing sledge, new and sharp.

ISAIAH 41:15

Around the turn of the twentieth century, a bar of steel was worth about $5. Yet when forged into horseshoes, it was worth $10; when made into needles, its value was $350; when used to make small pocketknife blades, its worth was $32,000; when made into springs for watches, its value increased to $250,000. What a pounding the steel bar had to endure to be worth this much! But the more it was shaped, hammered, put through fire, beaten, pounded, and polished, the greater its value.

May we use this analogy as a reminder to be still, silent, and long-suffering, for it is those who suffer the most who yield the most. And it is through pain that God gets the most out of us, for His glory and for the blessing of others.

Oh, give Your servant patience to be still,
And bear Your will;
Courage to venture wholly on Your arm
That will not harm;
The wisdom that will never let me stray
Out of my way;
The love that, now afflicting, yet knows best
When I should rest.

Our life is very mysterious. In fact, it would be totally unexplainable unless we believed that God was preparing us for events and ministries that lie unseen beyond the veil of the eternal world—where spirits like tempered steel will be required for special service.

The sharper the Craftsman's knives, the finer and more beautiful His work.

Oct 22nd

DAY 295

Whoever dwells in the shelter of the Most High
will rest in the shadow of the Almighty.

PSALM 91:1

It was my practice to rise at midnight for worship. God came to me at that precise time and awoke me from sleep that I might enjoy Him. He seemed to pervade my being. My soul became more and more attracted to Him like the waters of a river which pass into the ocean and after a time become one with it. Oh, unutterable happiness! Who could have thought that one should ever find happiness equal to this!

Hours passed like moments, when I could do nothing else but pray. It was a prayer of rejoicing, of possession, when the taste of God was so great, so pure, so unblended that it drew and absorbed the soul into a profound state of confiding and affectionate rest in God, without intellectual effort for I had no sight but of Jesus only. MADAME GUYON

A moment in the morning ere the cares of the day begin,
Ere the heart's wide door is open for the world to
enter in;
Ah, then, alone with Jesus, in the silence of the morn,
In heavenly sweet communion, let your happy day be born;
In the quietude that blesses with a prelude of repose,
Let your soul be soothed and softened as the dew revives the rose.

Two men were confessing to each other the causes of their failure in the ministry. "I let my hand slip out of God's hand," said one. The other said, "My soul-life raveled at the point where I ceased to pray, because there were things in my life I could not speak to God about." Prayer is a handclasp with God.

Take time for prayer if you have to take it by violence. Take time to behold Him!

DAY 296

Until now you have not asked for anything in my name.
Ask and you will receive, and your joy will be complete.

JOHN 16:24

During the American Civil War, a certain man had a son who enlisted in the Union army. The father was a banker, and although he gave his consent to his son, it seemed as if it would break his heart to let him go.

Once his son had left, he became deeply interested in the plight of soldiers, and whenever he saw one in uniform, his heart went out to him as he thought of his own dear boy. Often to the neglect of his business, he began spending his time and money to care for the soldiers who came home disabled. His friends pleaded with him not to neglect his business in this way, by spending so much time and energy on the soldiers. So he decided to give it all up, taking his friends' advice.

After he had made this decision, however, a young private in a faded, worn uniform stepped into the bank. It was easy to discern from the wounds on his face and hands that he had been in the army field hospital. The poor young man was fumbling in his pocket to find something, when the banker saw him. Perceiving his purpose for coming into the bank, he said to the soldier, "My dear man, I cannot help you today. I am extremely busy. You will have to go to the army headquarters, where the officers will take care of you."

The poor wounded soldier still stood there, not seeming to fully understand what was being said to him. He continued to fumble in his pockets and finally pulled out a scrap of dirty paper. He laid the filthy page before the banker, who read the following words written in pencil:

Dear Father,

This is one of my friends, who was wounded in the last battle and is coming to you directly from the hospital. Please receive him as you would me.

Charlie

All the banker's previous resolve to focus solely on his business instead of soldiers quickly flew away. He took the young man to his own magnificent home and gave him Charlie's room and seat at the dinner table. He cared for him until the food, rest, and love had returned him to health, and then sent him back to his place of service to again risk his life for his country's flag.

"Now you will see what I will do." EXODUS 6:1

Oct 24th

DAY 297

Because this widow keeps bothering me, I will see that she gets justice.

LUKE 18:5

We should be careful about what we ask from God; but when once we begin to pray for a thing we should never give up praying for it until we receive it, or until God makes it very clear and definite that it is not His will to grant it. R. A. TORREY

It is said of John Bradford that he had a peculiar art in prayer. When asked his secret, he said: "When I know what I want, I always stop on that prayer until I feel that I have pleaded it with God, and until God and I have had dealings with each other upon it. I never go on to another petition until I have gone through the first."

To the same point Mr. Spurgeon said: "Do not try to put two arrows on the string at once—they will both miss. He that would load his gun with two charges cannot expect to be successful. Plead once with God and prevail, and then plead again. Get the first answer and then go after the second. Do not be satisfied with running the colors of your prayers into one another until there is no picture to look at, but just a huge daub—a smear of colors badly laid on."

Far better would it be to know what our real needs are, and then concentrate our earnest supplications upon those definite objects, taking them thoughtfully one at a time.

"Ask what I shall give thee" (1 Kings 3:5 KJV).

Oct. 25th

DAY 298

He went up on a mountainside by himself to pray.
Later that night, he was there alone.

MATTHEW 14:23

Christ Jesus, in His humanity, felt the need of complete solitude—to be entirely by Himself, alone with Himself. Each of us knows how draining constant interchange with others can be and how it exhausts our energy. As part of humankind, Jesus knew this and felt the need to be by Himself in order to regain His strength. Solitude was also important to Him in order to fully realize His high calling, His human weakness, and His total dependence on His Father.

As a child of God, how much more do we need times of complete solitude—times to deal with the spiritual realities of life and to be alone with God the Father. If there was ever anyone who could dispense with special times of solitude and fellowship, it was our Lord. Yet even He could not maintain His full strength and power for His work and His fellowship with the Father without His quiet time. God desires that every servant of His would understand and perform this blessed practice, that His church would know how to train its children to recognize this high and holy privilege, and that every believer would realize the importance of making time for God alone.

Oh, the thought of having God all alone to myself and knowing that God has me all alone to Himself! ANDREW MURRAY

Lamartine, the first of the French Romantic poets and a writer of the nineteenth century, in one of his books wrote of how his mother had a secluded spot in the garden where she spent the same hour of each day. He related that nobody ever dreamed of intruding upon her for even a moment of that hour. It was the holy garden of the Lord to her.

Pity those people who have no such Beulah land! (See Isa. 62:4.) Jesus said, “Go into your room, close the door and pray” (Matt. 6:6), for it is in quiet solitude that we catch the deep and mysterious truths that flow from the soul of the things God allows to enter our lives.

A MEDITATION

My soul, practice being alone with Christ! The Scripture says, “When he was alone with his own disciples, he explained everything” (Mark 4:34). Do not wonder about the truth of this verse, for it can be true of your life as well. If you desire to have understanding, then dismiss the crowd, just as Jesus did. (See Matt. 14:22.) Let them “go away one at a time . . . until only Jesus [is] left” (John 8:9) with you. Have you ever pictured yourself as the last remaining person on earth, or the only person left in the entire universe?

If you were the only person remaining in the universe, your every thought would be, “God and I . . . ! God and I . . . !” And yet He is already as close to you as that. He is as near as if no heart but His and yours ever beat throughout the boundlessness of space.

O my soul, practice that solitude! Practice dismissing the crowd! Practice the stillness of your heart! Practice the majestic song “God and I! God and I!” Let no one come between you and your wrestling angel! You will receive conviction yet pardon, when you meet Jesus alone! GEORGE MATHESON

Oct 26th

DAY 299

God spoke.

GENESIS 46:2

Any man may hear the voice of God.

When man will listen, God speaks. When God speaks, men are changed. When men are changed, nations are changed.

In the ancient days God spoke, and the wonderful things which He told Moses on the mountaintop have inspired mankind for centuries.

Down through the years men of God have heard His voice. God spoke to George Müller, and he became the modern apostle of faith. Hudson Taylor heard Him speak, as he walked by the seashore on a memorable Sabbath morning, and in obedience to that Voice he launched forth into inland China, establishing Mission Stations in every province of that vast country.

God spoke to Dr. A. B. Simpson and he stepped aside from a well-beaten path, and like Abraham of old "obeyed and went, even though he did not know where he was going" (Heb. 11:8). Today, The Christian and Missionary Alliance, operating in more than twenty Mission Fields of the world, is the result of his obedience and untold numbers have been blessed through his ministry.

Charles Cowman heard the "soft and gentle Voice," when God spoke saying, "Get thee out of thy country, and from thy kindred, and from thy father's house, unto a land that I will shew thee" (Gen. 12:1 KJV). The result—One Mission Society, with hundreds of Mission Stations! And now its activities embrace the wide world.

God is not dumb that He should speak no more.
If thou hast wanderings in the wilderness
And find'st not Sinai, 'tis thy soul is poor:
There towers the mountain of the Voice no less,
Which whoso seeks shall find; but he who bends
Intent on manna still, and mortal ends,
Sees it not, neither hears its thundering lore.

LOWELL

Oct 27th

DAY 300

All your waves and breakers have swept over me.

PSALM 42:7

They are His waves, whether they break over us,
Hiding His face in smothering spray and foam;
Or smooth and sparkling, spread a path before us,
And to our haven bear us safely home.
They are His waves, whether for our sure comfort
He walks across them, stilling all our fear;
Or to our cry there comes no aid nor answer,
And in the lonely silence none is near.
They are His waves, whether we are hard-striving
Through tempest-driven waves that never cease,
While deep to deep with turmoil loud is calling;
Or at His word they hush themselves in peace.
They are HIS waves, whether He separates them,
Making us walk dry ground where seas had flowed;
Or lets tumultuous breakers surge about us,
Rushing unchecked across our only road.
They are His waves, and He directs us through them;
So He has promised, so His love will do.
Keeping and leading, guiding and upholding,
To His sure harbor, He will bring us through.

ANNIE JOHNSON FLINT

Stand firmly in the place where your dear Lord has put you, and do your best there. God sends us trials or tests, and places life before us as a face-to-face opponent. It is through the pounding of a serious conflict that He expects us to grow strong. The tree planted where the fierce winds twist its branches and bend its trunk, often nearly to the point of breaking, is commonly more firmly rooted than a tree growing in a secluded valley where storms never bring any stress or strain.

The same is true of human life. The strongest and greatest character is grown through hardship.

Oct 28th

DAY 301

You have made your way around this hill country long enough; now turn north.

DEUTERONOMY 2:3

Last summer a party of us lost our way among the lakes of Ontario. A violent storm came up, but we found shelter under a great rock till the storm raged past. Then we resumed our hunt dispiritedly until one said, "Let us climb this rock; we may spy the trail from the top." It was a hard climb, but the challenge of the rock restored our courage. As we conquered the heights we gained confidence and mastery, and the hilltop gave us a vision of our way out.

Get high enough up, you will be above the fog; and while the men down in it are squabbling as to whether there is anything outside the mist, you from your sunny station will see the far-off coasts, and haply catch some whiff of perfume from their shores, or see some glinting of glory upon the shining turrets of "a city which hath foundations" (Heb. 11:10 KJV).

The soul which hath launched itself forth upon God is in a free place, filled with the fresh air of the hills of God.

Oh, there are heavenly heights to reach
In many a fearful place,
While the poor, timid heir of God
Lies blindly on his face;

Lies languishing for light Divine
That he shall never see
'Till he goes forward at Thy sign,
And trusts himself to Thee.

C. A. FOX

We are continually retreating behind our limitations and saying, "Thus far and no farther can I go." God is ever laying His hand upon us and thrusting us into the open, saying, "You can be more than you are; you must be more than you are."

Are the hills of God thine atmosphere?

DAY 302

Because of his great love for us, God, who is rich in mercy, made us alive with Christ even when we were dead in transgressions. . . . And God raised us up with Christ and seated us with him in the heavenly realms in Christ Jesus.

EPHESIANS 2:4–6

This is our rightful place—"Seated . . . with him in the heavenly realms in Christ Jesus," yet seated and still. But how few of us actually experience this! In fact, most of us believe it is impossible to sit still "in the heavenly realms" while living our everyday life in a world so full of turmoil.

Oh, we believe it may be possible to visit these "heavenly realms" on Sundays or now and then during times of great spiritual emphasis and praise, but to actually be "seated" there all day, every day, is a completely different matter. Yet it is clear from the Scriptures that it is meant not only for Sundays but for weekdays as well.

A quiet spirit is of priceless value when performing outward activities. Nothing so greatly hinders the work of God's unseen spiritual forces, upon which our success in everything truly depends, as the spirit of unrest and anxiety.

There is tremendous power in stillness. A great believer once said, "All things come to him who knows how to trust and to be silent." This fact is rich with meaning, and a true understanding of it would greatly change our ways of working. Instead of continuing our restless striving, we would "sit down" inwardly before the Lord, allowing the divine forces of His Spirit to silently work out the means to accomplish our goals and aspirations.

You may not see or feel the inner workings of His silent power, but rest assured it is always mightily at work. And it will work for you, if you will only quiet your spirit enough to be carried along by the current of its power.

HANNAH WHITALL SMITH

There is a point of rest
At the great center of the cyclone's force,
A silence at its secret source;
A little child might slumber undisturbed,
Without the ruffle of one fair curl,
In that strange, central calm, amid the mighty whirl.

Make it your business to learn to be peaceful and safe in God through every situation.

DAY 303

We will flee on horses.

ISAIAH 30:16

God is never slow from His standpoint, but He is from ours, because impetuosity and doing things prematurely are universal weaknesses.

God lives and moves in eternity, and every little detail in His working must be like Himself, and have in it the majesty and measured movement, as well as the accuracy and promptness of infinite wisdom. We are to let God do the swiftness and we do the slowness.

The Holy Spirit tells us to "be quick to listen, slow to speak and slow to become angry" (James 1:19), that is, quick to take in from God, but slow to give out the opinions, the emotions of the creature.

We miss a great many things from God by not going slow enough with Him. Who would have God change His perfections to accommodate our whims? Have we not had glimpses into God's perfections, insight into wonderful truths, quiet unfoldings of daily opportunities, gentle checks of the Holy Spirit upon our decisions or words, sweet and secret promptings to do certain things?

There is a time for everything in the universe to get ripe—and to go slow with God is the heavenly pace that gathers up all things at the time they are ripe.

> What they win, who wait for God, is worth waiting for!
> Going slow with God is our greatest safety!

DAY 304

He will sit as a refiner and purifier of silver.

MALACHI 3:3

Our Father, who seeks to perfect His saints in holiness, knows the value of the refiner's fire. It is with the most precious metals that a metallurgist will take the greatest care. He subjects the metal to a hot fire, for only the refiner's fire will melt the metal, release the dross, and allow the remaining, pure metal to take a new and perfect shape in the mold.

A good refiner never leaves the crucible but, as the above verse indicates, "will sit" down by it so the fire will not become even one degree too hot and possibly harm the metal. And as soon as he skims the last bit of dross from the surface and sees his face reflected in the pure metal, he extinguishes the fire. ARTHUR TAPPAN PIERSON

He sat by a fire of sevenfold heat,
As He looked at the precious ore,
And closer He bent with a searching gaze
As He heated it more and more.
He knew He had ore that could stand the test,
And He wanted the finest gold
To mold as a crown for the King to wear,
Set with gems with a price untold.
So He laid our gold in the burning fire,
Though we would have asked for delay,
And He watched the dross that we had not seen,
And it melted and passed away.
And the gold grew brighter and yet more bright,
But our eyes were so dim with tears,
We saw but the fire—not the Master's hand,
And questioned with anxious fears.
Yet our gold shone out with a richer glow,
As it mirrored a Form above,
That bent o'er the fire, though unseen by us,
With a look of unspeakable love.
Should we think that it pleases His loving heart
To cause us a moment's pain?
Not so! for He saw through the present cross
The joy of eternal gain.
So He waited there with a watchful eye,
With a love that is strong and sure,
And His gold did not suffer a bit more heat,
Than was needed to make it pure.

Nov 15th

DAY 305

Not yours, but God's.

2 CHRONICLES 20:15

There are times when doing nothing is better than doing something. Those are the times when only God can do what is needed. True faith trusts Him then, and Him alone, to do the miracle. Moses and Jehoshaphat knew this secret; they knew the same Lord and the same Divine grace.

As the pursuing Egyptians trapped the helpless Israelites at the Red Sea, Moses said: "Do not be afraid. Stand firm and you will see the deliverance the LORD will bring you. . . . The LORD will fight for you; you need only to be still" (Ex. 14:13–14).

As the Moabites and the Ammonites, a vast multitude, closed in on Judah, King Jehoshaphat said to the helpless people: "Do not be afraid or discouraged because of this vast army. For the battle is not yours, but God's. . . . You will not have to fight this battle. Take up your positions; stand firm and see the deliverance the LORD will give you" (2 Chron. 20:15, 17, emphasis added).

When God alone can win the victory, faith lets God do it all. It is better to trust than to try. SUNDAY SCHOOL TIMES

"FAITH IS THE VICTORY THAT OVERCOMES"

The battle is not yours, but God's;
Therefore why fight?
True faith will cease from struggling,
And rest upon His might:
Each conflict into which you come
Was won on Calvary,
'Tis ours to claim what Christ has done,
And "hold" the victory.

H. E. JESSOP

"Hold thee still." "And this," says Saint Jerome, "is the hardest precept that is given to man: inasmuch as the most difficult precept of action sinks into nothingness when compared with this command to inaction."

DAY 306

Let us run with patience.

HEBREWS 12:1 KJV

Running "with patience" is a very difficult thing to do. The word "running" itself suggests the absence of patience, or an eagerness to reach the goal. Yet we often associate patience with lying down or standing still. We think of it as an angel who guards the bed of the disabled. Yet I do not believe that the kind of patience a disabled person may have is the hardest to achieve.

There is another kind of patience that I believe is harder to obtain—the patience that runs. Lying down during a time of grief, or being quiet after a financial setback, certainly implies great strength, but I know of something that suggests even greater strength—the power to continue working after a setback, the power to still run with a heavy heart, and the power to perform your daily tasks with deep sorrow in your spirit. This is a Christlike thing!

Many of us could tearlessly deal with our grief if only we were allowed to do so in private. Yet what is so difficult is that most of us are called to exercise our patience not in bed but in the open street, for all to see. We are called upon to bury our sorrows not in restful inactivity but in active service—in our workplace, while shopping, and during social events—contributing to other people's joy. No other way of burying our sorrow is as difficult as this, for it is truly what is meant by running "with patience."

Dear Son of Man, this was Your kind of patience. It was both waiting and running at one time—waiting for the ultimate goal while in the meantime doing lesser work. I see You at Cana of Galilee, turning water into wine so the marriage feast would not be ruined. I see You in the desert, feeding the multitude with bread, simply to relieve a temporary need. Yet all the time, You were bearing a mighty grief—not shared or spoken. Others may ask for a "rainbow in the clouds" (Gen. 9:13), but I would ask for even more from You. Make me, in my cloud, a rainbow bringing the ministry of joy to others. My patience will only be perfect when it works in Your vineyard. GEORGE MATHESON

When all our hopes are gone,
It is best our hands keep toiling on
For others' sake:
For strength to bear is found in duty done;
And he is best indeed who learns to make
The joy of others cure his own heartache.

Nov 3rd

DAY 307

Then he lay down under the bush and fell asleep.
All at once an angel touched him.

1 KINGS 19:5

God does not chide His tired child when that weariness is a result of toil for Him: "I know . . . your hard work" (Rev. 2:2)—the Greek is "labor to weariness." And what happened? "All at once an angel touched him." There is no wilderness without its angels. Though Elijah knew it not, angels guarded him round about in his blackest depression and were actually placing bread and water at his head while he was asking for death.

A man may have to cry in the midst of an apostate community, "I am the only one left" (1 Kings 19:10); but he is always companied by legions of holy angels. But more than that. Who is this angel? It is the Angel of the Lord, the Jehovah Angel; the One who, centuries later in Gethsemane, had to have an angel to strengthen Him. He touched His exhausted child. Blessed exhaustion that can bring such a touch!

As the psalmist has said (Ps. 127:2), "he grants sleep to those he loves." And God does not chide His tired child. THE DAWN

Dear child, God does not say today, "Be strong";
He knows your strength is spent; He knows how long
The road has been, how weary you have grown,
For He who walked the earthly roads alone,
Each bogging lowland, and each rugged hill,
Can understand, and so He says, "Be still,
And know that I am God." The hour is late,
And you must rest awhile, and you must wait
Until life's empty reservoirs fill up
As slow rain fills an empty upturned cup.
Hold up your cup, dear child, for God to fill.
He only asks today that you be still.

GRACE NOLL CROWELL

Nov 4th

DAY 308

In the same way, the Spirit helps us in our weakness. We do not know what we ought to pray for, but the Spirit himself intercedes for us through wordless groans. And he who searches our hearts knows the mind of the Spirit, because the Spirit intercedes for God's people in accordance with the will of God.

ROMANS 8:26–27

This is a deep mystery of prayer. It is a delicate, divine tool that words cannot express and theology cannot explain, but the humblest believer knows, even when he does not understand.

Oh, the burdens we lovingly bear but cannot understand! Oh, the inexpressible longings of our hearts for things we cannot comprehend! Yet we know they are an echo from the throne of God, and a whisper from His heart. They are often a groan rather than a song, and a burden rather than a floating feather. But they are a blessed burden, and a groan whose undertone is praise and unspeakable joy. They are "wordless groans." We cannot always express them ourselves, and often all we understand is that God is praying in us for something that only He understands and that needs His touch.

So we can simply pour from the fullness of our heart the burden of our spirit and the sorrow that seems to crush us. We can know that He hears, loves, understands, receives, and separates from our prayer everything that is in error, imperfect, or wrong. And then He presents the remainder, along with the incense of the great High Priest, before His throne on high. We may be assured that our prayer is heard, accepted, and answered in His name. A. B. SIMPSON

It is not necessary to be continually speaking to God, or always hearing from God, in order to have communion or fellowship with Him, for there is an unspeakable fellowship that is sweeter than words. A little child can sit all day long beside his mother, totally engrossed in his playing, while his mother is consumed by her work, and although both are busy and few words are spoken by either, they are in perfect fellowship. The child knows his mother is there, and she knows that he is all right.

In the same way, a believer and his Savior can continue many hours in the silent fellowship of love. And although the believer may be busy with the ordinary things of life, he can be mindful that every detail of his life is touched by the character of God's presence, and can have the awareness of His approval and blessing.

Then when troubled with burdens and difficulties too complicated to put into words and too puzzling to express or fully understand, how sweet it is to fall into the embrace of His blessed arms and to simply sob out the sorrow that we cannot speak!

DAY 309

Therefore, the promise comes by faith, so that it may be . . . guaranteed.

ROMANS 4:16

The great devotional teacher of the past century, Dr. Andrew Murray, said, "When you get a promise from God it is worth just as much as fulfillment. A promise brings you into direct contact with God. Honor Him by trusting the promise and obeying Him." Worth just as much as fulfillment. Do we grasp the truth often? Are we not frequently in the state of trying to believe, instead of realizing that these promises bring us into contact with God? "God's promise is as good as His presence." To believe and accept the promise of God is not to engage in some mental gymnastics where we reach down into our imaginations and begin a process of auto-suggestion, or produce a notional faith in which we argue with ourselves in an endeavor to believe God. It is absolute confidence in and reliance upon God through His Word.

By a naked faith in a naked promise I do not mean a bare assent that God is faithful, and that such a promise in the Book of God may be fulfilled in me, but a bold, hearty, steady venturing of my soul, body, and spirit upon the truth of the promise with an appropriating act. FLETCHER

"The faith that will shut the mouths of lions must be more than a pious hope that they will not bite."

DAY 310

When the cloud remained . . . the Israelites . . . did not set out.

NUMBERS 9:19

This was the ultimate test of obedience. It was relatively easy to fold up their tents when the fleecy cloud slowly gathered over the tabernacle and began to majestically float ahead of the multitude of the Israelites. Change normally seems pleasant, and the people were excited and interested in the route, the scenery, and the habitat of the next stopping place.

Yet having to wait was another story altogether. "When the cloud remained," however uninviting and sweltering the location, however trying to flesh and blood, however boring and wearisome to those who were impatient, however perilously close their exposure to danger—there was no option but to remain encamped.

The psalmist said, "I waited patiently for the LORD; he turned to me and heard my cry" (Ps. 40:1). And what God did for the Old Testament saints, He will do for believers down through the ages, yet He will often keep us waiting. Must we wait when we are face to face with a threatening enemy, surrounded by danger and fear, or below an unstable rock? Would this not be the time to fold our tents and leave? Have we not already suffered to the point of total collapse? Can we not exchange the sweltering heat for "green pastures . . . [and] quiet waters" (Ps. 23:2)?

When God sends no answer and "the cloud remain[s]," we must wait. Yet we can do so with the full assurance of God's provision of manna, water from the rock, shelter, and protection from our enemies. He never keeps us at our post without assuring us of His presence or sending us daily supplies.

Young person, wait—do not be in such a hurry to make a change! Minister, stay at your post! You must wait where you are until the cloud clearly begins to move. Wait for the Lord to give you His good pleasure! He will not be late!

An hour of waiting!
Yet there seems such need
To reach that spot sublime!
I long to reach them—but I long far more
To trust His time!
"Sit still, My children"—
Yet the heathen die,
They perish while I stay!
I long to reach them—but I long far more
To trust His way!
It's good to get,
It's good indeed to give!
Yet it is better still—
O'er breadth, through length, down depth, up height,
To trust His will!

F. M. N.

DAY 311

Your path led through the sea, your way through the mighty waters.

PSALM 77:19

God's path led through the sea"—just where you would not expect it to be! So when He leads us out by unexpected ways, off the strong solid land, out upon the changing sea, then we may expect to see His ways. We are with One who finds a path already tracked out, for it makes us perfectly independent of circumstances.

There is an infinite variety in the paths God makes, and He can make them anywhere! Think you not that He, who made the spider able to drop anywhere and to spin its own path as it goes, is not able to spin a path for you through every blank, or perplexity, or depression? God is never lost among our mysteries. He sees the road, "the end from the beginning."

Mystery and uncertainty are only to prepare us for deeper discipline. Had we no stormy sea we should remain weaklings to the end of our days. God takes us out into the deeps; but He knows the track! He knows the haven! and we shall arrive.

And with Jesus through the trackless deep move on! C. A. FOX

"Oh, the depth of the riches of the wisdom and knowledge of God! How unsearchable his judgments, and his paths beyond tracing out!" (Rom. 11:33).

Nov 8th

DAY 312

Peter was kept in prison, but the church was earnestly praying to God for him.

ACTS 12:5

Prayer is the link that connects us with God. It is the bridge that spans every gulf and carries us safely over every chasm of danger or need.

Think of the significance of this story of the first-century church: Everything seemed to be coming against it, for Peter was in prison, the Jews appeared triumphant, Herod still reigned supreme, and the arena of martyrdom was eagerly awaiting the next morning so it could drink the apostle's blood. "But the church was earnestly praying to God for him." So what was the outcome? The prison was miraculously opened, the apostle freed, the Jews bewildered, and as a display of God's punishment, wicked King Herod "was eaten by worms and died." And rolling on to even greater victory, "the word of God continued to spread and flourish" (vv. 23–24).

Do we truly know the power of our supernatural weapon of prayer? Do we dare to use it with the authority of a faith that not only asks but also commands? God baptizes us with holy boldness and divine confidence, for He is looking not for great people but for people who will dare to prove the greatness of their God! "But the church was earnestly praying." A. B. SIMPSON

In your prayers, above everything else, beware of limiting God, not only through unbelief but also by thinking you know exactly what He can do. Learn to expect the unexpected, beyond all that you ask or think.

So each time you intercede through prayer, first be quiet and worship God in His glory. Think of what He can do, how He delights in Christ His Son, and of your place in Him—then expect great things. ANDREW MURRAY

Our prayers are God's opportunities.

Are you experiencing sorrow? Prayer can make your time of affliction one of strength and sweetness. Are you experiencing happiness? Prayer can add a heavenly fragrance to your time of joy. Are you in grave danger from some outward or inward enemy? Prayer can place an angel by your side whose very touch could shatter a millstone into smaller grains of dust than the flour it grinds, and whose glance could destroy an entire army.

What will prayer do for you? My answer is this: Everything that God can do for you. "Ask for whatever you want me to give you" (2 Chron. 1:7). FREDERICK WILLIAM FARRAR

Wrestling prayer can wonders do,
Bring relief in dire straits;
Prayer can force a passage through
Iron bars and heavy gates.

DAY 313

[Jesus'] life may also be revealed in our mortal body.

2 CORINTHIANS 4:11

We may have two lives. First, our own life inherited from our parents and given us by our Creator. That life has some value, but how soon it fails and feels the forces of disease, decay, and approaching death!

But we may have another life, or rather the Life of Another—the life also of Jesus. How much more valuable and transcendent is this life! It has no weakness nor decay nor limitation. Jesus has a physical life as real as ours, and infinitely greater; He is an actual man with a glorified body and a human spirit. And that life belongs to us just as much as the precious blood He shed and the spiritual grace He bestows. He has risen and ascended as our living Head and He is ever saying to us, "Because I live, ye shall live also" (John 14:19 KJV).

Why should we limit Him to what we call the spiritual realm? His resurrection body has in it all the vitality and strength that our mortal frame can ever need. Someday He is to raise us from the dead by virtue of that resurrection life. Why should it be thought a strange thing if faith may now foredate its inheritance and claim in advance part of its physical redemption—a little handful of the soil of that better country—just as a seed is to bring forth more glorious fruit?

This was Paul's experience. Why may it not be ours? There was a day at Lystra when under a shower of stones Paul's life was ebbing out and he was left for dead outside the city gates. Then it was that the life also of Jesus asserted itself, and, calmly rising up in the strength of his Master, he walked back through the streets whose stones were stained by his own blood, and quietly went on his way preaching the Gospel as if nothing had happened.

The secret of this life is to live so close to Jesus that we shall breathe His very breath and ever be in touch with His life and love. So let us live by Him.

Healing is in His living body. We receive it as we abide in Him. We keep it only as we abide in Him. A. B. SIMPSON

There are miraculous possibilities for the one who depends on God.

DAY 314

You who bring good news to Zion, go up on a high mountain.

ISAIAH 40:9

Toys and trinkets are easily earned, but the most valuable things carry a heavy price. The highest places of power are always bought with blood, and you can attain those pinnacles if you have enough blood to pay. That is the condition of conquering holy heights everywhere. The story of true heroics is always the story of sacrificial blood. The greatest values and character in life are not blown randomly across our path by wayward winds, for great souls experience great sorrows.

Great truths are dearly bought, the common truths,
Such as we give and take from day to day,
Come in the common walk of easy life,
Blown by the careless wind across our way.
Great truths are greatly won, not found by chance,
Nor wafted on the breath of summer dream;
But grasped in the great struggle of our soul,
Hard buffeting with adverse wind and stream.
But in the day of conflict, fear, and grief,
When the strong hand of God, put forth in might,
Plows up the subsoil of our stagnant heart,
And brings the imprisoned truth seed to the light.
Wrung from the troubled spirit, in hard hours
Of weakness, solitude, and times of pain,

Truth springs like harvest from the well-plowed field,
And our soul feels it has not wept in vain.

Our capacity for knowing God is enlarged when we are brought by Him into circumstances that cause us to exercise our faith. So when difficulties block our paths, may we thank God that He is taking time to deal with us, and then may we lean heavily on Him.

DAY 315

Burst into song.

ISAIAH 49:13

There is a beautiful story which tells of songbirds being brought over the sea. There were thirty-six thousand, mostly canaries. The sea was very calm when the ship first sailed, and the little birds were silent. They kept their little heads under their wings and not a note was heard. But the third day out at sea, the ship struck a furious gale. The passengers were terrified. Children wept. Then a strange thing happened. As the tempest reached its height, the birds began to sing, first one, then another, until the thirty-six thousand were singing as if their little throats would burst.

When the storm rises in its fury, do we then begin to sing? Should not our song break forth in tenfold joy when the tempest begins?

I can hear the songbirds singing their refrain
It is morning in my heart;
And I know that life for me begins again,
It is morning in my heart.
It is morning, it is morning in my heart,
Jesus made the gloomy shadows all depart;

Songs of gladness now I sing,
For since Jesus is my King,
It is morning, it is morning in my heart.

O God, wilt Thou teach us to begin the music of heaven! Grant us grace to have many rehearsals of eternal Hallelujahs! "Bless the LORD, O my soul: and all that is within me, bless his holy name" (Ps. 103:1 KJV)!

Try singing! Singing in the storm!

Nov 12th

DAY 316

I was among the exiles by the Kebar River, the heavens were opened and I saw visions of God. . . . There the hand of the LORD was on [me].

EZEKIEL 1:1, 3

There is nothing that makes the Scriptures more precious to us than a time of "captivity." The old psalms of God's Word have sung for us with compassion by our stream at Babel and have resounded with new joy as we have seen the Lord deliver us from captivity and "restore our fortunes, . . . like streams in the Negev" (Ps. 126:4).

A person who has experienced great difficulties will not be easily parted from his Bible. Another book may appear to others to be identical, but to him it is not the same. Over the old and tear-stained pages of his Bible, he has written a journal of his experiences in words that are only visible to his eyes. Through those pages, he has time and again come to the pillars of the house of God and "to Elim, where there were . . . palm trees" (Ex. 15:27). And each of those pillars and trees have become a remembrance for him of some critical time in his life.

In order to receive any benefit from our captivity, we must accept the situation and be determined to make the best of it. Worrying over what we have lost or what has been taken from us will not make things better but will only prevent us from improving what remains. We will only serve to make the rope around us tighter if we rebel against it.

In the same way, an excitable horse that will not calmly submit to its bridle only strangles itself. And a high-spirited animal that is restless in its yoke only bruises its own shoulders. Everyone will also understand the analogy that Laurence Sterne, a minister and author of the eighteenth century, penned regarding a starling and a canary. He told of the difference between a restless starling that broke its wings struggling against the bars of its cage and continually cried, "I can't get out! I can't get out!" and a submissive canary that sat on its perch and sang songs that surpassed even the beauty of those of a lark that soared freely to the very gates of heaven.

No calamity will ever bring only evil to us, if we will immediately take it in fervent prayer to God. Even as we take shelter beneath a tree during a downpour of rain, we may unexpectedly find fruit on its branches. And when we flee to God, taking refuge beneath the shadow of His wing, we will always find more in Him than we have ever before seen or known.

Consequently, it is through our trials and afflictions that God gives us fresh revelations of Himself. Like Jacob, we must cross "the ford of the Jabbok" (Gen. 32:22) if we are ever to arrive at Peniel, where he wrestled with the Lord, was blessed by Him, and could say, "I saw God face to face, and yet my life was spared" (Gen. 32:30).

Make this story your own, dear captive, and God will give you "songs in the night" (Job 35:10) and will turn your "midnight into dawn" (Amos 5:8).

NATHANIEL WILLIAM TAYLOR

Submission to God's divine will is the softest pillow on which to rest.

It filled the room, and it filled my life,
With a glory of source unseen;
It made me calm in the midst of strife,

And in winter my heart was green.
And the birds of promise sang on the tree
When the storm was breaking on land and sea.

Nov 13 '47

DAY 317

When Joseph saw Benjamin with them, he said to the steward of his house, "Take these men to my house, slaughter an animal and prepare a meal; they are to eat with me at noon."

GENESIS 43:16

When their brother, who was to be their savior, saw that they had brought with them the dearest treasure of their family, there went forth the instant word for a king's feast to be prepared for them.

That is all that my Savior is waiting for that He may lavish the fullness of His bounty upon me: my bringing to Him the dearest possession of my life—myself—in unconditional surrender to His mastery, confessing my helplessness and awful need. Then He gives the word that I may come into His own house and eat at His table the best food of which He Himself partakes.

The surrender of Benjamin, their dearest possession, was the key to all the treasures of the kingdom—yes, even to the recognition of Joseph by the brothers and Jacob. The surrender of the costliest possession of my life is the key to the treasures of the Kingdom for me—yes, even to the full recognition and appropriation of Christ as my whole and only life.

Oh, Lord Jesus, show me more that I may give up, that I may have more of Thee! MESSAGES FOR THE MORNING WATCH

My friend, beware of me
Lest I should do

The very thing I'd sooner die than do,
In some way crucify the Christ in you.
If you are called to some great sacrifice,
And I should come to you with frightened eyes
And cry, "Take care, take care, be wise, be wise!"
See through my softness then a fiend's attack,
And bid me get me straight behind your back;
To your own conscience and your God be true,
Lest I play Satan to the Christ in you.
And I would humbly ask of you in turn
That if someday in me Love's fires should burn
To whiteness, and a Voice should call
Bidding me leave my little for God's all,
If need be, you would thrust me from your side—
So keep love loyal to the Crucified.

Nov 14th

DAY 318

Is anything too hard for the LORD?

GENESIS 18:14

This is God's loving challenge to you and me each day. He wants us to think of the deepest, highest, and worthiest desires and longings of our hearts. He wants us to think of those things that perhaps were desires for ourselves or someone dear to us, yet have gone unfulfilled for so long that we now see them as simply lost desires. And God urges us to think of even the one thing that we once saw as possible but have given up all hope of seeing fulfilled in this life.

That very thing, as long as it aligns with what we know to be His expressed will—as a son was to Abraham and Sarah—God intends to do for us. Yes, if we will let Him, God will do that very thing, even if we know it is such an utter impossibility that we would simply laugh at the absurdity of anyone ever suggesting it could come to pass.

"Is anything too hard for the LORD?" No, nothing is too difficult when we believe in Him enough to go forward, doing His will and letting Him do the impossible for us. Even Abraham and Sarah could have blocked God's plan if they had continued to disbelieve.

The only thing "too hard for the LORD" is our deliberate and continual disbelief in His love and power, and our ultimate rejection of His plans for us. Nothing is impossible for Jehovah to do for those who trust Him. MESSAGES FOR THE MORNING WATCH

DAY 319

But even if I am being poured out like a drink offering on the sacrifice and service coming from your faith, I am glad and rejoice with all of you. So you too should be glad and rejoice with me.

PHILIPPIANS 2:17–18

The leading symbol of our Christian faith is not an easy chair, or a feather-bed: it is a Cross. If we would be His disciples, let us be prepared to live dangerously; to take up the Cross and carry it into the teeth of opposition.

God is at perfect liberty to waste us if He chooses.

When the fight seems fierce, and you are tempted to be weary and disconsolate, remember that in the interest of His cause your Leader expects you to turn a glad face to the world—to rejoice and be exceeding glad!

I have shamed Thee; craven-hearted
I have been Thy recreant knight;

Own me yet, O Lord, albeit
Weeping whilst I fight!
"Nay," He said, "Wilt thou yet shame Me?
Wilt thou shame thy knightly guise?
I would have my angels wonder
At thy gladsome eyes."
Need'st thou pity, knight of Jesus?
Pity for thy glorious hest?
Oh, let God and men and angels
See that thou are blest!

SUSO

DAY 320

Those whom I love I rebuke and discipline.

REVELATION 3:19

God selects the best and most notable of His servants for the best and most notable afflictions, for those who have received the most grace from Him are able to endure the most afflictions. In fact, an affliction hits a believer never by chance but by God's divine direction. He does not haphazardly aim His arrows, for each one is on a special mission and touches only the heart for whom it is intended. It is not only the grace of God but also His glory that is revealed when a believer can stand and quietly endure an affliction. JOSEPH CARYL

If all my days were sunny, could I say,
"In His fair land He wipes all tears away"?
If I were never weary, could I keep
This blessed truth, "He gives His loved ones sleep"?

If no grave were mine, I might come to deem
The Life Eternal but a baseless dream.
My winter, and my tears, and weariness,
Even my grave, may be His way to bless.
I call them ills; yet that can surely be
Nothing but love that shows my Lord to me!

Christians with the most spiritual depth are generally those who have been taken through the most intense and deeply anguishing fires of the soul. If you have been praying to know more of Christ, do not be surprised if He leads you through the desert or through a furnace of pain.

Dear Lord, do not punish me by removing my cross from me. Instead, comfort me by leading me into submission to Your will and by causing me to love the cross. Give me only what will serve You best, and may it be used to reveal the greatest of all Your mercies: bringing glory to Your name through me, according to Your will. CAPTIVE'S PRAYER

DAY 321

Every place that the sole of your foot shall tread upon, that have I given unto you.

JOSHUA 1:3 KJV

This blessed inspiring word greeted Israel as they faced the Promised Land. They had the promise of it before; now they must go forward into it and place their feet upon it. The promise is in the perfect tense and denotes an act just now completed—"That have I given unto you."

Our Joshua gives us the same incentive for conquest: every promise in the New Testament that we put our feet upon is ours! The upland of spiritual power is yours though Anak may live there! It is yours if you will but go against him and drive him out of his strongholds, in the might of The Name.

If we dare to place our foot on anything God has promised He makes it real to us. So take Him as the supply for all your need: believe He is yours and never doubt it from this moment.

It may be your need is for spiritual cleansing. His promise covers this: "Now ye are clean through the word which I have spoken unto you" (John 15:3 KJV). If you can believe this you shall be sanctified and kept.

Take the promise that suits your need, and step out on it; not touching it timidly on tiptoe, but placing your foot flat down upon it. Do not be afraid it will not hold your weight. Put your whole need on the Word of the eternal God for your soul, for your body, for your work, for the dear ones for whom you are praying, for any crisis in your life: then stand upon it forever!

All the blessed promises of the Old Book are yours, and why are you so slack to go up and possess your land? The size of your inheritance depends upon how much land you have trodden underfoot, really stood on or walked over. Between you and your possessions that huge mountain looms up. March up to it and make it yours! Go in this thy might and God will get glory; and you, victory. A. B. SIMPSON

Footprints mean possession, but it must be your own footprints.

DAY 322

Nov 18th

Whatever were gains to me I now consider loss for the sake of Christ.

PHILIPPIANS 3:7

When George Matheson, the blind Scottish preacher, was buried, they lined his grave with red roses commemorating his life of love and sacrifice. And it was Matheson, this man who was so beautifully and significantly honored, who wrote the following hymn in 1882. It was written in five minutes, during a period he later called "the most severe mental suffering," and it has since become known around the world.

O Love that wilt not let me go,
I rest my weary soul in Thee,
I give Thee back the life I owe,
That in thine ocean depths its flow
May richer, fuller be.
O Light that followest all my way,
I yield my flickering torch to Thee,
My heart restores its borrowed ray,
That in Thy sunshine's glow its day
May brighter, fairer be.
O Joy that seekest me through pain,
I cannot close my heart to Thee,
I trace the rainbow through the rain,
And feel the promise is not vain,
That morn shall tearless be.
O Cross that liftest up my head,
I dare not ask to hide from Thee,
I lay in dust life's glory dead,
And from the ground there blossoms red,
Life that shall endless be.

There is a legend of an artist who had found the secret of a wonderful red that no other artist could imitate. He never told the secret of the color, but after his death an old wound was discovered over his heart. It revealed the source of the matchless hue in his pictures.

The moral of the legend is that no great achievement can be made, no lofty goal attained, nor anything of great value to the world accomplished, except at the cost of the heart's blood.

DAY 323

"In that day," declares the LORD, "you will call me 'my husband.'"

HOSEA 2:16

The coming of the Comforter is a holy thing, a solemn act, and must be preceded by an intelligent and solemn covenant between the soul and God. It is the marriage of the soul to the Redeemer, and it is not a "trial marriage." No true marriage is rushed into carelessly. It is carefully considered, and it is based upon complete separation and consecration and the most solemn pledges and vows. So, if the Comforter is come to abide, to be with us and in us evermore, we must come out and be separate for Him, we must consecrate ourselves to Jesus fully and forever, and we must covenant to be the Lord's "for better or for worse," and we must trust Him. The soul that thus truly and solemnly dedicates itself to Him becomes His, and He will come to that soul to abide forever, to be its "shield, and . . . exceeding great reward" (Gen. 15:1 KJV).

Take not back the gift you have voluntarily laid on the altar.

Jesus, Thy life is mine!
Dwell evermore in me;
And let me see
That nothing can untwine
Thy life from mine.
Thy life in me be shown!
Lord, I would henceforth seek
To think and speak
Thy thoughts, Thy words alone,
No more my own.
Thy fullest gift, O Lord,
Now at Thy word I claim,

Through Thy dear Name,
And touch the rapturous chord
Of praise forth-poured.
Jesus, my life is Thine,
And evermore shall be
Hidden in Thee!
For nothing can untwine
Thy life from mine.

FRANCES RIDLEY HAVERGAL

"Thou shalt abide [live] for me many days; . . . thou shalt not be for another man: so will I also be for thee" (Hos. 3:3 KJV).

DAY 324

He took Peter, John and James with him and went up onto a mountain to pray. As he was praying, the appearance of his face changed, and his clothes became as bright as a flash of lightning. . . . Peter and his companions . . . saw his glory.

LUKE 9:28–29, 32

If you are pleased with me, teach me your ways.

EXODUS 33:13

When Jesus took these three disciples up onto the mountain alone, He brought them into close communion with Himself. They "saw his glory" and said, "It is good for us to be here" (Luke 9:32–33). Heaven is never far from those who linger on a mountain with their Lord.

Who of us in certain moments of meditation and prayer has not caught a glimpse of the heavenly gates? Who has not in the secret place of holy communion felt a surging wave of emotion—a taste of the blessed joy yet to come?

The Master had special times and places for quiet conversation with His disciples. He met with them once on Mount Hermon but more often on the sacred slopes of the Mount of Olives. Every Christian should have his own Mount of Olives. Most of us today, especially those of us in cities, live under great stress. From early morning until bedtime we are exposed to the whirlwind of life. Amid all the turmoil, there is little opportunity for quiet thought, God's Word, prayer, and fellowship of the heart!

Even Daniel needed to have his Mount of Olives in his room amid the roar of idolatrous Babylon. Peter found a rooftop in Joppa, and Martin Luther found an "upper room" in Wittenberg, a place that is still considered sacred.

Joseph Parker, an English Congregationalist preacher of the nineteenth century, once said, "If we, as the church, do not get back to spiritual visions, glimpses of heaven, and an awareness of a greater glory and life, we will lose our faith. Our altar will become nothing but cold, empty stone, never blessed with a visit from heaven." And this is the world's need today—people who have seen their Lord. THE LOST ART OF MEDITATION

Come close to Him! Perhaps He will take you today to the mountaintop—the same place He took Peter with his blundering, and James and John, the "sons of thunder" (Mark 3:17), who time and again totally misunderstood their Master and His mission. There is no reason why He will not take you, so do not shut yourself out by saying, "Oh, these wonderful visions and revelations of the Lord are only for certain people!" They may be for you! JOHN THOMAS MCNEILL

Nov 21st

DAY 325

God has made the one as well as the other.

ECCLESIASTES 7:14

Too often we see life's prose, but not its poetry. Too often we miss the inspiration of the songs. How manifold are our sorrows, but how manifold are His gifts!

Sin is here, but so is boundless grace; the devil is here, but so is Christ; the sword of judgment is crossed by Mercy's scepter.

"Judgment and Mercy," according to a lovely Jewish legend, "were sent forth together after the Fall to minister to the sinning but redeemed race," and together they still act. One afflicts, the other heals; where one rends, the other plants a flower; one carves a wrinkle, the other kindles a smile; the rainbow succeeds the storm; the succoring wing covers our naked head from the glittering sword.

Gethsemane had its strengthening Angel!

God everlastingly sets Mercies over against Miseries! His interventions are never mistimed. He never comes at the wrong season. God has the affairs of the world in His hands. In your blackest crises the angel presences are doubtless in your neighborhood!

God never strikes the wrong note; never sings the wrong song. If God makes music, the music will prove medicinal. JOSEPH PEARCE

With mercy and with judgment
My web of time He wove.
And aye the dews of sorrow
Were lustered with His love,
I'll bless the Hand that guided,
I'll bless the Heart that planned,
When throned where glory dwelleth,
In Immanuel's land.

Deep waters crossed life's pathway,
The hedge of thorns was sharp;
Now, these lie all behind me—
Oh! For a well-tuned harp!
Oh! to join Hallelujahs
With your triumphant band,
Who sing, where glory dwelleth
In Immanuel's land.

SAMUEL RUTHERFORD

Listen for the night-songs of God!

Nov. 22nd

DAY 326

People will dwell again in his shade; they will flourish like the grain, they will blossom like the vine.

HOSEA 14:7

The day ended with heavy showers, and the plants in my garden were beaten down by the pelting storm. I looked at one plant I had previously admired for its beauty and had loved for its delicate fragrance. After being exposed to the merciless storm, its flowers had drooped, all its petals were closed, and it appeared that its glory was gone. I thought to myself, I suppose I will have to wait till next year to see those beautiful flowers again.

Yet the night passed, the sun shone again, and the morning brought strength to my favorite plant. The light looked at its flowers and the flowers looked at the light. There was contact and communion, and power passed into the flowers. They lifted their heads, opened their petals, regained their glory, and seemed more beautiful than before. I wondered how this took place—these feeble flowers coming into contact with something much stronger, and gaining strength!

I cannot explain exactly how we are able to receive the power to serve and to endure through communion with God, but I know it is a fact. Are you in danger of being crushed by a heavy and difficult trial? Then seek communion with Christ and you will receive strength and the power to be victorious, for God has promised, "I will strengthen you" (Isa. 41:10).

YESTERDAY'S GRIEF

The falling rain of yesterday is ruby on the roses,
Silver on the poplar leaf, and gold on willow stem;
The grief that fell just yesterday is silence that encloses
God's great gifts of grace, and time will never trouble them.
The falling rain of yesterday makes all the hillsides glisten,
Coral on the laurel and beryl on the grass;
The grief that fell just yesterday has taught the soul to listen
For whispers of eternity in all the winds that pass.
O faint of heart, storm-beaten, this rain will shine tomorrow,
Flame within the columbine and jewels on the thorn,
Heaven in the forget-me-not; though sorrow now is sorrow,
Yet sorrow will be beauty in the magic of the morn.

KATHERINE LEE BATES

Nov. 23rd

DAY 327

Righteousness goes before him and prepares the way for his steps.

PSALM 85:13

How I ascertain the will of God:

I seek at the beginning to get my heart into such a state that it has no will of its own in regard to a given matter.

Nine-tenths of the trouble with people is right here. Nine-tenths of the difficulties are overcome when our hearts are ready to do the Lord's will, whatever it may be. When one is truly in this state it is usually but a little way to the knowledge of what His will is.

Having surrendered my own will, I do not leave the result to feeling or simply impressions. If I do so, I make myself liable to great delusions.

I seek the will of the Spirit of God through, or in connection with, the Word of God.

The Spirit and the Word must be combined. If the Holy Ghost guides us at all, He will do it according to the Scriptures, and never contrary to them.

Next I take into account providential circumstances. These often plainly indicate God's will in connection with His Word and Spirit.

I ask God in prayer to reveal His will to me aright.

Thus, through prayer to God, the study of His Word, and reflection, I come to a deliberate judgment, and if my mind is thus at peace, and continues so after two or three more petitions, I proceed accordingly. In trivial matters, and in transactions involving most important issues, I have found this method always effective. GEORGE MÜLLER

Nov 24th

DAY 328

Against all hope, Abraham in hope believed.

ROMANS 4:18

Abraham's faith seemed to be in complete agreement with the power and constant faithfulness of Jehovah. By looking at the outer circumstances in which he was placed, he had no reason to expect the fulfillment of God's promise. Yet he believed the Word of the Lord and looked forward to the time when his descendants would be "as numerous as the stars in the sky" (Gen. 26:4).

Dear soul, you have not been given only one promise, like Abraham, but a thousand promises. And you have been given the example of many faithful believers as a pattern for your life. Therefore it is simply to your advantage to rely with confidence upon the Word of God. And although He may delay in sending His help, and the evil you are experiencing may seem to become worse and worse, do not be weak. Instead, be strong and rejoice, for God usually steps forward to save us when we least expect it, fulfilling His most glorious promises in a miraculous way.

He generally waits to send His help until the time of our greatest need, so that His hand will be plainly seen in our deliverance. He chooses this method so we will not trust anything that we may see or feel, as we are so prone to do, but will place our trust solely on His Word—which we may always depend upon, no matter our circumstance. C. H. VON BOGATZKY

Remember, the very time for faith to work is when our sight begins to fail. And the greater the difficulties, the easier it is for faith to work, for as long as we can see certain natural solutions to our problems, we will not have faith. Faith never works as easily as when our natural prospects fail. GEORGE MUELLER

Nov 25th

DAY 329

But he was pierced for our transgressions, he was crushed for our iniquities; the punishment that brought us peace was on him, and by his wounds we are healed.

ISAIAH 53:5

He was led like a lamb to the slaughter.

ISAIAH 53:7

Yet it was the LORD's will to crush him.

ISAIAH 53:10

I came alone to my Calvary,
And the load I bore was too great for me;

The stones were sharp and pierced my feet,
And my temples throbbed with the withering heat.
But my heart was faint with the toil that day,
So I sat down to think of an easy way;
Loomed sharply before me that tortuous trail—
No use to try—I would only fail.
I turned back in sorrow, clothed with defeat,
For my load was too heavy; I would retreat
To easier highways, with scenery more fair—
Yet a moment I lingered watching there.
As I held my gaze on that flinty side,
A man came up to be crucified;
He toiled all the way of that painful road,
And the cross that he bore far surpassed my load:
His brow with thorns was pierced and torn;
His face had a look of pain and was worn;
He stopped for a moment and looked on me—
And I followed in rapture to Calvary!

"MY CALVARY," BY MATTHEW BILLER

Haunt the place called Calvary.

DAY 330

May he be like rain falling on a mown field.

PSALM 72:6

Amos tells of "the king's mowings" (Amos 7:1 KJV). Our King also has many scythes and is constantly using them to mow His lawns. The bell-like sound of the whetstone against the scythe foretells of the cutting down of countless blades of grass, daisies, and other flowers. And as beautiful as they were in the morning, within a few hours they will lie in long, faded rows.

In human life, we try to take a brave stand before the scythe of pain, the shears of disappointment, or the sickle of death. And just as there is no way to cultivate a lawn like velvet without repeated mowings, there is no way to develop a life of balance, tenderness, and sympathy for others without enduring the work of God's scythes.

Think how often the Word of God compares people to grass, and God's glory to its flower. But when the grass is cut, when all the tender blades are bleeding, and when desolation seems to reign where flowers once were blooming, the perfect time has come for God's rain to fall as delicate showers so soft and warm.

Dear soul, God has been mowing you! Time and again the King has come to you with His sharp scythe. But do not dread His scythe—for it is sure to be followed by His shower. F. B. MEYER

When across the heart deep waves of sorrow
Break, as on a dry and barren shore;
When hope glistens with no bright tomorrow,
And the storm seems sweeping evermore;
When the cup of every earthly gladness
Bears no taste of the life-giving stream;
And high hopes, as though to mock our sadness,
Fade and die as in some restless dream,
Who will hush the weary spirit's chiding?
Who the aching void within will fill?
Who will whisper of a peace abiding,
And each surging wave will calmly still?
Only He whose wounded heart was broken
With the bitter cross and thorny crown;
Whose dear love glad words of joy had spoken,
Who His life for us laid meekly down.

Blessed Healer, all our burdens lighten;
Give us peace. Your own sweet peace, we pray!
Keep us near You till the morn does brighten,
And all the mists and shadows flee away!

DAY 331

Even though refined by fire.

1 PETER 1:7

"What makes this set of china so much more expensive than that?" asked the customer.

"It has more work on it. It has been put through the fire twice. See, in this one the flowers are in a yellow band; in that one they are on the white background. This had to be put through the fire a second time to get the design on it."

"Why is the pattern on this vessel so blurred and marred—the design not brought out clearly?"

"That one was not burned enough. Had it remained in the furnace longer the dark background would have become gold—dazzling gold, and the pattern would have stood out clear and distinct."

Perhaps some of those who seem to have more than their share of suffering and disappointment are, like the costly china, being doubly tried in the fire, that they may be more valuable in the Master's service.

The potter never sees his clay take on rich shades of silver, or red, or cream, or brown, or yellow, until after the darkness and the burning of the furnace. These colors come—after the burning and darkness. The clay is beautiful—after the burning and darkness. The vase is made possible—after the burning and darkness.

How universal is this law of life! Where did the bravest man and the purest woman you know get their whitened characters? Did they not get them as the clay gets its beauty—after the darkness and the burning of the furnace? Where did Savonarola get his eloquence? In the darkness and burning of the furnace wherein God discovered deep things to him. Where did Stradivari get his violins? Where did Titian get his color? Where did Angelo get his marble? Where did Mozart get his music, and Chatterton his poetry, and Jeremiah his sermons? They got them where the clay gets its glory and its shimmer—in the darkness and the burning of the furnace. ROBERT G. LEE

Thou who didst fashion man on earth, to be
Strong in Thy strength, and with Thy freedom free,
Complete at last Thy great design in me.
Cost what it may of sorrow and distress,
Of empty hands, of utter loneliness,
I dare not, Lord, be satisfied with less.
So, Lord, reclaim Thy great design in me, Give or reclaim
Thy gifts, but let me be
Strong in Thy strength, and with Thy freedom free.
Let us not rebel at the second breath of the flame if He
sends it.

Nov 28th

DAY 332

These were the potters, and those that dwelt among plants and hedges: there they dwelt with the king for his work.

1 CHRONICLES 4:23 KJV

We may dwell "with the king for his work" anywhere and everywhere. We may be called to serve Him in the most unlikely places and under the most adverse conditions. It may be out in the countryside, far away from the King's many activities in the city. Or it may be "among plants and hedges" of all kinds—hindrances that surround us, blocking our way. Perhaps we will be one of "the potters," with our hands full of all types of pottery, accomplishing our daily tasks.

It makes no difference! The King who placed us "there" will come and dwell with us. The hedges, or hindrances, are right for us, or He will quickly remove them. And doesn't it stand to reason that whatever seems to block our way may also provide for our protection? As for the pottery—it is exactly what He has seen fit to place in our hands and is for now "his work." FRANCES RIDLEY HAVERGAL

Go back to your garden plot, sweetheart!
Go back till the evening falls,
And tie your lilies and train your vines,
Till for you the Master calls.
Go make your garden fair as you can,
You will never work alone;
Perhaps he whose plot is next to yours
Will see it and mend his own.

Brightly colored sunsets and starry heavens, majestic mountains and shining seas, and fragrant fields and fresh-cut flowers are not even half as beautiful as a soul who is serving Jesus out of love, through the wear and tear of an ordinary, unpoetic life. FREDERICK WILLIAM FABER

The most saintly souls are often those who have never distinguished themselves as authors or allowed any major accomplishment of theirs to become the topic of the world's conversation. No, they are usually those who have led a quiet inner life of holiness, having carried their sweet bouquets unseen, like a fresh lily in a secluded valley on the edge of a crystal stream. KENELM DIGBY

Nov. 29th

DAY 333

To him who is able to keep you from stumbling and to present you before his glorious presence without fault and with great joy.

JUDE V. 24

Take that word keep and hold it close to your heart tonight and tomorrow. It is one of the great and magnificent messages of the Gospel—He "is able to keep you from stumbling." Put into the word you all the weakness, all the unworthiness, all the sinfulness which belongs to man since the Fall; yet, He is able to keep you. He does not underrate the disadvantage of its being you when He bids His messengers say He is "able to keep you from stumbling." It would be impossible, utterly impossible, were it not undertaken by Infinite love. Look out, and up, then. Look up "from the depth"—the vast depth of your weakness, perhaps of your mysteriously inherited weakness. Look out of your failure under some temptation, inward or outward, inherited so to speak from yourself, from your own unfaithfulness in the past. Look up, out of your ruined purposes—unto Himself.

Being what He is, Keeper of Israel, God of the promises, Lord of the Sacrifice, Prince of life, present Savior, indwelling Power, He is able to keep you, that your feet shall not totter. They shall stand "in a large room" (Ps. 31:8 KJV); they shall hold on straight, until at last they enter, step by step—for it is one step at a time even then—"Through the gates into the city" (Rev. 22:14 KJV).

"He shall never give thy feet to tottering." H. C. G. MOULE

We may step firmly down upon the temptation which Another has crushed for us, and we are conquerors in Him.

Behind the dim unknown standeth God within the shadows keeping watch above His own.

Nov 30th

DAY 334

I have chosen him, so that he will direct his children.

GENESIS 18:19

God chooses people He can depend upon. He knew what to expect from Abraham and said of him, "I have chosen him, so that he will direct his children . . . that the LORD will bring about for Abraham what he has promised him." God knew Abraham would "direct his children." The Lord can be depended upon, and He desires for us to be just as reliable, determined, and stable. This is simply the meaning of faith.

God is looking for people on whom He can place the weight of His entire love, power, and faithful promises. And His engines are strong enough to pull any weight we may attach to them. Unfortunately, the cable we fasten to the engine is often too weak to handle the weight of our prayers. Therefore God continues to train and discipline us in His school of stability and certainty in the life of faith. May we learn our lessons well and then stand firm. A. B. SIMPSON

God knows that you can withstand your trial, or else He would not have given it to you. His trust in you explains the trials of your life, no matter how severe they may be. God knows your strength, and He measures it to the last inch. Remember, no trial has ever been given to anyone that was greater than that person's strength, through God, to endure it.

DAY 335

Enoch walked faithfully with God.

GENESIS 5:22

A day's walk with God will do more to awaken awe, wonder, and amazement in your soul than would a century of travel through the sights of the earth. He chooses for you a way you know not, that you may be compelled into a thousand intercourses with Him, which will make the journey ever memorable with glory to Him and blessing to you.

Jesus, these eyes have never seen
That radiant form of Thine;
The veil of sense hangs dark between
Thy blessed face and mine.
I see Thee not, I hear Thee not,
Yet art Thou oft with me;
And earth hath ne'er so dear a spot
As where I meet with Thee.
Like some bright dream that comes unsought
When slumbers o'er me roll,
Thine image ever fills my thought
And charms my ravished soul.
Yet though I have not seen, and still
Must rest in faith alone,
I love Thee, dearest Lord, and will,
Unseen but not unknown.

HYMNS OF CONSECRATION AND FAITH

··········DAY 336··········

Unless a kernel of wheat falls to the ground and dies, it remains only a single seed. But if it dies, it produces many seeds.

JOHN 12:24

In Northampton, Massachusetts, stands the old cemetery where David Brainerd is buried. Brainerd, a pioneer American missionary, died in 1747 at the age of twenty-nine after suffering from tuberculosis. His grave is beside that of Jerusha Edwards, the daughter of Jonathan Edwards, a Puritan theologian of that day. Brainerd loved Jerusha and they were engaged to be married, but he did not live until the wedding.

Imagine what hopes, dreams, and expectations for the cause of Christ were buried in the grave with the withered body of that young missionary. At that point, nothing remained but memories and several dozen Native American converts! Yet Jonathan Edwards, that majestic old Puritan saint, who had hoped to call Brainerd his son, began to write the story of that short life in a little book. The book took wings, flew across the sea, and landed on the desk of a Cambridge student by the name of Henry Martyn.

Poor Henry Martyn! In spite of his education, brilliance, and great opportunities, he—after reading that little book on the life of Brainerd—threw his own life away! Afterward, what had he accomplished once he set his course toward home from India in 1812? With his health then broken, he dragged himself as far north as the town of Tokat, Turkey, near the Black Sea. There he lay in the shade of a pile of saddles, to cool his burning fever, and died alone at the age of thirty-one.

What was the purpose behind these "wasted lives"? From the grave of a young David Brainerd, and the lonely grave of Henry Martyn near the shores of the Black Sea, have arisen a mighty army of modern missionaries.

LEONARD WOOLSEY BACON

Is there some desert, or some boundless sea,
Where You, great God of angels, will send me?
Some oak for me to rend,
Some sod for me to break,
Some handful of Your corn to take
And scatter far afield,
Till it in turn will yield
Its hundredfold
Of grains of gold
To feed the happy children of my God?
Show me the desert, Father, or the sea;
Is it Your enterprise? Great God, send me!
And though this body lies where ocean rolls,
Father, count me among all faithful souls.

DAY 337

Stay here and keep watch with me.

MATTHEW 26:38

When He needed God most in the greatest crisis of His life, Jesus sought a garden. Under the olive trees, with the Passover moon shining down upon Him, He prayed in agony for strength to do God's will. Only those who have been through such agony can realize even in part what that bleak hour of renunciation, for the sake of you and me, meant to Christ.

Are we willing that He should suffer Gethsemane and the Cross for us in vain?

"I go to pray," He said to the eight,
"Rest here at the gate."
But He spake to the three entreatingly,
"Will you watch with me as I pray

A stone's throw away?
I suffer tonight exceedingly."
The eight slept well at the garden gate
(As tired men will);
The three tossed fitfully within,
(Twice half-roused by His need of them)
But they slept—
Till the black in the East turned gray,
Till their garments were drenched with the tears of the day:
Slept
Till He called them—each one by his name—
The three within, and the eight at the gate.
The ground was hard where the eight had slept
(As hard as the road the soldiers stepped);
The grass was bent where the three had dreamt,
But red where the Lord had wept.

MIRIAM LEFEVRE CROUSE

"Couldn't you men keep watch with me for one hour?" (Matt. 26:40).

Dec 4th DAY 338

We were under great pressure.

2 CORINTHIANS 1:8

So that Christ's power may rest on me.

2 CORINTHIANS 12:9

God allowed the crisis in Jacob's life at Peniel to totally surround him until he ultimately came to the point of making an earnest and humble appeal to God Himself. That night, he wrestled with God and literally came to the place where he could take hold of Him as never before. And through his narrow brush with danger, Jacob's faith and knowledge of God was expanded, and his power to live a new and victorious life was born.

The Lord had to force David, through the discipline of many long and painful years, to learn of the almighty power and faithfulness of his God. Through those difficult years, he also grew in his knowledge of faith and godliness, which were indispensable principles for his glorious career as the King of Israel.

Nothing but the most dangerous circumstances in which Paul was constantly placed could ever have taught him, and thus the church through him, the full meaning of the great promise of God he learned to claim: "My grace is sufficient for you" (2 Cor. 12:9). And nothing but the great trials and dangers we have experienced would ever have led some of us to know Him as we do, to trust Him as we have, and to draw from Him the great measure of His grace so indispensable during our times of greatest need.

Difficulties and obstacles are God's challenges to our faith. When we are confronted with hindrances that block our path of service, we are to recognize them as vessels for faith and then to fill them with the fullness and complete sufficiency of Jesus.

As we move forward in faith, simply and fully trusting Him, we may be tested. Sometimes we may have to wait and realize that "perseverance [must] finish its work" (James 1:4). But ultimately we will surely find "the stone rolled away" (Luke 24:2) and the Lord Himself waiting to bestow a double blessing on us for our time of testing. A. B. SIMPSON

DAY 339

This love that surpasses knowledge.

EPHESIANS 3:19

We do not really see the ocean. To do that is beyond our power. Through that vista we glimpse a bit of blue water as though God has painted a picture and framed it with hills and trees. But southward and northward on distance-hidden shores stretches water we have never seen. Bays lie placid by sunlit rocks, and long surges roll in soothing rhythm on smoothly sloping sands. Inlets ripple under tropic moons, and warming currents bear springtime's promise to frozen arctic reefs. Beyond that curved blue line that limits our sight, there rolls an open plain of waters to realms where we have never been, leaving the strands of palmy islands of which we do not know. And this is but the surface! Beneath are miles of depth, fathomless with mysteries beyond the thoughts of men.

God's measureless love is like the ocean. Through the windows of earthly life we catch a gleam. From the valleys of trouble we glimpse it near the shore. On the sands of hope we see it, wave on wave. From the headlands of faith we view a broader tide to the line that blends eternity with time. Our happiest days are islands set in its boundless breadth. Yet, as with the ocean, we have never seen it all! Even eternity cannot reveal its greatness to the wondering hosts of heaven, nor all the universe exhaust the fountains whence it flows.

We can only see a little of the ocean,
Just a few miles distant from the rocky shore,
But out there—far beyond our eyes' horizon,
There's more—immeasurably more.
We can only see a little of God's loving—
A few rich treasures from His mighty store;
But out there—far beyond our eyes' horizon,
There's more—immeasurably more.

DAY 340

They triumphed over him by the blood of the Lamb . . . ; they did not love their lives so much as to shrink from death.

REVELATION 12:11

When James and John came to Christ with their mother, asking Him to give them the best place in His kingdom, He did not refuse their request. He told them that the place would be given to them if they could do His work, drink His cup, and be baptized with His baptism. (See Mark 10:38.)

Are we willing to compete for God's best, with the knowledge that the best things are always achieved by the most difficult paths? We must endure steep mountains, dense forests, and the Enemy's chariots of iron, since hardship is the price of the victor's coronation. Arches of triumph are made not of rose blossoms and strands of silk but of hard blows and bloody scars. The very hardships you are enduring in your life today have been given to you by the Master, for the express purpose of enabling you to win your crown.

Therefore do not always look ahead to your tomorrows for some ideal situation, exotic difficulty, or faraway emergency in which to shine. Rise today to face the circumstances in which the providence of God has placed you. Your crown of glory is hidden in the heart of these things—the hardships and trials pressing in on you this very hour, week, and month of your life. Yet the most difficult things are not those seen and known by the world but those deep within your soul, unseen and unknown by anyone except Jesus. It is in this secret place that you experience a little trial that you would never dare to mention to anyone else and that is more difficult for you to bear than martyrdom.

Beloved, your crown lies there. May God help you to overcome and to wear it.

It matters not how the battle goes,
The day how long;
Faint not! Fight on!
Tomorrow comes the song.

DAY 341

Dec 7th

Lord, come to my aid!

ISAIAH 38:14

Are you feeling that life for you has become a tangled skein; tangled with problems that seem to be desperately hard to unravel? If so, examine them and see whether it be not true that somewhere in the tangle there is the golden thread of an obvious present duty. Commence with that thread: what ought you to do next? Now! Never mind tomorrow!

Father, my life is in tangle,
Thread after thread appears
Twisted and broken and knotted,
Viewed through the lapse of years.
I cannot straighten them, Father;
Oh, it is very hard;
Somehow or other it seemeth,
All I have done is marred.
I did not see they were getting
Into this tangled state;
How it has happened I know not—
Is it too late, too late?
Is it? "Ah, no!" Thou dost whisper,
"Out of this life of thine

Yet may come wonderful beauty
Wrought by My Power Divine."
Take then, the threads, O my Father,
Let them Thy mind fulfill,
Work out in love a pattern
After Thy holy will!

CHARLOTTE MURRAY

The case looks utterly hopeless. Hope is dead—yea, buried, and the bones are lying scattered at the grave's mouth. But the eye fixed on the living God can bring a resurrection. Hope may yet flourish again. The net of terrible entanglement may be broken by a Father's hand, and liberty and life abundant may yet be mine!

The Savior can solve every problem,
The tangles of life can undo,
There is nothing too hard for Jesus,
There is nothing that He cannot do.

OSWALD J. SMITH

Dec 8th

DAY 342

Listen to what the unjust judge says. And will not God bring about justice for his chosen ones, who cry out to him day and night? Will he keep putting them off? I tell you, he will see that they get justice, and quickly.

LUKE 18:6–8

God's timing is not ours to command. If we do not start the fire with the first strike of our match, we must try again. God does hear our prayer, but He may not answer it at the precise time we have appointed in our own minds. Instead, He will reveal Himself to our seeking hearts, though not necessarily when and where we may expect. Therefore we have a need for perseverance and steadfast determination in our life of prayer.

In the old days of flint, steel, and brimstone matches, people had to strike the match again and again, perhaps even dozens of times, before they could get a spark to light their fire, and they were very thankful if they finally succeeded. Should we not exercise the same kind of perseverance and hope regarding heavenly things? When it comes to faith, we have more certainty of success than we could ever have had with flint and steel, for we have God's promises as a foundation.

May we, therefore, never despair. God's time for mercy will come—in fact, it has already come, if our time for believing has arrived. Ask in faith without wavering, but never cease to petition the King simply because He has delayed His reply.

Strike the match again and make the sparks fly. Yet be sure to have your tinder ready, for you will get a fire before long. CHARLES H. SPURGEON

I do not believe there is such a thing in the history of God's eternal kingdom as a right prayer, offered in the right spirit, that remains forever unanswered. THEODORE L. CUYLER

Dec. 9th

DAY 343

But take heart!

JOHN 16:33

Jesus said, "Ye shall have tribulation" (v. 33 KJV)—not difficulties, but tribulation. But "tribulation worketh patience" (Rom. 5:3 KJV).

Millstones are used to grind the corn to powder, and typify the sacredness of the discipline of life.

"No man shall take the nether or the upper millstone to pledge: for he taketh a man's life to pledge" (Deut. 24:6 KJV).

You have been having a snug time in the granary; then God brings you out and puts you under the millstones, and the first thing that happens is the grinding separation of which our Lord spoke: "Blessed are you when people . . . exclude you and . . . reject your name as evil, because of the Son of Man" (Luke 6:22). Crushed forever is any resemblance to the other crowd.

Hands off! when God is putting His saints through the experience of the millstones. We are apt to want to interfere in the discipline of another saint. Do not hinder the production of the bread that is to feed the world!

In many parts of the world, people sing as they grind the corn between the millstones. "The sound of the millstones is music in the ears of God." It is not music to the worldling, but the saint understands that His Father has a purpose in it all.

Ill-tempered persons, hard circumstances, poverty, willful misunderstandings and estrangements are all millstones. Had Jesus any of these things in His life? Had He not! He had a devil in His company for three years! He was continually thwarted and misunderstood by the Pharisees. And is the disciple above his Master?

When these experiences come, remember that God has His eye on every detail.

But beware! lest the tiniest element of self-pity keeps God from putting us anywhere near the millstones. OSWALD CHAMBERS

Dec 16th

DAY 344

Blessed is he, whosoever shall not be offended in me.

LUKE 7:23 KJV

It is sometimes very difficult not to be offended in Jesus Christ, for the offense may be the result of my circumstances. I may find myself confined to narrow areas of service, or isolated from others through sickness or by taking an unpopular stance, when I had hoped for much wider opportunities. Yet the Lord knows what is best for me, and my surroundings are determined by Him. Wherever He places me, He does so to strengthen my faith and power and to draw me into closer communion with Himself. And even if confined to a dungeon, my soul will prosper.

The offense that causes me to turn from Christ may be emotional. I may be continually confused and troubled over questions I cannot solve. When I gave myself to Him, I had hoped that my skies would always be fair, but often they are overcast with clouds and rain. But I must believe that when difficulties remain, it is that I may learn to trust Him completely—to trust and not be afraid. And it is through my mental and emotional struggles that I am being trained to tutor others who are being tossed by the storm.

The offense causing me to turn away may be spiritual. I had imagined that once within His fold, I would never again suffer from the stinging winds of temptation. Yet it is best for me the way it is, for when I endure temptation His grace is magnified, my own character matures, and heaven seems sweeter at the end of the day.

Once I arrive at my heavenly home, I will look back across the turns and trials along my path and will sing the praises of my Guide. So whatever comes my way, I will welcome His will and refuse to be offended in my loving Lord.

ALEXANDER SMELLIE

Blessed is he whose faith is not offended,
When all around his way
The power of God is working out deliverance
For others day by day;
Though in some prison dark his own soul does fail,
Till life itself be spent,
Yet still can trust his Father's love and purpose,
And rest therein content.
Blessed is he, who through long years of suffering,
Not now from active toil,

Still shares by prayer and praise the work of others,
And thus "divides the spoil."
Blessed are you, O child of God, who does suffer,
And cannot understand
The reason for your pain, yet will gladly leave
Your life in His blest Hand.
Yes, blessed are you whose faith is "not offended"
By trials unexplained,
By mysteries unsolved, past understanding,
Until the goal is gained.

FREDA HANBURY ALLEN

DAY 345

If your son asks.

LUKE 11:11

Henry Gibbud was a mission worker in the city of New York. He was a man of great devotion and wonderful power in prayer. On one occasion he had been working all night in the slums of the great city.

Tired and sleepy at the end of his toil, he made his way in the dark of the morning to the Brooklyn ferry dock. He put his hand in his pocket to pay his fare homeward, but to his dismay he discovered that he did not have the three pennies needed. His heart sank in deep discouragement, but he closed his eyes and began to pray. "Lord, I have been toiling all night in Thy service, trying to bring lost men and women to Thee. I am hungry and sleepy and wish to go home, but I do not have even three pennies for my fare. Will You not help me?"

As he closed his simple prayer, he opened his eyes. They fell upon something shining in the dust at his feet. He reached down and picked up the glittering object and found it was a fifty-cent piece. He paid his fare and went on his way rejoicing.

What was the joy that flooded his heart? It was the fulfillment of the precious promise: "If a son shall ask" (KJV).

Have you taken your place in God's presence, not as a stranger, but as a son?

"If a son, then an heir" (Gal. 4:7 KJV).

Heir of a mighty King, heir to a throne,
Why art thou wandering sad and alone?
Heir to the love of God, heir to His grace,
Rise to thy privilege, claiming thy place.
Heir of a Conqueror, why dost thou fear?
Foes cannot trouble thee when He is near.
Child of the promises, be not oppressed,
Claim what belongs to thee, find sweetest rest.
Heir by inheritance! child of thy God!
Right to thy sonship is found in His Word;
Walk with the noble ones, never alone;
Prince of the Royal Blood, come to thy throne.
Heirs! we are joint-heirs with Jesus our Lord!
Heirs of the Covenant, found in His Word!
Rise to thy privilege, heir to His grace!
Heir to the love of God, rise, claim thy place!

Dec 12th

DAY 346

*Though you have made me see troubles, many
and bitter, you will restore my life again.*

PSALM 71:20

God makes you "see troubles." Sometimes, as part of your education being carried out, you must "go down to the depths of the earth" (Ps. 63:9), travel subterranean passages, and lie buried among the dead. But not for even one moment is the bond of fellowship and oneness between God and you strained to the point of breaking. And ultimately, from the depths, He "will restore [your] life again."

Never doubt God! Never say that He has forsaken or forgotten you or think that He is unsympathetic. He "will restore [your] life again." No matter how many twists and turns the road may have, there is always one smooth, straight portion. Even the longest day has a sunset, and the winter snow may stay quite some time, but it will finally melt.

Be steadfast, "because you know that your labor in the Lord is not in vain" (1 Cor. 15:58). He will turn to you again and comfort you. And when He does, your heart that has forgotten how to sing will break forth in thankful and jubilant song, just like the psalmist who sang, "My tongue will sing of your righteousness" (Ps. 51:14).

Though the rain may fall and the wind be blowing,
And chilled and cold is the wintry blast;
Though the cloudy sky is still cloudier growing,
And the dead leaves tell that the summer has passed;
My face is fixed on the stormy heaven,
My heart is as calm as the summer sea,
Glad to receive what my God has given,
Whate'er it be.

When I feel the cold, I can say, "He sends it,"
And His winds blow blessing, I surely know;
For I've never a need but that He will meet it;
And my heart beats warm, though the winds may blow.

Dec. 13th

DAY 347

Lord, I know that people's lives are not their own . . . to direct their steps.

JEREMIAH 10:23

We were at the foot of Mont Blanc in the village of Chamouni. A sad thing had happened the day before. A young physician had determined to reach the heights of Mont Blanc. He accomplished the feat and the little village was illuminated in his honor; on the mountainside a flag was floating that told of his victory.

After they had ascended, and descended as far as the hut, he wanted to be released from his guide; he wanted to be free from the rope, and insisted on going on alone.

The guide remonstrated with him, telling him it was not safe; but he tired of the rope, and declared that he would be free. The guide was compelled to yield. The young man had gone only a short distance when his foot slipped on the ice and he could not stop himself from sliding down the icy steeps. The rope was gone, so the guide could not hold him nor pull him back. Out on the shelving ice lay the body of the young physician.

The bells had been rung, the village had been illumined in honor of his success; but alas, in a fatal moment he refused to be guided; he was tired of the rope.

Do you get tired of the rope? God's providences hold us, restrain us, and we get tired sometimes. We need a guide, and shall until the dangerous paths are over. Never get disengaged from your Guide. Let your prayer be "Lead

Thou me on," and sometime the bells of heaven will ring that you are safe at home! CHARLES H. SPURGEON

Oh, tame me, Lord! rebellious nature calm.
Oh, tame me, Lord!
This heart so tossed and filled with wild alarm;
Oh, tame me, Lord!
These human longings, let them end in Thee,
And let me be Thy bond-slave—
Even me.

THE MARECHAL

DAY 348

Blessed is the one who waits.

DANIEL 12:12

Waiting may seem like an easy thing to do, but it is a discipline that a Christian soldier does not learn without years of training. Marching and drills are much easier for God's warriors than standing still.

There are times of indecision and confusion, when even the most willing person, who eagerly desires to serve the Lord, does not know what direction to take. So what should you do when you find yourself in this situation? Should you allow yourself to be overcome with despair? Should you turn back in cowardice or in fear or rush ahead in ignorance?

No, you should simply wait—but wait in prayer. Call upon God and plead your case before Him, telling Him of your difficulty and reminding Him of His promise to help.

Wait in faith. Express your unwavering confidence in Him. And believe that even if He keeps you waiting until midnight, He will come at the right time to fulfill His vision for you.

Wait in quiet patience. Never complain about what you believe to be the cause of your problems, as the children of Israel did against Moses. Accept your situation exactly as it is and then simply place it with your whole heart into the hand of your covenant God. And while removing any self-will, say to Him, "Lord, 'Not my will, but yours be done' [Luke 22:42]. I do not know what to do, and I am in great need. But I will wait until You divide the flood before me or drive back my enemies. I will wait even if You keep me here many days, for my heart is fixed on You alone, dear Lord. And my spirit will wait for You with full confidence that You will still be my joy and my salvation, 'for you have been my refuge, [and] a strong tower against the foe' [Ps. 61:3]." MORNING BY MORNING

Wait, patiently wait,
God never is late;
Your budding plans are in Your Father's holding,
And only wait His grand divine unfolding.
Then wait, wait,
Patiently wait.
Trust, hopefully trust,
That God will adjust
Your tangled life; and from its dark concealings,
Will bring His will, in all its bright revealings.
Then trust, trust,
Hopefully trust.
Rest, peacefully rest
On your Savior's breast;
Breathe in His ear your sacred high ambition,
And He will bring it forth in blest fruition.
Then rest, rest,
Peacefully rest!

MERCY A. GLADWIN

Dec 13th

DAY 349

I was left alone, gazing at this great vision.
DANIEL 10:8

What lonely men were the great prophets of Israel! John the Baptist stood alone from the crowd! Paul had to say, "Everyone deserted me" (2 Tim. 4:16). And, who was ever more alone than the Lord Jesus?

Victory for God is never won by the multitude. The man who dares to go where others hold back will find himself alone, but he will see the glory of God, and enter into the secrets of eternity. GORDON WATT

I go alone
Upon the narrow way that leads
Through shadowed valleys, over rocky heights,
To glorious plains beyond;
And sometimes when the way is very lone
I cry out for companionship, and long
For fellow-travelers on the toilsome path,
Until a Voice of sweetest music whispers,
"My grace sufficient is, no other guide thou needst but Me."
And then the path grows brighter as
I go alone.
My Savior knows
The way I take. Himself has trod
The selfsame road. He knows each stone,
Temptations, pitfalls hid by blossoms fair,
The hour of darkness that my life must share,
The wilderness of sorrow, doubt, and fear,
Renunciation's agony, and every pang
Of loneliness and labor's wear; enough for me

That He has known it all, that now He stays
To strengthen, guide and help me. I am glad
My Savior knows.
Thy will be done
Whether on pleasant paths I walk along,
Or crouch amid the lightnings of the storm,
Whether for me the larks of springtime sing,
Or winter's icy blasts my being sting;
Whatever Thou dost send is best for me,
With joyful heart I take it all from Thee,
Rejoicing in Thy sovereignty, and pray
That Thou wilt lead me on my upward way;
The road grows smoother as I travel on.
Thy will be done.

AMY L. PERSON

The lone wolf travels a lonely path, but he beats the pack to the kill!

Dec 16th

DAY 350

Commit your way to the Lord.

PSALM 37:5

Talk to God about whatever may be pressuring you and then commit the entire matter into His hands. Do this so that you will be free from the confusion, conflicts, and cares that fill the world today. In fact, anytime you are preparing to do something, undergoing some trial, or simply pursuing your normal business, tell the Father about it. Acquaint Him with it; yes, even burden Him with it, and you will have put the concerns and cares of the matter behind you. From that point forward, exercise quiet, sweet diligence

in your work, recognizing your dependence on Him to carry the matter for you. Commit your cares and yourself with them, as one burden, to your God.
R. LEIGHTON

Build a little fence of trust
Around today;
Fill the space with loving work
And therein stay.
Look not through the protective rails
Upon tomorrow;
God will help you bear what comes
Of joy or sorrow.

MARY BUTTS

You will find it impossible to "commit your way to the LORD," unless your way has met with His approval. It can only be done through faith, for if there is even the slightest doubt in your heart that your way is not a good one, faith will refuse to have anything to do with it. Also, this committing of your way to Him must be continuous, not just one isolated action. And no matter how unexpected or extraordinary His guidance may seem and no matter how close to the edge of the cliff He may lead you, never snatch the guiding reins from His hands.

Are you willing to submit all your ways to God, allowing Him to pass judgment on them? There is nothing a Christian needs to more closely examine than his own confirmed views and habits, for we are so prone to taking God's divine approval of them for granted. And that is why some Christians are so anxious and fearful. They have obviously not truly committed their way to the Lord and left it with Him. They took it to Him but walked away with it again.

DAY 351

God does all these things to a person.

JOB 33:29

In a certain old town was a great cathedral. And in that cathedral was a wondrous stained-glass window. Its fame had gone abroad over the land. From miles around people pilgrimaged to gaze upon the splendor of this masterpiece of art. One day there came a great storm. The violence of the tempest forced in the window, and it crashed to the marble floor, shattered into a hundred pieces. Great was the grief of the people at the catastrophe which had suddenly bereft the town of its proudest work of art. They gathered up the fragments, huddled them in a box, and carried them to the cellar of the church. One day there came along a stranger and craved permission to see the beautiful window. They told him of its fate. He asked what they had done with the fragments; and they took him to the vault and showed him the broken morsels of glass. "Would you mind giving these to me?" said the stranger. "Take them along," was the reply, "they are no longer of any use to us." The visitor carefully lifted the box and carried it away in his arms. Weeks passed by; then one day came an invitation to the custodians of the cathedral. It was from a famous artist, noted for his master-skill in glass-craft. It summoned them to his study to inspect a stained-glass window, the work of his genius. Ushering them into his studio he stood them before a great veil of canvas. At the touch of his hand upon a cord the canvas dropped. And there before their astonished gaze shone a stained-glass window surpassing in beauty all their eyes had ever beheld. As they gazed entranced upon its rich tints, wondrous patterns, and cunning workmanship the artist turned and said: "This window I have wrought from the fragments of your shattered one, and it is now ready to be replaced."

Once more a great window shed its beauteous light into the dim aisles of the old cathedral, but the splendor of the new far surpassed the glory of the old, and the fame of its strange fashioning filled the land.

Do you say that your plans have been crushed? Then know this: Jesus Christ is a matchless life-mender. Try Him! JAMES H. MCCONKEY

DAY 352

Do you believe that I am able to do this?

MATTHEW 9:28

God deals with impossibilities. It is never too late for Him to do so, as long as that which is impossible is brought to Him in complete faith by the person whose life and circumstances would be impacted if God is to be glorified. If we have experienced rebellion, unbelief, sin, and ruin in our life, it is never too late for God to deal triumphantly with these tragic things, if they are brought to Him in complete surrender and trust.

It has often been said, and truthfully so, that Christianity is the only religion that can deal with a person's past. God "will repay you for the years the locusts have eaten" (Joel 2:25), and He is trustworthy to do it unreservedly. He does so not because of what we are but because of who He is. God forgives and heals and restores, for He is "the God of all grace" (1 Pet. 5:10). May we praise Him and trust Him. SUNDAY SCHOOL TIMES

Nothing is too hard for Jesus
No man can work like Him.

We have a God who delights in impossibilities and who asks, "Is anything too hard for me?" (Jer. 32:27). ANDREW MURRAY

DAY 353

These are those who. . . . follow the Lamb wherever he goes.

REVELATION 14:4

There are three classes in the Christian life; the men of the wing, the men of the couch, and the men of the road.

The first are those who fly before; they are the pioneers of progress; they are in advance of their fellows.

The second are those who stand still, or rather lie still; they are the invalids of the human race—they come not to minister, but to be ministered unto.

The third are those who follow; they are the ambulance corps of humanity; they are the sacrificial souls that come on behind. I think with John that these last are the most beautiful souls of all. They are lovely in their unobtrusiveness; they do not wish to lead, choosing rather to be in the rear; they come forward only when others are driven backward. They want no glory from the battle, no wreath for the victory, no honorable mention among the heroes. They seek the wounded, the dying, the dead; they anoint for life's burial; they bring spices for the crucified; they give the cup of cold water; they wash the soiled feet. They break the fall of Adam; of Magdalene. They are lured by every form of helplessness.

They come out to meet the shadows: they go in the track not of the lark, but of the nightingale; they follow the Lamb.

Give me the trouble without the glitter, O Lord! Let others lead! I am content to follow. Help me to serve Thee in the background! Is it not written they that tarry at home divide the spoil? I cannot fight Thy battles, but I can nurse Thy wounded. I cannot repel Thy foes, but I can repair Thy fortress. I cannot conduct Thy marches, but I can succor those who have fainted by the way.

Write my name amongst those who follow Thee!

O Captain of my Salvation, put me with the ambulance corps! GEORGE MATHESON

What though the hindmost place is thine,
And thou art in the rear?
This need not cause thy heart a pang,
Nor cost thine eye a tear.
The post of duty is the place
Where oft the Captain shows His face.
All cannot charge or lead the van,
All can be brave and true;
And where the Captain's standards wave
There's work for all to do;
And work from which thou may'st not flee,
Which must be done, and done by thee.
Among the stragglers, faint and few,
Thou dost thy march pursue;
This need not make thy heart to droop,
The weak may yet be true;
Through many a dark and stormy day
The Captain thus holds on His way.

"They will set out last, under their standards" (Num. 2:31).

DAY 354

You have shown your people desperate times.

PSALM 60:3

I have always been glad that the psalmist said to God that certain times of life are desperate or difficult. Make no mistake about it, there are difficult things in life.

This summer someone gave me some beautiful pink flowers, and as I took them, I asked, "What kind are they?" My friend answered, "They are rock flowers. They grow and bloom only on rocks where you can see no soil." Then I thought of God's flowers growing in desperate times and hard places, and I somehow feel that He may have a certain tenderness for His "rock flowers" that He may not have for His lilies and roses. MARGARET BOTTOME

The trials of life are sent to make us, not to break us. Financial troubles may destroy a person's business but build up his character. And a direct blow to the outer person may be the greatest blessing possible to the inner person. So if God places or allows anything difficult in our lives, we can be sure that the real danger or trouble will be what we will lose if we run or rebel against it. MALTBIE D. BABCOCK

Heroes are forged on anvils hot with pain,
And splendid courage comes but with the test.
Some natures ripen and some natures bloom
Only on blood-wet soil, some souls prove great
Only in moments dark with death or doom.

God finds His best soldiers on the mountain of affliction.

Dec. 21st

DAY 355

"For I know the plans I have for you," declares the LORD, "plans to prosper you and not to harm you, plans to give you hope and a future.

JEREMIAH 29:11

The love of God a perfect plan
Is planning now for thee,
It holds "a future and a hope,"
Which yet thou canst not see.

Though for a season, in the dark,
He asks thy perfect trust,
E'en that thou in surrender "lay
Thy treasure in the dust,"
Yet He is planning all the while,
Unerringly He guides
The life of him, who holds His will
More dear than all besides.
Trust were not trust if thou couldst see
The ending of the way,
Nor couldst thou learn His songs by night,
Were life one radiant day.
Amid the shadows here He works
The plan designed above,
"A future and a hope" for thee
In His exceeding love.
"A future"—abiding fruit,
With loving kindness crowned;
"A hope"—which shall thine own transcend,
As Heaven the earth around.
Though veiled as yet, one day thine eyes
Shall see His plan unfold,
And clouds that darkened once the path
Shall shine with Heaven's gold.
Enriched to all eternity
The steadfast soul shall stand,
That, "unoffended," trusted Him
Who all life's pathway planned.
I have an heritage of bliss,
Which yet I may not see;
The Hand that bled to make it mine,
Is keeping it for me.

FREDA HANBURY ALLEN

Dec 22nd

DAY 356

Be still, and know that I am God.

PSALM 46:10

Is there any note in all the music of the world as mighty as the grand pause? Is there any word in the Psalms more eloquent than the word "Selah," meaning pause? Is there anything more thrilling and awe-inspiring than the calm before the crashing of the storm, or the strange quiet that seems to fall upon nature before some supernatural phenomenon or disastrous upheaval? And is there anything that can touch our hearts like the power of stillness?

For the hearts that will cease focusing on themselves, there is "the peace of God, which transcends all understanding" (Phil. 4:7); "quietness and trust" (Isa. 30:15), which is the source of all strength; a "great peace" that will never "make them stumble" (Ps. 119:165); and a deep rest, which the world can never give nor take away. Deep within the center of the soul is a chamber of peace where God lives and where, if we will enter it and quiet all the other sounds, we can hear His "gentle whisper" (1 Kings 19:12).

Even in the fastest wheel that is turning, if you look at the center, where the axle is found, there is no movement at all. And even in the busiest life, there is a place where we may dwell alone with God in eternal stillness.

There is only one way to know God: "Be still, and know." "The LORD is in his holy temple; let all the earth be silent before him" (Hab. 2:20).

All-loving Father, sometimes we have walked under starless skies that dripped darkness like drenching rain. We despaired from the lack of light from the sun, moon, and stars. The gloomy darkness loomed above us as if it would last forever. And from the dark, there spoke no soothing voice to mend our broken hearts. We would gladly have welcomed even a wild clap of thunder, if only to break the torturing stillness of that mournfully depressing night.

Yet Your soft whisper of eternal love spoke more sweetly to our bruised and bleeding souls than any winds that breathe across a wind harp. It was Your "gentle whisper" that spoke to us. We were listening and we heard You, and then we looked and saw Your face, which was radiant with the light of Your love. And when we heard Your voice and saw Your face, new life returned to us, just as life returns to withered blossoms that drink the summer rain.

DAY 357

Take your son . . . whom you love. Take now thy son . . . whom thou lovest.

GENESIS 22:2 NIV; KJV

God's command is "Take now," not presently. To go to the height God shows can never be done presently. It must be done now.

"Sacrifice him there as a burnt offering on a mountain I will show you" (v. 2). The mount of the Lord is the very height of the trial into which God brings His servant. There is no indication of the cost to Abraham; his implicit understanding of God so far outreaches his explicit knowledge that he trusts God utterly and climbs the highest height on which God can ever prove him, and remains unutterably true to Him.

There was not conflict; that was over. Abraham's confidence was fixed; he did not consult with flesh and blood—his own or anyone else's; he instantly obeyed. The point is, that though all other voices should proclaim differently, obedience to the dictates of the Spirit of God at all costs is to be the attitude of the faithful soul.

Always beware when you want to confer with your own flesh and blood—-i.e., your own sympathies, your own insight. When our Lord is bringing us into personal relationship with Himself, it is always the individual relationship He breaks down.

If God has given the command, He will look after everything; your business is to get up and go! OSWALD CHAMBERS

"The Holy Spirit says: 'Today'" (Heb. 3:7).

Not of the sunlight,
Not of the moonlight,
Not of the starlight!
O young Mariner,
Down to the haven
Call your companions,
Launch your vessel and crowd your canvas,
And, ere it vanishes
Over the margin,
After it, follow it,
Follow the Gleam.

TENNYSON

DAY 358

"Take the arrows. . . . Strike the ground." He struck it three times and stopped. The man of God was angry with him and said, "You should have struck the ground five or six times."

2 KINGS 13:18–19

How striking and powerful is the message of these words! Jehoash, king of Israel, thought he had done quite well when he struck the ground "three times and stopped." To him, it seemed to be an extraordinary act of his faith, but the Lord and the prophet Elisha were deeply disappointed, because he had stopped halfway.

Yes, he did receive something; in fact, he received a great deal—exactly what he had believed God for, in the final analysis. Yet Jehoash did not receive everything that Elisha meant for him to have or that the Lord wanted to bestow on him. He missed much of the meaning of the promise, and the fullness of the blessing. He did receive more than any human could have offered, but he did not receive God's best.

Dear believer, how sobering is the truth of this story! How important it is for us to learn to pray through our circumstances and to fully examine our hearts with God's message to us!

Otherwise, we will never claim all the fullness of His promise or all the possibilities that believing prayer offers. A. B. SIMPSON

"To him who is able to do immeasurably more than all we ask or imagine, according to his power that is at work within us, to him be glory" (Eph. 3:20–21).

In no other place does the apostle Paul use these seemingly redundant words: "immeasurably more than all." Each word is packed with God's infinite love and power "to do" for His praying believers. Yet there is the following limitation: "according to his power that is at work within us." He will only do as much for us as we will allow Him to do in us. The same power that saved us, washed us with His blood, filled us with the power of His Holy Spirit, and protected us through numerous temptations will work for us to meet every emergency, every crisis, every circumstance, and every adversary. THE ALLIANCE

DAY 359

Dec 25th

Come with me by yourselves to a quiet place and get some rest.

MARK 6:31

There is one pause in music of which the untrained singer does not know the value—the pause: it is not the cessation of the music; it is a part of it.

Before the tide ebbs or flows there is always a time of poise when it is neither ebbing nor flowing.

In a Christian life that is to be effective, there will always be the pause and the poise.

The desert has been God's training school for many of His prophets—Abraham, Moses, Elijah, Paul. But not all who come from Arabia are prophets; and God has other schools. Before the years of witness, there were the years of stillness. Every witness with a great message has these years. Let not the saints shrink from the discipline and training! The sightless days will mean a grander vision; the silent years, the sweeter song. If the Lord puts you in the dark, it is but to strengthen your eyes to bear the glory that He is preparing for you; if He bids you be silent, it is but to tune your tongue to His praise. Remember that the pause is part of the music.

The great Composer writes the theme
And gives us each a part to play;
To some a sweet and flowing air,
Smooth and unbroken all the way;
They pour their full heart's gladness out
In notes of joy and service blent;
But some He gives long bars of "rests,"
With idle voice and instrument.
He who directs the singing spheres,
The music of the morning stars,
Needs, for His full creation's hymn,
The quiet of the soundless bars.
Be silent unto God, my soul,
If this the score He writes for thee,
And "hold the rest," play no false note
To mar His perfect harmony.
Yet be thou watchful for thy turn,
Strike on the instant, true and clear,
Lest from the grand, melodious whole
Thy note be missing to His ear.

ANNIE JOHNSON FLINT

Dec 26th

DAY 360

Caleb asked her, "What can I do for you?" She replied, "Do me a special favor. Since you have given me land in the Negev, give me also springs of water." So Caleb gave her the upper and lower springs.

JOSHUA 15:18–19

There are both "upper and lower springs" in life, and they are springs, not stagnant pools. They are the joys and blessings that flow from heaven above, through the hottest summer and through the most barren desert of sorrow and trials. The land belonging to Acsah was in the Negev under the scorching sun and was often parched from the burning heat. But from the hills came the inexhaustible springs that cooled, refreshed, and fertilized all the land.

These springs flow through the low places, the difficult places, the desert places, the lonely places, and even the ordinary places of life. And no matter what our situation may be, these springs can always be found. Abraham found them amid the hills of Canaan. Moses found them among the rocks of Midian. David found them among the ashes of Ziklag, when his property was gone and his family had been taken captive. And although his "men were talking of stoning him . . . David found strength in the LORD his God" (1 Sam. 30:6).

Isaiah found them in the terrible days when King Sennacherib of Assyria invaded Judah, when the mountains themselves seemed to be thrown into the midst of the sea. Yet his faith could still sing: "There is a river whose streams make glad the city of God, the holy place where the Most High dwells. God is within her, she will not fall" (Ps. 46:4–5).

The Christian martyrs found them amid the flames, the church reformers amid their enemies and struggles, and we can find them each day of the year if we have the Comforter in our hearts and have learned to say with David, "All my springs of joy are in you" (Ps. 87:7 NASB).

How plentiful and how precious these springs are, and how much more there is to be possessed of God's own fullness! A. B. SIMPSON

I said, "The desert is so wide!"
    I said, "The desert is so bare!
What springs to quench my thirst are there?
    Where will I from the tempest hide?"
I said, "The desert is so lone!
    No gentle voice, nor loving face
To brighten any smallest space."
    I paused before my cry was done!
I heard the flow of hidden springs;
    Before me palms rose green and fair;
The birds were singing; all the air
    Was filled and stirred with angels' wings!
And One asked softly, "Why, indeed,
    Take overanxious thought for what
Tomorrow brings you? See you not
    The Father knows just what you need?"

Dec. 27th

DAY 361

Pure nard, an expensive perfume.

JOHN 12:3

Love's reckoning will always be unusual. It was by no means the ordinary thing to do for the homeless Savior; that breaking of the alabaster and that lavish anointing were quite out of the usual way.

Did Mary's heart beat painfully as she glided in with her hoarded treasure? Did she intuitively hide her purpose from all eyes but His, who read its irrepressible meaning? Perhaps she thought only of Him who was her all.

Apparently she obtained her spikenard for the very purpose that she might anoint the Lord's body in burial. Possibly it was only an impulse which made her decide to anoint Him beforehand. Let us rejoice that she made the Master's heart glad before it was too late.

One tiny violet of encouragement will mean more to those with whom we live today than will acres of orchids when their pulses are stilled in death.

There were four women who set out later with their spices, only to find the empty tomb.

The opportunity for anointing had passed.

It is passing today! Not in realms of glory will we be able to share in His sufferings, to help in bearing the Cross. Here, and here alone such service may be ours.

O soul of mine, be extravagant in love of Jesus!

There is no fragrance like that of my alabaster box—the box I break for Him!

I shall not pass this way again,
But far beyond earth's "where and when,"
May I look back along the road
Where on both sides good seed I sowed.
I shall not pass this way again;
May wisdom guide my tongue and pen,
And love be mine, that so I may
Plant roses all along the way.
I shall not pass this way again;
Grant me to soothe the hearts of men, Faithful to
friends, true to my
God; A fragrance on the path I trod.

Dec. 28th

DAY 362

For no word from God will ever fail.

LUKE 1:37

High in the snow-covered Alpine valleys, God works one of His miracles year after year. In spite of the extremes of sunny days and frozen nights, a flower blooms unblemished through the crust of ice near the edge of the snow. How does this little flower, known as the soldanelle plant, accomplish such a feat?

During the past summer the little plant spread its leaves wide and flat on the ground in order to soak up the sun's rays, and it kept that energy stored in its roots throughout the winter. When spring came, life stirred even beneath its shroud of snow, and as the plant sprouted, it amazingly produced enough warmth to thaw a small dome-shaped pocket of snow above its head.

It grew higher and higher, and as it did, the small dome of air continued to rise just above its head until its flower bud was safely formed. At last the icy covering of the air compartment gave way, and the blossom burst into the sunshine. The crystalline texture of its mauve-colored petals sparkled like the snow itself, as if it still bore the marks of the journey it had endured.

This fragile flower sounds an echo in our hearts that none of the lovely flowers nestled in the warm grass of the lower slopes could ever awaken. Oh, how we love to see impossible things accomplished! And so does God.

Therefore may we continue to persevere, for even if we took our circumstances and cast all the darkness of human doubt upon them and then hastily piled as many difficulties together as we could find against God's divine work, we could never move beyond the blessedness of His miracle-working power. May we place our faith completely in Him, for He is the God of the impossible.

Dec. 29th

DAY 363

He remains faithful forever.

PSALM 146:6

God never forgets His Word. Long ago He promised a Redeemer; and although He waited four thousand years, the promise at last was most surely fulfilled.

He promised Abraham a son; and although a quarter of a century of testing intervened, the promise at last came literally true. He promised Abraham the Land of Promise as an inheritance; and although four hundred years of trial intervened, at last the land was possessed. He promised Jeremiah that after seventy years the captives should return from Babylon; and on the very hour, the action answered to the Word. He promised Daniel that at a definite time Messiah should appear; and the most extraordinary evidence that we have to offer to the doubting Hebrew today that Jesus is his Messiah, is the literal fulfillment of the prophecy of Daniel.

Just as true are God's promises to the believer. They are all "Yea and Amen" in Christ Jesus. He has guaranteed them. The promises of God form a great checkbook. Every one is endorsed by the Mediator, and His word and honor are pledged to their fulfillment. To make them "Yea and Amen" you must sign your name upon the back of the promise and then personally appropriate it.

"Anyone who believes in him will never be put to shame." (Rom. 10:11).

Dec 30th

DAY 364

Where morning dawns, where evening fades, you call forth songs of joy.

PSALM 65:8

Have you ever risen early, climbed a hill, and watched God make a morning? The dull gray gives way as He pushes the sun toward the horizon, and then the tints and hues of every color begin to blend into one perfect light as the full sun suddenly bursts into view. As king of the day, the sun moves majestically across the sky, flooding the earth and every deep valley with glorious light. At this point, you can hear the music of heaven's choir as it sings of the majesty of God Himself and of the glory of the morning.

In the holy hush of the early dawn
I hear a Voice—
"I am with you all the day,
Rejoice! Rejoice!"

The clear, pure light of the morning made me yearn for the truth in my heart, which alone could make me pure and clear as the morning itself and tune my life to the concert pitch of nature around me. And the breeze that blew from the sunrise made me hope in God, who had breathed into my nostrils the breath of life. He had so completely filled me with His breath, mind, and Spirit that I would only think His thoughts and live His life. Within His life I had found my own, but now it was eternally glorified.

What would we poor humans do without our God's nights and mornings! GEORGE MACDONALD

In the early morning hours,
'Twixt the night and day,
While from earth the darkness passes
Silently away;

Then it's sweet to talk with Jesus
In your bedroom still—
For the coming day and duties
Ask to know His will.
Then He'll lead the way before you,
Laying mountains low;
Making desert places blossom,
Sweet'ning sorrow's flow.
Do you want a life of triumph,
Victory all the way?
Then put God in the beginning
Of each coming day.

DAY 365

From this day on I will bless you.
HAGGAI 2:19

God has certain dates from which He begins to bless us. On the day of consecration (Gen. 22:16–17), the day when our all is surrendered to Him—on that day untold blessing begins.

Have we come to that date?

"It was on the 22nd of July, 1690, that happy day," says Madame Guyon, "that my soul was delivered from all its pains. On that day I was restored, as it were, to perfect liberty. I was no longer depressed, no longer borne down under the burden of sorrow. I had thought God lost, and lost forever; but I found Him again. And He returned to me with unspeakable magnificence and purity. In a wonderful manner difficult to explain, all that which had been taken from me was not only restored, but restored with increase and new advantages. In Thee, O my God, I found it all, and more than all! The peace which I now possessed was all holy, heavenly, inexpressible. What I had possessed some years before, in the period of my spiritual enjoyment, was consolation, peace—the gifts of God, but now that I was fully yielded to the will of God, whether that will was consoling or otherwise, I might now be said to possess not merely consolation, but the God of consolation; not merely peace, but the God of peace.

"One day of this happiness, which consisted in simple rest or harmony with God's will, whatever that will might be, was sufficient to counterbalance years of suffering.

"Certainly it was not I, myself, who had fastened my soul to the Cross and, under the operations of a providence just but inexorable, had drained, if I may so express it, the blood of the life of nature to the last drop. I did not understand it then; but I understand it now. It was the Lord who did it. It was God that destroyed me, that He might give me true life."

Oh, the Spirit-filled life may be thine, may be thine,
    In thy soul evermore the Shechinah may shine;
It is thine to live with the tempests all stilled,
    It is thine with the blest Holy Ghost to be filled;
It is thine, even thine, for thy Lord has so willed.

NOTES

NOTES

NOTES

NOTES

NOTES